T0289586

JUSTICE BY MEANS OF DEMOCRACY

JUSTICE

BY MEANS OF

Democracy

DANIELLE ALLEN

The University of Chicago Press

Chicago and London

The University of Chicago Press, Chicago 60637
The University of Chicago Press, Ltd., London
© 2023 by Democratic Knowledge, LLC
Published 2023
Printed in the United States of America

32 31 30 29 28 27 26 25 24   5

ISBN-13: 978-0-226-77709-2 (cloth)
ISBN-13: 978-0-226-77712-2 (e-book)
DOI: https://doi.org/10.7208/chicago/9780226777122.001.0001

Library of Congress Cataloging-in-Publication Data

Names: Allen, Danielle S., 1971–, author.
Title: Justice by means of democracy / Danielle Allen.
Description: Chicago : The University of Chicago Press, 2023. |
    Includes bibliographical references and index.
Identifiers: LCCN 2022037786 | ISBN 9780226777092 (cloth) |
    ISBN 9780226777122 (ebook)
Subjects: LCSH: Equality—Political aspects. | Democracy. | Justice.
Classification: LCC JC575 .A48 2023 | DDC 320.01/1—dc23/eng/20220816
LC record available at https://lccn.loc.gov/2022037786

♾ This paper meets the requirements of ANSI/NISO Z39.48-1992
(Permanence of Paper).

In every human society, there is an effort continually tending to confer on one part the height of power and happiness, and to reduce the other to the extreme of weakness and misery. The intent of good laws is to oppose this effort and to diffuse their influence universally and equally.

—CESARE BECCARIA

Justice is the end of government. It is the end of civil society. It ever has been and ever will be pursued until it be obtained, or until liberty be lost in the pursuit. In a society under the forms of which the stronger faction can readily unite and oppress the weaker, anarchy may as truly be said to reign as in a state of nature, where the weaker individual is not secured against the violence of the stronger; and as, in the latter state, even the stronger individuals are prompted, by the uncertainty of their condition, to submit to a government which may protect the weak as well as themselves; so, in the former state, will the more powerful factions or parties be gradually induced, by a like motive, to wish for a government which will protect all parties, the weaker as well as the more powerful.

—FEDERALIST, NO. 51,
JAMES MADISON/ALEXANDER HAMILTON

As I would not be a slave, so I would not be a master. This expresses my idea of democracy. Whatever differs from this, to the extent of the difference, is not democracy.

—ABRAHAM LINCOLN

I tell my students, "When you get these jobs that you have been so brilliantly trained for, just remember that your real job is that if you are free, you need to free somebody else. If you have some power, then your job is to empower somebody else. This is not just a grab-bag candy game."

—TONI MORRISON

Contents

PART I

A Theory of Justice Revised

Prologue

ON SURPRISE AND THE PURPOSE
OF POLITICAL PHILOSOPHY

Surprised by Politics

The Great Recession of 2008; Thomas Piketty's *Capital in the Twenty-First Century*; earthshaking elections in the past eight years in the US and Britain, in South America, and across Europe; a global pandemic; and the Russian invasion of Ukraine have put questions of political economy, social stability, governance, and their entanglement on the map for everyone, not just economists. Prior to the arrival of the COVID-19 pandemic, many wondered whether the political surprises of recent years flowed from the dramatic increases in income and wealth inequality in developed countries, and from the suddenly diverging fates of those with and without university education. Many were the calls to revisit our approach to political economy. With the pandemic, in developed democracies like the US and the UK, we also witnessed profound failures of governance, coupled with economic ruin for many, even as the well-off sailed along relatively untouched. The need for a reinvented political economy has become only more pressing. Yet reinventing political economy actually requires stepping outside the domain of economics. Economists have, I think, been answering the questions set for them by political philosophers. If we wish for different answers, we have to devise different questions.[1]

The purpose of this book is to propose some fresh questions—in particular, questions about political equality. The road to proposing fresh questions for economists lies through a reconsideration of the basic foundations of justice. I will propose in this book that the surest path to justice is the protection of political equality; that justice is therefore best, and perhaps only, achieved by means of democracy; and that the social ideals and organizational design principles that flow from a recognition of the fundamental importance to human well-being of political equality and democracy provide an alternative framework within which economists might do their work.

To ask an audience—or readers—to think about political equality, a highly abstract concept, is like scheduling your course lectures at 8 a.m: you ensure, in some sense, that those who read beyond the introduction are ready for something serious. In this case, I hope to offer a journey into political philosophy and a reflection on some of the basic concepts that define justice, democracy, and democratic aspirations. In my view, important features of our contemporary experience across multiple domains—political, social, and economic—flow from intellectual mistakes that have been made consistently over the past few decades and that have their origins even earlier in the tradition of political philosophy. I would like to correct these mistakes. Understanding recent events and building foundations for a new political economy will require us to journey back to see where things went wrong. I will lead us on this journey but will do so mainly to return to concrete political and economic realities. This itself is a method: the journey from epistemic failures in the present to a reconsideration of underlying theoretical paradigms and back to the present to revisit our understandings of current realities with fresh eyes.

What is the relationship between political economy, political philosophy, and a theory of justice? As economic theorists from Adam Smith to Karl Marx to John Maynard Keynes to Friedrich Hayek have recognized, any given economic system is built out of a set of underlying rules for human interaction. For Smith and Hayek, the rules that undergird a healthy market economy were the products of long processes of social evolution generating a conventional morality anchored in practices like honesty, promise-keeping, property, and contract. For Marx, the relevant rules were designed by those with power in order to preserve their power and support their capacity to extract value from others. All recognized that the rules of the game structuring human interaction and those generating particular forms of economy embodied distinctive sets of social ideals and could be redesigned. Hayek expected improvement could be achieved at the margins through modest and restrained forms of experimentalism; he believed that innovations could be made to stick through processes of human imitation and adaptation. Marx thought the rules could be comprehensively reorganized and made to stick from the top down. Hayek recognized the power in self-organizing systems; Marx recognized operations of power in the institutions of human governance and believed they could be redirected in a wholesale fashion.

More modestly, the American founders—authors of the Declaration of Independence, the Constitution, and the Federalist Papers—also saw the power and value in intentionally designed institutions of human governance. Their goal was a set of institutions that recognized the natural dynamics of human interaction—both of competition and of cooperation—and worked to guide those dynamics in directions supportive of the "safety and happiness of the people" and its "general welfare." Both self-organizing evolution and intentional governance can bring benefit to human society; both can also bring ill effects.[2]

A theory of justice does not seek to describe the rules that have come to be in human society—whether as a result of the emergence of self-organizing systems of human cooperation or as a result of intentional efforts to organize human governance.[3] Instead, a theory of justice seeks to identify the parameters for determining which among possible sets of rules for human interaction yields the best prospects for human flourishing, at both an individual and a species level.[4] These parameters would then be relevant to political economy in setting directions for and bounds to our experimentalism, as we seek to identify which economic policies count as redesigns that improve, rather than worsen, human prospects.

Readers will initially be skeptical that an ideal of political equality can enrich our understanding of justice generally or help us renovate political economy. In our contemporary world, invocations of political equality most immediately call to mind topical challenges such as voting rights, campaign finance reform, and felon re-enfranchisement in the US; or the issues of party functioning and membership within nations and democratic deficits in the operations of the European Union in Europe. A few years ago, if you had asked someone what political equality was mainly about, I think those are the sorts of issues they would have offered in reply. The topics are precise and technical. Yet that was before we were all so seriously surprised by events—the election of Donald Trump and the Brexit vote, for example; the upending of German politics by the migration crisis; the governance crises emerging in the US with the pandemic and in Europe with the Russian attack on Ukraine. At stake in understanding political equality are deeper issues of the strength and health of human societies and their ability to advance the general welfare by building collaborative institutions and practices that deliver safety and happiness to all.

As it happens, our best route to understanding what political equality fundamentally is will involve an investigation into why we were so surprised by those events. Such an inquiry brings to light how policy paradigms in use for the past few decades—and economic paradigms in particular—contain a blind spot that explains our surprise. This blind spot has arisen, I will argue, from the dependence of much recent economic thought on underlying, implicit theories of justice that have shortchanged political equality and democracy, sometimes even despite their authors' best intentions. I will suggest that a shift of our attention to political equality, and to a richer conception of political equality, will help us eliminate that blind spot.

With a fresh approach to a theory of justice, this book seeks to lay a foundation to reorganize policy debates around the value of political equality and the idea that justice at home is best pursued by means of democracy at home.

Pragmatism and the Purposes of Political Philosophy

Before beginning, I want to say a few more words about myself and my methods as a political philosopher. People often ask me what kind of political philosopher I am. I answer that I am a eudaemonist democratic pragmatist. But what on earth does that mean? *Eudaemonist* is the ancient Greek word for someone who focuses on how human beings can best flourish and who takes that flourishing as the overall goal of all thought and effort. I think that there are better and worse ways for human beings to live, and the better ways support our flourishing, and that makes me a eudaemonist. But at the same time, I think human beings can figure out how they will best flourish only by putting their heads together, collectively, through democratic practices of deliberation and decision-making. I don't think we get our answers about how to flourish from on high or from sources external to human judgment or from any individual human being. That makes me a democrat. Finally, I believe the surest way we can determine our best path to flourishing is by making judgments about what is and isn't working, given what we understand about our purposes—our hopes and aspirations for our own well-being—and knowing that our judgments will be fallible and will need correction. Commitment to this ongoing practice of experimentalism and judgment makes me a pragmatist, and even more technically, a fallibilist, corrigibilist pragmatist. But to keep it (relatively!) simple, I just label my approach that of a eudaemonist democratic pragmatist.

To help readers orient themselves to my argument, let me provide a fuller explanation of the method I deploy. My pragmatist method stands in contrast to metaphysical approaches. My method is more Deweyan or Wittgensteinian than Platonist or Kantian. "Beliefs are rules for action," the late nineteenth-century philosopher and psychologist William James famously wrote. With that comment, he identified a framework for testing the content of ideas that was an alternative to what, say, Platonic metaphysics or Kantian deontology had long provided. James meant that we can fully understand the content of an idea, a value, or a normative claim only after we have begun to see how it affects the world. Once someone tries to act on the basis of a normative claim, what changes around them? What practical effects do their beliefs have? If new beliefs secure a better set of experiences for those impacted by the actions stemming from them, then those new beliefs are good.

Conversely, when our beliefs leave us surprised by the world, we should investigate where and why they fail to have traction with realities, and experiment with new beliefs, developed with a view to improving the fit between belief, reality, and desired outcome. To focus on how well our beliefs deliver to us the world we hope to live in is not a narrowly consequentialist view. As we consider whether our beliefs are serving us well, we are also asking whether we are building worlds in which it is possible for us to be the kinds of people that we wish to be. Pragmatism can look like either consequentialism or virtue ethics. It differs from both in drawing the basis for judgment about the states of being its principles usher into existence not from external and fixed metrics (whether those are deontological or teleological) but rather from ongoing practices of judgment about well-being and what is effectively hypothesis testing of those judgments.

Or put it this way: How are we to know whether a set of experiences emerging from new ideas is "better" than the experiences the relevant group of people had previously? We have to count on those people to make judgments, based on conversation among themselves, about their own flourishing. Pragmatism, like Aristotelian eudaemonism, rests on the belief that human beings can fare better or worse; they can flourish or not. Aristotle sought a once-and-for-all account of that flourishing by studying nature. Pragmatists, in contrast, achieve accounts of flourishing through democratic means.

Like John Stuart Mill, pragmatists recognize all individuals as engaged in the business of determining whether they are happy.[5] Pragmatists recognize that because none of us *can* know the minds of others, other than partially, hazily, and wishfully, none of us is in a position to make a sound determination of what will count as happiness for another.[6] Each of us must do that for ourselves. Understanding what counts as human flourishing therefore requires two things. First, it requires social practices and organizations that permit individualized explorations by each person of their own happiness. Second, it requires democratic conversations that permit the cohabitants of a community, of a nation, of the globe to seek solutions—for all decisions that we must necessarily make together—that best permit us to bring our multiple views about flourishing into alignment. Democratic eudaemonism shares some features with Aristotelianism, but it is fundamentally pragmatist, rather than neo-Aristotelian, because on this account, the question of what makes us happy can be answered only through democratic means.

The second sentence of the Declaration of Independence provides a particularly profound statement of this pragmatist approach to democratic eudaemonism. Here it is in full:

> We hold these truths to be self-evident, that all men are created equal, that they are endowed by their Creator with certain unalienable Rights, that among these are Life, Liberty and the pursuit of Happiness,—That to secure these rights, Governments are instituted among Men, deriving their just powers from the consent of the governed,—That whenever any Form of Government becomes destructive of these ends, it is the Right of the People to alter or to abolish it, and to institute new Government, laying its foundation on such principles and organizing its powers in such form, as to them shall seem most likely to effect their Safety and Happiness.

The final clause is the most important for our purposes. From generation to generation, we must survey our circumstances, "the course of human events," and *judge* whether our government, whose purpose is to secure our rights to life, liberty, and an individualized pursuit of happiness, currently succeeds. Where it does not, we must revisit the basic terms of our social arrangements and reorganize them "as to us shall seem *most likely* to effect our Safety and Happiness" (emphasis added). The best we can do is make a probabilistic judgment about the joint structures that are "most likely" to achieve flourishing for all of us, a collective "safety and happiness." Moreover, we make this judgment, conceding our own fallibility as we make it. We know, as we act and as we do our best to judge rightly, that another generation will come along and correct us. The greatest philosophical contribution of the Declaration of Independence is its articulation of a species of pragmatism— this fallibilist, corrigibilist democratic eudaemonism.

Pragmatism assists our move into the future and helps us determine what to do by cultivating the practice of judgment and refining the terms of what counts as a good judgment. It gives us intellectual and normative tools for inching our way toward individual and collective flourishing. Yet pragmatism works backward, too. That is, we can use it to probe past historical practices for the values and normative commitments around which they were organized, and we can affirm those that have succeeded in delivering well-being and reject those that have undermined it.

Let's return again to William James's idea that beliefs are rules for action. A feature of a rule is that if it is applied consistently over time, it generates patterned behavior. Over the past three decades, in the United States, a rule has been introduced that children must be buckled into car seats. The result of this rule is that families have, on the whole, needed bigger cars to accommodate multiple car seats for their children; this has presumably contributed to the market shift over the past two decades toward SUVs and away from sedans, a shift that has to some degree offset improvements in fuel economy over the same period. To find the logic in a set of practices, as I deploy that idea, is to seek out the beliefs that led to the habitual behaviors that give a practice its patterned look.

This approach to studying sociopolitical phenomena is also similar to Pierre Bourdieu's method in *Outline of a Theory of Practice* (Bourdieu

1977). In Bourdieu's analysis of practices, they are not stable, not static, as in a structuralist account. Instead, any given actor faces a set of social rules and may or may not decide to deploy them in the way they have been most recently used by those who preceded that actor on the stage. The rules are made and remade through these ongoing pragmatist re-engagements. As the poet Frank Bidart writes, "We fill pre-existing forms and when we fill them, we change them and are changed" ("Borges and I" in Bidart 1997). Rules can be remade, and as they are remade, beliefs evolve along with them. Nonetheless, some social phenomena do coalesce with more durable rules. State formation is a type of human development that has effected a near freezing into place of some norms—particularly those that pertain to political decision-making, marriage and membership, markets and property, war and punishment, and education.

In inviting people to scrutinize patterns of social difference, as I will do throughout this book, I invite us to become aware of how long-standing customary "rules of action" define social, economic, and political phenomena. First, I want to ascertain where those rules for action represent things that we still value and perhaps need to work harder to protect. Second, I want to identify where those rules represent beliefs that we might want to shift.

The argument in this book is therefore eudaemonistic, in an Aristotelian spirit, but that eudaemonism is linked to pragmatism, not metaphysics. This means it is linked to practices of judgment, not permanently fixed to algorithmically accessible metrics of well-being, whether established deontologically or teleologically.

In the book's argument, I start from John Rawls's *Theory of Justice* because it was in reading that book that I first had my own intuitions about where common conceptions of justice had lost traction with our realities (cf. Honneth 2014). No political philosopher of the past quarter century has had a more significant impact on political discourse in the English-speaking world than Rawls. He has given us many of our common and conventional "rules for action." A pragmatist inevitably starts from the reigning intellectual paradigms. As I pulled on the threads in Rawls's *Theory of Justice* that discomfited me and made me anxious about a lack of fit between the theory, our circumstances, and our aspirations, I came to see a pathway to an alternative set of beliefs about justice that might give us alternative rules for action.

New Rules for Action

As we will see, "rules for action" is a broad concept covering beliefs about what our ideals or goals should be, strategic design principles for specific organizational domains, and the tactical choices about rules and norms that can bring those design principles to life in practical, on-the-ground applications. This book tackles all of these subsets of rules for action: our ideals and goals, design principles that tether them to practice, and specific rules and norms for practice that flow from those design principles. While in this book I use these ideals, principles, and practical norms to sketch policy paths we might adopt going forward, we can also use them to look backward historically and sharpen our understanding of how reigning theories of justice and of political economy have synched up together over time. Table 1 provides a review of how classical liberalism, Keynesian social democracy, and neoliberalism forged links among theories of justice and broad social ideals, design principles for economic policy, and specific rules and norms for concrete applications of economic policy.

In this book, I offer a detailed set of rules for action that are alternatives to those that Rawls offered and to those that dominated in earlier paradigms of political economy. I offer this set of rules for action as a hypothesis about the pathway to human well-being. I provide an account of justice anchored by democracy and political equality, specify the ideals characterizing justice understood this way, identify subsidiary ideals that pertain to political, social, and economic realms, and clarify some of the design principles and context-specific rules and norms that emerge from those ideals. This set of alternative rules for action constitutes a road map of how we might make our way toward

TABLE 1 Rules for action: Examples from the history of political economy

Paradigm of political economy	Ideals	Guiding design principles for policy	Context-specific rules and norms in emblematic policies
Classical liberalism	• Order • Rule • Utilitarianism • Antipaternalistic liberty • Autonomy (contra social hierarchies)	• Division of labor • Specialization • Competitive markets • Comparative advantage • Ricardian growth • Precursors of mechanism design • Cardinal utility	• Free trade • Antimonopoly • Complementarity of state-provided infrastructure and private investment
Keynsian social democracy	• Solidarity • Security • Fairness	• Aggregate demand • Paradox of thrift • Solidarity wages • Theory of second best	• Demand management • Tax transfer and public goods redistribution • Egalitarian supply-side policies
Neoliberalism	• Negative (formal) freedom • Procedural justice	• Self-interest (individuals and government officials) and competitive markets • No interpersonal comparisons of utility	• Laissez-faire economics • School vouchers • "Negative income" tax

Source: Adapted from Bowles and Carlin (2021).

human flourishing by pursuing justice by means of democracy. This approach to justice anchors a political economy that might be thought of as "power-sharing liberalism."

Tables 2–4 provide an overview of where we are headed. These tables will not be fully accessible yet; I haven't defined the basic terms that populate their cells. The goal of this book is to make these tables, and the forward pathway they map, understandable to readers. If I am able to do that, then I hope others will consider this pathway soundly enough judged to be worth testing out.

TABLE 2 Core principles of justice

Domain	Overarching ideal	Guiding design principles	Rules and norms
Human life	Justice and human flourishing	• Non-sacrificeability of both positive and negative liberties for protection of human purpose • Political equality (defined by five facets) as first principle of flourishing • Difference without domination	Further rules for action flow from subsidiary ideals for each domain of human life. The subsidiary ideals are domain-specific versions of the guiding design principles of political equality first, non-sacrificeability, and difference without domination. The subsidiary ideals direct the strategic and tactical work involved in organizing the powers of government and other social institutions.

TABLE 3 Subsidiary ideals of justice, their guiding design principles, and consequent rules for action

Subdomain	Subsidiary ideals	Guiding design principles	Rules and norms
Political	• Egalitarian participatory constitutional democracy	• Energy • Republican safety • Inclusion	• Achieve equilibrium between minority-protecting mechanisms and majority-protecting mechanisms and voice and representation for all
Social	• Connected society • Polypolitanism	• Maximize bridging relationships while supporting polypolitan bonding relationships	• Reorganize authority and responsibility as well as organizational processes in civil society organizations to support bridging opportunities and power sharing
Economic	• Empowering economies: economic policy should support people's ability to function as citizens	• Free labor, democracy-supporting firms, and a good-jobs economy • Investments in bridging relationships • Democratic steering of the economy • Charters and rules that protect equal basic liberties, both positive and negative	• Use a relational lens to analyze the economy • Use a strict scrutiny standard to review practices and processes for domination, with the goal of achieving non-domination

TABLE 4 Power-sharing liberalism: Justice by means of democracy as basis for political economy

Paradigm of political economy	Ideals	Guiding design principles	Rules and norms
Power-sharing liberalism	• Human flourishing • Political equality first • Difference without domination • Egalitarian participatory constitutional democracy • Connected society • Polypolitanism • Empowering economies	• Social preferences and principal agent models • "Identity economics" • Increasing returns and multiple equilibria • Networked economy • Enhanced mechanism design • Cardinal utility • Lived-experience policy making • Iterative co-design • Power sharing • Social discovery of solutions	• Investment in realm of pre-production and infrastructure of productive economy • End to wage theft • Workplace rights and voice, including control of scheduling/time • Good-jobs economy • Competition *for* the market via corporate governance reform • Civil society, market, and public sector partnerships to align natural and actual polities • Antimonopoly policies and practices

1

Justice That Sacrifices Democracy

AN ERROR

A Twentieth-Century Blind Spot: A First Look

We have been blindsided by events and living in a state of intellectual surprise for much of the past decade and a half. This has occurred, I suggest, because of a blind spot in dominant liberal policy-making paradigms and in the political philosophies on which they rest: something has been occurring outside our field of vision. Theories, often implicitly or tacitly held, provide the lenses through which we interpret events around us. When our interpretations cease to have traction on the world as we experience it—and thereby cause us surprise—we ought to revisit our undergirding theories.

The dominant liberal policy paradigm, emerging from places like Harvard's Kennedy School of Government and operating in Washington think tanks and policy-making spaces, fuses two things: utilitarian economic welfarism and what might be considered a knockoff variant of Rawlsianism. I will call this knockoff "quasi-Rawlsian welfarism." Quasi-Rawlsian welfarism focuses on economic redistribution with reference to John Rawls's difference principle, as articulated in his landmark 1971 work, *Theory of Justice*.

In the utilitarian model, the goal of policy is to maximize societal happiness or, better, utility, as the economists label it. In its crudest forms, the effort to maximize aggregate utility relies on cost-benefit analyses, linked to preferences typically cast in terms of material goods. Much modeling of utility maximization in relation to preferences has abstracted away from the contextual, social, psychological, and cultural particularities of individual economic actors.[1] The pursuit of utilitarian welfare maximization has typically focused on maximizing aggregate growth—in terms of income and wealth—and on using redistributive policies to spread the benefit of that growth.

When philosopher John Rawls published *Theory of Justice* in 1971, one of his main goals was to overturn utilitarianism. He sought to prioritize the right over the good, establishing as the purpose of political order the protection of a framework of right, not the pursuit of any particular good, even utility or happiness. Yet even as, philosophically, he sought to overturn utilitarianism, in many ways the quasi-Rawlsianism that emerged in the wake of his work has reinforced utilitarianism's practical applications.

In the Rawlsian framework, the goal of a just society is twofold. First, there is a goal to protect a set of basic liberties (rights). Those basic liberties include things like the right of association, the right to free expression, and the right to participate politically. Second, there is a goal to pursue social and economic structures—within the constraint of protecting the above basic rights—that secure fair equal opportunity throughout the society and that benefit the least well-off in society. Rawls calls the obligation to benefit the least well-off the "difference principle."

In Rawls's own argument, the difference principle applies to income and wealth *and* also to the social bases of respect and positions of responsibility and power. In his view, the latter social and political resources should also be objects of distributive concern. Yet the difference principle has been applied by Rawls's interpreters most commonly in the domains of income and wealth. This focus reflects that fact that interpreting the difference principle in material terms is the more natural interpretation of the principle, even if such an interpretation runs contrary to Rawls's express intent. Since Rawls's innovative and influential difference principle has anchored the major part of the reception of his work, this habit of interpretation has led to a dominant focus, in philosophical discussions of justice, on the economic questions of distributive justice.[2] Relatedly, in the policy world, quasi-Rawlsianism, understood as a presumptive focus on redistributive taxation, has emerged as a common starting point for policy frameworks.

Without intending to, Rawls reinforced the utilitarian paradigm precisely by splitting off consideration of basic rights from his treatment of social and economic spheres, which were addressed via the difference principle.[3] He provided support for the utilitarian focus on growth, so long as it was tethered to redistribution.

In both utilitarian welfarism and quasi-Rawlsian welfarism, as expressed in the policy world, the core question for justice was long one of material distribution. That this is the case is clear from the implications of common parlance. When someone invokes the concept of social justice, the first thing that comes to mind tends to be matters of economic distribution and welfarist social rights. Similarly, when a speaker invokes the concept of inequality, the relevant kind of inequality the speaker has in mind is almost invariably economic inequality.[4] Only more recently has that conceptual association begun to widen to matters of social and political equality, thanks to the efforts of scholars working in feminist and critical race theory.[5] More broadly, economic inequality is what many scholars and the general public know how to talk about most comfortably, thanks to the intellectual support provided by policy paradigms coming out of utilitarian and Rawlsian welfarism.[6]

Two features of this fused utilitarian/quasi-Rawlsian policy paradigm merit attention. The first is that the utilitarian and the quasi-Rawlsian paradigms are both universalizing; they abstract away from the contextual specifics of any given society to develop overarching policy guidelines (utility maximization on the one hand and the difference principle on the other). Here quasi-Rawlsianism is in tune with Rawls himself. For instance, in *Theory of Justice*, Rawls seeks the definition of the "right" by asking us to imagine stepping behind "a veil of ignorance," where we no longer know anything about our own social situation; from that perspective in the imagination, we are to try to identify the principles that would constitute a just society, one that we would consider just regardless of whether we turned out to be one of the society's wealthier or poorer; male, female, or transgender; black, white, or brown; Christian, Buddhist, Muslim, Jewish, Hindu, atheist, or agnostic members; and so forth. The principles of justice are to be devised without taking into account any underlying demographic features of a society. Moreover, they are understood to apply universally, to any social context.

In the context of utilitarianism, the move to abstract away from social particularity is less a matter of the intentional design of the theory and more a necessary consequence of its mathematization. In principle, utility is a concept that can embrace not only a given actor's preferences for material outcomes but also his or her values and norms. But the project of "maximizing" utility effectively requires that we convert preferences into something arithmetic. Financial interests are conventionally used as a proxy for utility, thus flattening the particularities of preference that may in fact give meaning and shape to the life of any particular agent. The move to treat material gain, or money, as a proxy for utility permits universalization. Financial stakes can be translated into a currency and compared across countries and contexts without reference to the underlying demographic facts or situations on the ground in any given country. In other words, one of the things both of these intellectual paradigms do is turn our attention away from the underlying demographic and institutional arrangements of a society. We train our minds away from questions such as "Who has power and on account of what sorts of institutional structures and according to what sorts of allocations of resources and opportunities?"[7] Prices dominate our mental landscape, at the expense of the protocols of organization and the tokens of authority and obligation (social capital) that structure human cooperation in contexts of political and social governance. To give you a concrete example of the kind of abstraction I am trying to pinpoint, think about how the World Bank operated throughout the late twentieth century. The bank applied a set of boilerplate require-ments for economic liberalization to developing economies as condi-tions for receiving loans.[8] The reigning welfarist policy paradigms have more generally taught us to overlook social and political phenomena that underlie economic conditions; this is their blind spot.

The development of a field of vision where economic questions are treated without reference to underlying political issues has also stemmed from the transition, over the course of the twentieth century, from law to economics as the primary academic influence on public pol-icy. Sociologist Elizabeth Popp Berman (2014) has written well about the variety of factors—including new capacities for computation—that drove that change. Much could be said about this transition of influ-ence, but suffice it here to note that it underscores the point I'm making. Legal thinking is fundamentally about the institutions of *specific* socie-ties and about the consequences of those institutions' particularities for the specific societies in which they are found. Even subdisciplines like comparative law that compare legal systems in different places must begin by seeing the specificity of the legal institutions in each place under comparison. When law dominated the policy-making universe, universalizing policy approaches that abstracted from demographic and social specificity were not broadly available.

The abstracting, universalizing features of the fused utilitarian/quasi-Rawlsian welfarism that dominated policy-making of the late twen-tieth century produced theories with a distinctive field of vision occlud-ing society, politics, and political rights. They left us vulnerable to being surprised not only by 2008 but also by Brexit, Trump, Bolsonaro, Orban, the resurgence of a far right in Germany, and the aggression of Russia. Of course, this policy paradigm has its own historical backstory, deriv-ing from the history of political philosophy. I turn to that next.

Our Twentieth-Century Blind Spot: The Backstory

The twentieth-century blind spot I am describing rested on an underly-ing philosophical orientation away from positive liberty; it originates from a small philosophical mistake made in the early nineteenth century that has characterized most variants of liberalism ever since. The mistake was to draw a distinction between two halves of the set of basic rights protected by liberalism. An early nineteenth-century French thinker, Benjamin Constant, was among the first to divide basic human rights into two categories. He called them the "rights of the ancients" and the "rights of the moderns." The rights of the ancients embraced rights to participate in politics and to shape a society's collective life. We now call these positive liberties. The rights of the moderns, in contrast, comprise a right to property and the right to be left alone in order, among other things, to take your property and to engage in commercial transactions in pursuit of your own well-being as you see fit. We call these negative liberties. I introduced the concept of basic rights in describing Rawls's *Theory of Justice* and provided as examples freedom of association, freedom of expression, and the right to participate in politics. With these three examples, I was limning the full spectrum of basic rights, including both halves as distinguished by Constant. But, as we shall see, the result of this distinction between the two sets of rights has been to reduce attention to matters political.

The rights of the ancients were political rights, the right to be a part of a society that was working together to steer itself through collective decision-making. The rights of the moderns, for Constant, were about private autonomy—steering your own life and being more or less left alone by any collective decision-making. These latter rights are the ones—thanks also to the work of Immanuel Kant and John Stuart Mill—that are understood to make the exercise of autonomy (Kant) and individualism (Mill) possible and to provide each individual the chance to develop and implement a conception of the good life, with minimal interference from others.[9] Constant endorsed the latter set of negative liberties as the priority focus and recommended redirection of energy away from the positive, political liberties.

That distinction has worked its way into the philosophical tradition and was extended by Isaiah Berlin in the early twentieth century. Berlin introduced the terms "negative" and "positive" liberties and also prioritized the former.[10] Similarly, we might see Hayek, with his rejection of "primitive" morality, as providing a more sophisticated structure than Constant's for repudiating the liberty of the ancients. In other words, in the mid-twentieth century, both left-leaning liberals and right-leaning advocates of the market economy combined in rejecting the positive liberties of the ancients.[11]

Recognizing this development, Rawls in *Theory of Justice* affirmed the need to protect the whole set of basic rights and claimed to have put the two sets of rights back together. Yet comprehensively reversing the dominant tendency of a century and a half of political philosophy was harder than he might have thought. Although he asserted a commitment to political as well as private rights, to positive as well as negative liberties, Rawls's execution of his argument does not live up to the initial intentions he laid out for it. At important points in *Theory of Justice*, the political rights become sacrificeable in his argument.

Rawls's list of the basic liberties is an amalgam of the two categories of rights.[12] He writes: "The basic liberties of citizens are, roughly speaking, political liberty (the right to vote and to be eligible for public office) together with freedom of speech and assembly; liberty of conscience and freedom of thought; freedom of the person along with the right to hold (personal) property; and freedom from arbitrary arrest and seizure as defined by the concept of the rule of law" (Rawls 1971, 61).[13] Here, at the start of the book, he does indeed appear to embrace political equality and to put the liberties of the ancients and of the moderns on an equal footing. Yet this listing does not then align with the structure of the argument throughout *Theory of Justice*. For instance, when he first introduces the basic structure and key examples of major social institutions, he includes "the legal protection of freedom of thought and liberty of conscience," but he leaves out protection of political liberty.[14] And indeed, in the discussion of liberty in parts 2 and 3 of his book, liberty of conscience is given first place and routinely elevated for its intrinsic value.[15] Political liberty is treated second, and Rawls repeatedly makes the case that conditions may obtain where political liberty should be sacrificed for the sake of fulfilling material needs.[16] Rawls acknowledges that the prioritization of negative over positive liberties has been a feature of classical liberalism since Constant, and through his argument's structure he also embraces that prioritization. While he acknowledges that some would want to put greater weight on positive liberties than he does, he also clearly makes his own choice to prioritize negative liberties.[17]

The consequences of this prioritization appear most pointedly when Rawls argues that while "historical situations" and "historical limitations" (his phrases) might sometimes justify lesser political liberty, they can never justify "the loss of liberty of conscience and the rights defining the integrity of the person" (sec. 39, 247). The "various liberties are not all on a par," he writes (sec. 39, 247). In other words, while the political liberties would never be sacrificed in an ahistorical well-ordered society, reduced political liberty may be justified in some nonideal historical circumstances; yet even in those nonideal circumstances, the negative liberties require absolute protection.

In the revised edition of *Theory of Justice*, Rawls goes further: "Under conditions that cannot be changed at present, there may be no way to institute the effective exercise of these freedoms [political liberties]; but if possible the *more central ones* should be realized first" (sec. 39; emphasis added).[18] Rawls's introduction in the revised edition of the phrase "more central ones" to refer to the negative liberties concedes the point. It's a throwaway comment, and the concept of centrality is not explicitly worked out in his argument. Yet the comment establishes a clear prioritization within the list of basic liberties. Although Rawls never explicitly names the "more central" freedoms, in his argument these are clearly the rights supporting personal, not public, autonomy: the rights of the moderns, not of the ancients.[19]

This is a tiny moment in Rawls's vast corpus—one that he himself probably did not consider central to the architecture of his argument— but it anchors and clarifies the structure of the argument about the basic liberties in *Theory of Justice*. I take it to be a ramifying mistake. That which we seek to protect absolutely, even in nonideal circumstances, as non-sacrificeable provides the content of our most fundamental ideals;

it is that which we insist on using to shape the world willy-nilly. For Rawls, within his list of prioritized basic liberties, only the negative liberties had the status of non-sacrificeable.[20] If one established the positive and negative liberties, political equality and autonomy-securing rights, as genuinely co-original and co-equal, in nonideal conditions neither set would be clearly more sacrificeable than the other, and the theory of justice—a theory that should guide us from specific nonideal situations toward improved situations—would change dramatically. Contra Berlin's argument that pluralism of values means inevitable conflict among them, analysis of real political choices would begin with the project of seeking alignment between the protection of negative and of positive liberties. Only after a project of pursuing alignment had been exhausted would one turn to debating a trade-off between these two categories of liberties. Moreover, trade-offs would be debated in the decision-making context with reference to the particulars of the occasion;[21] victory would not be preawarded to the negative liberties. In other words, the assignment of a status of non-sacrificeability to both positive and negative liberties means *there are no a priori answers to be had about potential trade-offs, only existentially consequential judgments to be made in the moment about what liberties to preserve in the face of a tragic dilemma.*

But Rawls chose for us. He chose negative over positive liberties. As a result, over the whole arc of *Theory of Justice*, we end up mainly focusing on the conjunction of our private rights (to autonomy, association, expression, and so forth) with questions of economic justice—the wealth associated with autonomous pursuits of excellence and the need for redistribution that comes from the unequal flow of the gains of productivity across a population. Although Rawls does not abandon the question of political liberty altogether, he does across his corpus performatively embrace what he calls "one of the tenets of classical liberalism," namely, "that the political liberties are of less intrinsic importance than liberty of conscience and freedom of the person" (Rawls 1971, 229). And remember, the entire purpose of the original distinction formulated by Constant was to split off those rights that supported economic activity from the others and to focus on them. When you de-emphasize the political rights and focus primarily on the private rights or negative liberties, you can easily come to focus exclusively on economic questions and lose sight of political questions. Then, when politics rears its head, you will be surprised. That is the deeper historical backstory for what happened with the intellectual paradigms that dominated liberal democratic policy-making in the late twentieth century.

Anatomy of an Error

To move past the intellectual blind spot of the twentieth century, however, we need to understand not only the historical progression of theories through which it came about but also the analytical error that sustained it within Rawls's *Theory of Justice*. It is his book that really delivered the blind spot to late twentieth-century policy-making. Developing a better theory of justice will require avoiding repetition of the same error. For this reason, we need to dig still deeper into Rawls's argument and clarify the anatomy of his error.

Despite the clear prioritization of negative over positive liberties across his corpus, as I have laid out above, Rawls believed, and argued, that in his theory of justice he had consistently treated the liberties of the ancients and the moderns as co-original and co-equal.[22] In *Political Liberalism*, he writes, "The ancient and the modern liberties are co-original and of equal weight with neither given pride of place over the other. The liberties of both public and private autonomy are given side by side and unranked in the first principle of justice. These liberties are co-original for the further reason that both kinds of liberty are rooted in one or both of the two moral powers, respectively in the capacity for a sense of justice and the capacity for a conception of the good" (413). Yet, as we have seen, in imagining moments when the two categories of liberties come into conflict, Rawls routinely prioritized the liberties of the moderns over those of the ancients. There is no room in his account for people whose mantra, behind the veil of ignorance, might be "Give me liberty, or give me death," where liberty means political liberty.

Nor is there room for people who would make the existential choice between the two categories of liberty only when there was truly no alternative and all potential pathways to alignment had been exhausted—and not a moment before.

Why did Rawls, in contrast to the Patrick Henrys among us, default to protection of negative liberties and material well-being above political liberties when imagining conflicts between the two categories of liberties and between material needs and public autonomy? Why did he consider sacrifices of political liberty appropriate in particular conditions? Why did he apply this view not only to political liberty generally but also to equal political liberty and the equal worth of political liberty? These positions reflect the fact that for Rawls, the negative liberties, the basic liberties that operate in the service of personal autonomy, are intrinsically valuable to a fully flourishing human life because autonomy itself is intrinsically valuable and the heart of human flourishing. In contrast, he conceives public autonomy as primarily providing instrumental value, with political participation being a means to protect the negative liberties.

In his argument, the exercise of public autonomy or political equality does provide at least one element of intrinsic value—namely, self-respect—but this is only one of the elements of intrinsic value necessary to a fully flourishing human life. And so the instrumental value of political liberty comes first in his argument. Indeed, he contends that only some will orient their conception of the good around the limited source of intrinsic value that he attributes to the positive liberties. He writes, "In a well-governed state, only a small fraction of persons may devote much of their time to politics. There are many other forms of human good" (sec. 36).[23] Rather than seeing political equality as an intrinsic good that also has instrumental value in bringing about the conditions for those many other forms of human good, Rawls sees the good of political equality as competing with other goods that might be chosen via the exercise of private autonomy. Yet political equality is a multivalent intrinsic good, not merely one good among many from which one might choose. It can deliver the conditions for all goods—an instrumental value—but it is also fully a part of the experience of autonomy, intrinsically valuable as such. It is just as intrinsically necessary to full human flourishing as the negative liberties. Indeed, private and public autonomy are so mutually dependent that they cannot be disentangled.

Yet Rawls sought to achieve just such a disentanglement. This aspiration is imaginable only in contexts of great social homogeneity or for those who have a lived experience of cultural alignment between themselves and those who hold decision-making power. As Rawls sees it, people need political equality in the original position (i.e., the hypothetical moment where people work together to form a social contract) to establish the principles of justice and a basic constitutional structure that will make it possible for each to pursue their own definition of the good life in the context of civil society associations (sec. 36). The result of this constitutional strategy, he hopes, will be a state that does *not* impose on our efforts to shape a way of life, thereby respecting our personal autonomy. In other words, private autonomy would be protected by default and completely, through the structure of the constitution. Public autonomy—or political participation—was not necessary as an extension of private autonomy because private autonomy could be expected to be so well protected in the just society.

Despite anticipating a level of protection for private autonomy that seemed to disentangle it from the need for public autonomy, Rawls does have one concern about how collective decisions might impose on our experience of autonomy. Rawls primarily sees this as a problem inhering in our life within the associations of civil society. He also thinks it is easily solved. He writes,

> The basic structure is then to secure the free internal life of the various communities of interests in which persons and groups seek to achieve, in forms of social union consistent with equal liberty, the ends and excellences to which they are drawn. People want to exercise control over the laws and rules that govern their association, either by directly taking part themselves in its affairs or indirectly through representatives with whom they are affiliated by ties of culture and social situation. (sec. 82)

Here, when Rawls talks about the goods that we derive from our social associations, he comes closest to recognizing the permanent entanglement of personal and public autonomy. He acknowledges that our autonomy requires our ability to exercise control over the laws and rules that govern our associations in "various communities of interest." Participation—or public autonomy—is the solution that mitigates the experience of imposition from collective decisions on personal autonomy. Rawls can see this with respect to the organizations of civil society. His mistake is in not extending this insight to political participation broadly.

The intrinsic value of participation extends beyond self-respect: there is no cure for the experience of imposition on private autonomy other than participation in the crafting of public decisions. The value here, however, is not merely instrumental protection of one's private autonomy but also the intrinsically valuable experience of autonomy itself, the public autonomy that is to be had when one functions as a coauthor of the restraints imposed on private autonomy. To be a coauthor in this way, a cocreator of a community's agenda, is an intrinsic, not an instrumental good. It is the sort of good captured by W. E. B. Du Bois when he invokes an aspiration to be a cocreator in the kingdom of culture. Being that cocreator feels good; in that activity of cocreation people flourish. Rawls captures this basic dynamic in his description of how participation in our civil associations and their cultural life is a direct expression of our pursuit of autonomy, and he recognizes but fails to explicate how this description also captures the relationship between citizens and the polity as a whole, not merely their relationship to their own associational groups.

In other words, he envisages a state that can do all the things that states do—make decisions about whether and how to go to war, adjudicate contests when the rights of adversarial parties come into conflict, tax and distribute state revenues in the form of public goods—without tilting the playing field in favor of some conceptions of the good rather than others. But no such state exists—a point being driven home now by controversies over secularism and the veil in France, and vaccine mandates, abortion, marriage equality, and limits on freedom for religious minorities in the United States. A hypothetical "neutral" state, in which participation and the opportunity for influence constitute a discretionary, sacrificeable value rather than a necessary good is imaginable only when the cultural universe of those who hold the levers of power in a state is reasonably close to the cultural universe that characterizes the population governed by the state. In such circumstances, public decisions read as "minimalist" or "neutral" not because they are or aren't minimalist but because they implicitly track the conceptions of the good that predominate within the population.[24] Rawls more or less admits this in his analysis of the problem of the impositions brought about by social decisions in the passage quoted above. There he argues that we will want to participate in shaping the rules that govern our associations and our communities of interest unless that work is done for us by "representatives with whom [we] are affiliated by ties of culture and social situation" (sec. 82). Cultural homogeneity can make the status of participation as a necessary and intrinsic good harder to see.

Given the necessary fact of diversity in all polities, however, citizens cannot exercise their autonomy only through private action. The exercise of autonomy also requires both participation in civil society and political participation. Conditions of heightened diversity make the theoretical point especially visible, but it is a broader human point: the political liberties are intrinsically valuable insofar as autonomy is intrinsically valuable. They are the form autonomy takes.[25] To make a mistake here is to make a mistake about fundamentals of justice. The twentieth-century blind spot flows from this deep, fundamental mistake. In the wake of a long history of interpreting Rawls in directions that prioritize material and economic issues of inequality, and of the inconsistencies in Rawls's own argument around protections afforded to political liberties, it is time for us to take a new perspective and to think afresh. The goal is not to tinker with Rawls's theory but to initiate consideration of justice from another starting point altogether.

Can we identify an alternative paradigm for political economy that would not similarly leave us so vulnerable to surprises of the kind we have recently experienced? I think we can, particularly if we pursue an alternative political philosophy and theory of justice. Our thinking about justice would be improved, I believe, if we began from political equality, recognizing that it has the same intrinsic importance for justice and human flourishing as liberty of conscience and freedom of the person.[26] It should be equally non-sacrificeable. It should take its place as one of the necessary design principles specifying the content of justice. Answers about how to achieve justice in the social and economic domains change once one restores equal priority in a theory of justice to protection of political equality (equal political liberty) alongside protection of the traditional negative liberties: freedom of conscience, freedom of association, and the right to bodily integrity. To see how a view of justice in the social and economic domains must change given a fundamental commitment to the non-sacrificeability of political liberties and political equality, we must elaborate more fully the nature of an analytical starting point in which political equality and public autonomy, on the one hand, and the rights relevant to private autonomy, on the other, are genuinely co-equal.

We will have to return to basics. If justice consists of forms of human organization necessary to support human flourishing, our job is to clarify the design principles needed for that work. I propose that we begin with two: the non-sacrificeability of *both negative and positive liberties* and, deriving from that, a commitment to political equality. In the next chapter, I will argue that an ideal of justice, understood as the route to human flourishing, depends on these two design principles, as well as a third, called "difference without domination." I will then make the case for why these principles in turn mean that justice is best achieved by means of democracy.

2

Justice by Means of Democracy

AN IDEAL AND ITS DESIGN PRINCIPLES

An Alternative Ideal for the Twenty-First Century

Let's start from scratch: Justice consists of those forms of human inter-action and social organization necessary to support human flourishing. The design principles needed to implement justice will flow from our understanding of human flourishing. Importantly, the defining pur-poses of specific human lives that can count as examples of flourishing are various; there is no single picture of the flourishing life. What is shared, however, across cases of human flourishing is that human beings are creatures who need to chart their own courses in life. They thrive on autonomy, the opportunity for self-creation and self-governance. Their flourishing also depends on their cultivation of the capacity (of habits, dispositions, virtues, and character) to direct the opportunity of autonomy toward their own flourishing. But that is a theme for another day. Here I focus only on the social conditions that deliver the auton-omy necessary for human flourishing and justice.

That autonomy is made real in our political institutions via the pro-tection of both negative and positive liberties. Negative liberties are those rights of free speech, association, freedom of religion, and so forth, that permit us to chart our own course toward happiness, based on our own definitions of the good. Positive liberties and rights are those opportunities that we have to participate in our political institutions as decisionmakers, as voters, as elected officials, as people who contribute to the deliberations of our public bodies. Through our positive liberties, or political equality, we have the chance to shape our collective world together. The autonomy that delivers human flourishing requires shared autonomy through political institutions in order to reach its fullest form. This makes democracy necessary to the achievement of human flourishing and justice.

But it is worth expanding on precisely why positive liberties and political equality are intrinsically valuable and share a status with negative liberties as non-sacrificeable. To understand this fully, we have to take a moment to rethink the concept of equality and its different types. My experience is that very few of us typically take the time to ascertain how different kinds of equality relate to each other. Let's begin with a basic list. There's moral human equality; there's political equality; there's social equality, or economic equality, or economic egalitarianism. The list goes on. There's also racial equality and gender equality, and so forth. What are the relations among all these categories of equality?

The relationship I'd like to propose among them is that human moral equality is the fundamental concept (see also Waldron 2017). Human moral equality names the existence of the need—stated above, distinctive of members of the human species, and fundamental to our flourishing—to be an author of one's own life, coupled with a capacity, also distinctive of members of the human species, to make evaluative judgments (Williams 2009). At the core of the idea of human equality lies our purposiveness and our capacity for autonomy. Also at the core is the need to have that capacity recognized as a necessary element of well-being, worth, and dignity. Yet a complication immediately rears its head. Well-being resting on autonomy cannot emerge simply from being the author of one's own life as an individual operating in an autonomously controlled space. None of us lives on such a private island. Each of us lives inside a set of societal constraints. As we pursue our purposes, and shape our lives in relation to them, there is no way to proceed through the world without recognizing and submitting to a set of limits that come from laws, shared cultural practices, social norms, and organizational protocols. Consequently, the only way to be maximally autonomous and to achieve fulfillment of one's purposiveness is to be a cocreator of those social constraints, both politically and culturally. The argument, then, is that human flourishing is a matter of both private autonomy and public autonomy, with the latter entailing meaningful participation in collective decision-making, both through participation in the evolution of cultural practices and the structure of civil society and through participation in the institutions of political governance. Only such participation as brings genuine and equally shared opportunities for influence meets the standard of "meaningful" participation. Full human flourishing therefore entails an experience of political equality, and our positive liberties are intrinsically, not merely instrumentally, valuable (cf. Mansbridge 1980; Williams 2009; LeBron 2014; Waldron 2017). To support both private and public autonomy, and fulfillment of human purpose, we need both our negative and our positive liberties, welded together. Finally, democracy is the only governance form that can deliver political equality. An ideal democracy comprises a population of free and equal citizens, whose equality must first and foremost be understood as a matter of both political equality and equality in the rights constituting private autonomy.[1] I draw a line of this kind from human purposiveness and basic human flourishing to political equality and democracy, and I take both to be simultaneously instrumentally and intrinsically valuable.[2] Insofar as the job of justice is to secure human flourishing, we can fully achieve justice only by means of democracy.

Understanding what it means to pursue justice by means of democracy next requires clarifying just how our negative and positive liberties are welded together. They are not merely independently non-sacrificeable but also dependent on each other. To sacrifice either set of liberties is in fact to jeopardize the other set. These two bodies of rights are co-original in further ways that have not yet been specified. For instance, the right to association is not just a right of private autonomy, one of the sacred rights of the moderns. If anything, its earliest appearances on the historical register show it fully conjoined to efforts to secure rights of public autonomy. In seventeenth-century England, dissenters gathered not merely to celebrate religious rites but also to raise challenges to the legitimate authority of the monarch (Green 1985). They laid claim to a right to association to protect not only freedom of thought but also their political power. In the Bill of Rights to the US Constitution, the right to assemble was closely conjoined to the right to petition political authorities for changes in policies. In our own era, the Chinese government currently imposes great restrictions on the freedom of association not (or not only) to limit freedom of conscience but (also) to minimize the likelihood that political solidarities will form that are capable of challenging the government's authority (Allen 2012a). Some rights, in other words, that have been identified as elements of negative liberty should properly be reclassified as being components of positive liberty. This is the first adjustment that comes into view when we launch our investigation of justice from political equality. This adjustment already indicates how elements of the intrinsic value associated with the basic liberties also attach to political equality. The autonomy-satisfying right of association provides intrinsic value not only in its role as a contributor to negative liberty but also in its role as a power-activating element of positive liberty. When citizens have political equality, they have not only the instrumental value of democracy but also something of intrinsic value: empowerment.

Where Rawls offhandedly treats the pursuit of private autonomy as leading over time to the protection of the political liberties in addition to the "more central liberties," I see the connection flowing the other way around. The pursuit of democracy—which is to say of public autonomy—necessarily brings with it protection of the rights supporting private autonomy.[3] Those negative liberties must exist for the positive liberties to exist, so protection of the positive liberties is necessarily protection of the negative liberties. Because human beings generally have the capacity for autonomy as a property of their species—not merely choosing their own way of life but also shaping the necessarily shared aspects of life through participation in politics—democracy is a good thing for them. Democracy permits the full realization of a basic human capacity. This is an intrinsic good. Relatedly, human beings tend to grow morally and in other ways through political participation; this tendency is another species property. The fact that democracy activates this capacity is another aspect of its intrinsic value.[4] In both these ways, democracy supports the flourishing of human beings as the kind of being they are. In short, democracy rests on the underlying moral equality that resides in this general human capacity for autonomy, and it provides a vehicle for the full realization of this capacity. In *Political Liberalism*, Rawls describes this capacity for autonomy as consisting of "the two moral powers, respectively in the capacity for a sense of justice and the capacity for a conception of the good" (413). Democracy is the type of polity that most fully activates these capacities. While the justice of democracy as a type of polity therefore derives from its grounding in *human moral equality*, the realization of democracy as a political form depends on maximizing the trajectory toward *political equality*.

In sum, human moral equality—which resides in our capacity for autonomy—necessitates political equality (that is, democracy) so that human beings can flourish as the kind of creature that they are. This is how basic human moral equality—which undergirds any rights regime[5]—and political equality fit together to support the work of justice.

Political Equality: A Design Principle

As I have said, justice consists of those forms of human interaction and social organization necessary to support human flourishing, and the design principles needed to implement justice will flow from our understanding of human flourishing. Now we have two of those principles in hand: the shared non-sacrificeability of negative and positive liberties and the commitment to political equality. At this point, I'd like to spend some time specifying the content of that commitment to political equality. Given how fundamental I am making political equality for the work of justice, it will be clear that I don't think reference to issues like voting rights, campaign finance reform, and specific electoral mechanisms suffice as an account of what political equality consists of. Issues such as these tend to pick out some of the formal institutional mechanisms that we use to try to achieve political equality through participation in governance. But what sort of broader concept of political equality do these institutional mechanisms reflect or, if we are successful, actually operationalize?

I propose a concept of political equality with five facets. These five facets are elements of a definition for political equality, as an anchor for justice. The facets do not constitute a comprehensive account of the content of political equality. Instead, they serve as a conceptual starter set.[6] The first facet of political equality is a requirement for experiences of non-domination, both in social contexts and in the context of operating within political institutions. The second facet consists of equal access to the instruments of government, an equal chance to participate in decision-making within political institutions. The third facet is something that I call "epistemic egalitarianism." This is the notion that any well-functioning democracy needs to make good decisions based on good knowledge processes, that is, processes for gathering and sorting knowledge and making judgments on its basis. Successful democratic knowledge processes will require reliance on both expertise and the social knowledge that ordinary people have. In other words, epistemic egalitarianism requires the development of processes that unite experts and laypeople in strong partnerships so that decisions can be made based on the whole citizenry's knowledge banks. Epistemic egalitarianism makes room for all to participate in epistemic processes of problem identification and solution discovery, even as there are different roles in the process for those with formal expertise and those whose contribution comes from the perspective of routine social participation, in one context or another. The fourth facet of political equality is reciprocity. This concerns the relational ethic that citizens have with one another: the ability to look one another in the eye; the ability to propose the need for redress of grievances and to be secure in the expectation that redress will be possible within constraints of reasonableness and rights. Some of the controversies surrounding the issue of police violence, for instance, have tapped into the need of citizens for reciprocity expressed through actually responsive processes for redress of grievances. The fifth facet of political equality is something I call "co-ownership of political institutions." This involves recognizing that all the machinery of a democracy—all of the assemblies, congresses, and judicial offices at federal, state, county, and municipal levels—constitutes a valuable asset. This massive apparatus is a form of property that we own together. What does it mean for us to own that property together and to have co-ownership in relationship to it? The concept of co-ownership of our political institutions should help define some limits on usage of these institutions, for instance, ruling out the privatization of prisons or conversion of a military into an army of contractors. I take the concept of political equality, then, to embrace at least these five facets, guides for thinking about institutional design and cultural norms.[7] Before we move on, though, it's worth offering a deeper overview of each of them.[8]

FREEDOM FROM DOMINATION

To be free from domination, in the argument of Philip Pettit, is to be free from the prospect of arbitrary interference or "reserve control." In his brilliant book *Just Freedom*, Pettit explains freedom from domination with reference to the expression "free rein." If you give a horse free rein, it may be able to go where it wants, but the rider retains "reserve control" and can reassert constraint at any point. Or consider Nora in Henrik Ibsen's play *A Doll's House*. Nora's husband, Torvald, a late-nineteenth-century bourgeois gentleman, applies few restrictions to his wife, who is able to spend her time as she pleases. And yet she is unhappy. She is at liberty thanks only to his good graces; she is dominated by his reserve control.

To have freedom from domination requires more than just protection of the basic liberty to choose your religion, political party, associations, and employment. It also requires an equal share of control over the institutions—the laws, policies, procedures—that necessarily interfere with your life but that do so, ideally, only to protect each individual from domination by another, and any group from domination by other groups.[9]

Pettit offers three simple tests for assessing whether freedom from domination exists in a society: the straight-talk test, the tough-luck test, and the eyeball test. Can the people and their representatives speak forthrightly to one another and to other citizens, or do some find themselves bowing and scraping, for instance, to those with deep pockets? If the latter, domination exists. If your side loses a vote in a political dispute, do you have good reason to view it as tough luck rather than as the "sign of a malign will working against you or your kind"? If you do not, again there is domination. And, finally, can citizens look others in the eye "without reason for fear or deference"?

Importantly, a world without domination is neither a world without hierarchy nor one without constraints. Its hierarchy and constraints (for instance, law) must, however, be legitimate. Whether specific instances of hierarchy and constraint are legitimate depends on procedural questions and on the absence of patterns of domination from the interpersonal engagements that transpire within the framework of the hierarchical institution or legal system under consideration.[10]

EGALITARIAN ACCESS TO THE INSTRUMENT OF GOVERNMENT

A democracy consists of the establishment of impersonal forms of corporate decision-making. That is, group decision-making institutions are established whose legitimacy is tied to a conception of "the people" who authorize them and whom they represent. Decision-making power is not tied to any single individual. In antiquity, democracies were the first type of political form to achieve a depersonalization of power. In contrast to a monarchy or oligarchy, it could not be said that political power lay in the hands of this or that particular person or group of people.[11] Democracies can structure these "depersonalizing" institutions in a variety of ways. For instance, the world has seen the direct democracy of the ancient Athenians and the representative democracies of the moderns. We have seen forms both presidential and parliamentarian. The relevant decision-making institutions are typically legislative, executive, and judicial. Executive decision-making includes the regulatory apparatus of executive agencies.

A second important element of political equality is that all citizens have equal access to this decision-making apparatus. We are accustomed to arguing for such equal access in the context of protecting voting rights. The US is currently engaged in fierce debates about campaign finance law and whether one or another legal regime in this policy domain generates unequal access to the decision-making apparatus. The issue of pro bono provision of defense counsel for the indigent is also relevant here. So too is the question of ballot access—whether every nonfrivolous candidate has a right to get their name on the ballot for a competitive election. (The concept of proof of nonfrivolousness as a barrier to entry to the ballot is analogous to the concept of nonfrivolousness as a standard for bringing a lawsuit.) The question of precisely what institutional arrangements count as ensuring egalitarian access to legislative, executive (including regulatory), and judicial decision-making processes at all levels of government (federal, state, and local) is open to debate, but the ideal is clear: a pathway to pull the levers of power that is open to one should be, in fact as well as in principle, open to all, contingent on each individual's acquiring the legitimately established qualifications relevant to the use of that particular lever of power.[12]

EPISTEMIC EGALITARIANISM

Like all polities, democracies depend on successful collective learning and knowledge-management practices to make good decisions. In contrast to other regime types, democracies have access to a technique for strengthening collective decision-making by drawing on the knowledge resources of the whole citizenry. This feature of political equality is what I call "epistemic egalitarianism."

Human beings are sponges, taking in information from and about their environment. Some are better sponges than others, but all of us are absorbent. All people are created equal in that we are all born to absorb. Recognizing this fact, we can cultivate collective intelligence that is better than what any individual can achieve. Of course, to say everyone is an equal participant in the project of observing and interpreting the course of human events does not mean that everyone is equally good at it, only that everyone has the capacity to pick up some bit of information, some observation, that is relevant to the whole picture and that no one else will have noticed. Some people will pick up more than others, but everyone picks up something. Experts have a crucial role to play within the larger democratic community, but the value of their contributions should not obscure the fact that contributions are needed from every quarter to achieve a complete view.[13]

Democracies can strengthen our individual and collective capacities to analyze the relation between present and future, and to make related policy judgments, by drawing everyone into the work of understanding the course of human events. They can build a collective intelligence superior to what even a closed group of experts can achieve, by developing egalitarian approaches to knowledge cultivation. Experts are most valuable when they work hand in hand with a well-educated general population capable of supplying useful social knowledge to deliberations.[14]

This sort of egalitarian epistemic practice can strengthen democratic decision-making, supporting consideration of decisions from a 360-degree point of view, with all perspectives taken into account. Moreover, deploying such practices also reinforces political equality. When the knowledge and understanding that flow into a political decision are closely controlled by a limited few, their control of knowledge resources pulls decision-making power to them as well. Broadening the engagement of the citizenry in the discovery, analysis, and deliberation

processes that feed into policy-making decentralizes power, supporting political equality. The place of epistemic egalitarianism in political
equality thus underscores the need to treat education as a public good.
An effective educational system is necessary to maximize the potential of citizens to participate effectively in the knowledge-management
processes and deliberations of their democracy. It's not an accident that
forty-nine of the fifty US state constitutions include a right to education, or that many explicitly ground that right in preparing people for
citizenship (Rebell 2018, chap. 3). A good educational system is an important foundation for realizing political equality, precisely because of the
epistemic egalitarianism required of political equality.

RECIPROCITY

Justice in human relationships requires the kind of equality expressed
by principles of reciprocity. Such principles provide the basis for interaction through which both friends and fellow citizens can achieve
equality of agency in their relationships.

Whether in friendship or politics, each participant wants a sphere of
agency unfettered by others.[15] Each has the capacity to engage, through
talk, in a project of responsiveness to make sure that no one is encroaching on their own sphere of agency.[16] This is not to say that the spheres
of agency of different people never intersect; it's rather that the intersections need to be harmonizing, not encroaching or dominating. The
work of cocreation, discussed below in relation to co-ownership of
political institutions, is about bringing our spheres of agency into relationships with one another. But a key feature of achieving reciprocity
is that we are able both to name and to redress those moments where
our spheres of agency have been unduly imposed upon by others. The
achievement of freedom depends on this egalitarian engagement in a
constant recalibration to undo, or redress, or fix encroachments. A free
people grounds its problem-solving methods on this sort of egalitarian basis, via habits of reciprocity. Doing things with words is at the

heart of those egalitarian problem-solving methods and mutual responsiveness. Reciprocity—or mutual responsiveness—is at the heart of justice.

Two sets of practices define the reciprocity at the core of political equality: practices that make possible the redress of grievances and practices that make it possible to acknowledge and reciprocate benefits that have been supplied by one's fellow citizens.[17] No political decision is equally good for all members of the polity, even when all members of the polity have had equal access to the instruments of government and have been equally able to contribute their knowledge to group-decision-making practices. Even in these conditions, some members of the polity will incur losses. When settled patterns emerge in who bears the losses that result from political decision-making, political equality has come undone. The goal, instead, is to establish practices that result in political gains and losses circulating through the citizenry over time (Allen 2004, chaps. 3, 4, 8, and 9).

To some extent this is achieved through practices of redress for grievances, as in the civil legal system. To another extent this is achieved through legislative and deliberative practices, including well-developed habits of compromise and negotiation, that recognize and reciprocate sacrifices that some members of the polity bear on behalf of others. This idea of reciprocity identifies the kind of equality that needs to be in play in relations between people in order for freedom to obtain. This is an equality in which, when one person does injury to another, the other person can push back and achieve redress so that there can be a balancing of agency in their relations. Securing conditions in which no one dominates anyone else requires a form of conversational interaction that rests on and embodies equality in the relationships among the participants. It is not merely that the ideal of equality requires securing conditions free from domination—the first facet of equality that we looked at—but also that equality of agency, achieved through reciprocal responsiveness, itself provides the means for securing freedom. Equality of agency rests on citizens' ability to adopt habits of nondomination in their ordinary interactions with one another; these are habits that in *Talking to Strangers* I called "political friendship" (Allen 2004, chaps. 3, 4, 8, and 9). I will explore this idea further in chapter 7.

CO-OWNERSHIP OF POLITICAL INSTITUTIONS

The final component of political equality is cultivation, in all members of the polity, of an understanding that each has an equal ownership share in existing political institutions. Nobel Prize–winning economist Herbert Simon (2014) makes a similar argument that a democracy's political institutions constitute an asset owned by the people as a whole. Moreover, he argues that this commonly owned asset is the source of significant wealth generation in developed democracies, and that this wealth might consequently be allocated to a universal basic income on the grounds that the public owns the asset that generated it. While I don't advocate for a universal basic income, the point stands that the political institutions we share constitute a shared asset, the benefits of which should redound to all of us and ownership of which should remain with all of us. As I said above, the concept of co-ownership of our political institutions should help define some limits on usage of these institutions, for instance, ruling out the privatization of prisons or conversion of a military into an army of contractors. The topic of redistricting is also relevant here. Current approaches to redistricting often put that work in the hands of political parties rather than the people at large. This makes political institutions the possession of political elites. If, instead, those institutions were correctly understood as the possession of the people themselves, then control over their most basic and routine reorganization would be assigned to the people directly.

This focus on co-ownership of political institutions as a critical element of political equality also underscores the importance of political equality as cocreation, where many people participate equally in creating a world together. We are co-owners of our institutions because we are cocreators of them. Ideally, we carry out this work under conditions of mutual respect and accountability and by sharing intelligence and sacrifice. The point of political equality is not merely to secure spaces free from domination but also to engage all members of a community equally in the work of creating and constantly re-creating that community and to state clearly that the resulting institutions and shared practices are an asset that belongs to all.

This is not the end of an account of the elements of human practice that define political equality. I have offered, as I said, only a conceptual starter set. But this starter set is powerful enough to give us a framework for understanding how to design political institutions that support human flourishing.

*   *   *

In the expansive definition of political equality sketched above, protecting equal basic liberties, including the political liberties, requires securing (1) freedom from domination, (2) equal access to the instruments of government, (3) educational resources that support egalitarian participation by all in the polity's processes of knowledge management and deliberation, (4) a culture of reciprocity and turn-taking, and (5) an asset-based conception of political institutions that assigns the ownership stake in that asset to all citizens and blocks capture of those institutions by a subset of the population Realizing this picture of political equality via the political realm is not merely a matter of using majority vote for decision-making, nor of campaign finance regulation, but of working comprehensively to build egalitarian participatory constitutional democracy, as we shall see in chapter 3.[18] Egalitarian participatory constitutional democracy will turn out to be a subsidiary ideal that flows from the design principles for justice with which we've begun. And the five facets of political equality help bring further specification to the design principles needed for just political institutions. The goal is institutions wherein members of the polity are routinely obliged to share power in a variety of public contexts with unchosen others and are able to do so successfully.

But before we turn to the implications of this theory of justice for political institutions, we need to bring the social and economic realms fully into the frame. To achieve this, we have one more design principle to draw out. Once a commitment to political equality is seen as fundamental to the project of justice, what becomes of social and economic questions? Does justice collapse merely to the project of democracy? It does not. There is also work to do in civil society and the economy.

Difference without Domination: A Third Design Principle

I have launched our inquiry into justice by focusing on the intrinsic value of political equality and democracy to human flourishing. Contrary to how others have often approached concerns of justice, I have put economic questions to the side for a moment. It's time to bring them back into the frame. The next question to ask is what the implications are of the shared non-sacrificeability of negative and positive liberties and of a fundamental commitment to political equality for understanding the requirements of justice in the social and economic realms.

The important question for a theory of justice that begins from political equality is not only how political institutions function (or fail to function) to support political equality but also how economic and social domains do so.[19] In other words, questions of economic justice and social policy should be taken up from the point of view of how to develop a political economy and forms of civil society that support political equality. If we make economic and social policy in some sense secondary or instrumental to the goal of generating egalitarian empowerment and political equality, what's the result?

Once we ask this question, we find ourselves led toward a refinement of the idea of what it means to pursue justice by means of democracy. We uncover another design principle to guide this work across the three domains of political institutions, the economy, and civil society. There is more than one way to protect equal basic liberties, and some approaches are more likely than others to develop dynamics in the social and economic realms that support rather than undermine political equality. It turns out that the question we have to ask is this: What basic structure protects equal basic liberties (both positive and negative) in such a way as to generate social and economic dynamics that don't undermine those very liberties? Asking this will lead us, as we will see, to a new principle to assist with clarifying justice in the economic and social realms: "difference without domination." Our route to this additional principle is through a paradox that comes into view once one asks how economic and social domains can function in support of political equality and democracy.

The paradox goes like this. If societies protect basic rights like freedom of association and contract—which define both the social and economic domains and bring them into existence as evolutionary, self-governing systems based on free human interaction—they will necessarily end up with social difference. That's a great and beautiful result of freedom, but social difference also easily articulates with domination, caste society structures, and exploitation. There's no way to secure basic rights without also securing social difference, and so an obvious question emerges: How can we protect rights and foster the emergence of social difference yet avoid the articulation of that difference with structures of domination?[20] Similarly, if we protect the right to contract, the basic right to property, we will necessarily get economic structures that can articulate with domination, which is to say, with the kinds of inequalities that are disempowering of citizens. Protecting our basic rights quickly looks likely to result in undermining our pursuit of political equality. What are we going to do about that?

If we wish to unify protection of political equality and protection of the other basic liberties (on the principle of shared non-sacrificeability), we need to think about a principle to guide our rule-setting for the economic and social realms to avoid the emergence of domination. I call the relevant principle "difference without domination." In brief, the principle entails that we scrutinize our institutions to diagnose patterns of difference, work to ascertain whether they arise from or support domination, and, if they do, redesign the rules of governance through political institutions, the rules providing undergirding charters for the economy, the rules organizing the microinteractions of the economy,

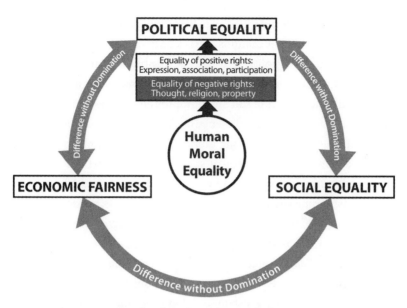

FIGURE 1 A virtuous circle: political equality as the ground of justice

or the organizational protocols of civil society, to remove or at least lessen the operating forces of domination. Many have debated whether discussions of justice should consist of substantive or procedural matters.[21] The argument I make here is that the job of rule-setting turns the procedural into the substantive, and that our rule-setting across all three domains (political, economic, and social) should be guided by the principle of difference without domination. This would permit us to establish a virtuous cycle linking political, social, and economic domains in support of the kind of human flourishing that rests on autonomy, both private and public.

Difference without Domination: A Deeper Dive into a Project of Vision Correction

The time has come to revisit the basic grounds for a theory of justice. As many have pointed out, Rawls's arguments are too dependent on an expectation of social homogeneity that drives key features of political life into the background of his consideration. That expectation is not merely a problem on the margins. It has a deep consequence. It supports Rawls's placement of political equality and public autonomy as secondary to the liberties supporting individual autonomy. As a theoretical matter, this is a nonviable starting point for any discussion of politics, defined as that activity is by dissensus.[22] As a practical matter, however, the insufficiency of this starting point shows itself with its most vivid immediacy in conditions of great social diversity, where public decisions will routinely impinge on most citizens' ability to deploy autonomy in fashioning their life courses. In such contexts, autonomy itself is accessible only through participation in the collective effort to shape the parameters of collective life. As W. E. B. Du Bois puts it in the first chapter of *The Souls of Black Folk*, "The power of the ballot we need in sheer self-defense—else what shall save us from a second slavery?" Du Bois's point is not merely instrumental. It is not merely that the power of the ballot blocks the re-emergence of a socioeconomic institution of slavery. It is also that the exercise of political power is itself an element of the intrinsically valuable experience of non-slavery, which is to say, of non-domination.

In my argument I depart from Rawls and follow Du Bois. I give the ancient and modern liberties equal weight, but this in turn means it is inadmissible for the dynamics in the social and economic realms to unfold in such a way as to abrogate the political liberties, or political equality, just as it is inadmissible for them to abrogate the rights that support private autonomy. We need a principle of strict scrutiny. When we protect the negative liberties of the moderns, are those protections compatible with simultaneous protection of the positive liberties of the ancients? The application of such a principle of strict scrutiny should permit us to bring the two kinds of liberty into alignment over time.

Here we reach the greatest challenge. It is precisely the type of rights protection that lies at the heart of protecting equal basic rights—and particularly the right to freedom of association—that generates forms of social and economic difference that often become a source of domination in any given society, ultimately coming to undermine pathways to political equality. We must confront the fact that our choices about *how* to protect the equal basic liberties always also affect the structure of the social and economic domains and vice versa.

Segregation is the easy, obvious example of the full entanglement of patterns of rights protection, the social sphere, and political economy. Jim Crow was defended on grounds of the need to protect freedom of association, an equal basic liberty. Yet from this ostensible protection of a basic liberty flowed a variety of forms of domination. A segregated society, for instance, undermines political equality by establishing patterns of domination and limited access to the levers of power. That said, it does not necessarily undermine private autonomy. This was in effect the meaning of the segregationists' argument that it should be possible to build two separate but equal worlds, an argument equally embraced by black power advocates. Surprisingly, and counter to Rawls's own stated view, the segregationist outlook is compatible with the Rawlsian notion that only the rights supporting private autonomy or liberty of conscience should be considered utterly sacrosanct. But once political liberties, and political equality, are also considered sacrosanct, then segregationist social structures are plainly revealed as antithetical to a just society. This example shows the importance of considering the political liberties as equal in importance to the liberties that protect private autonomy.

Moreover, Jim Crow's effects on the social structure of the United States in the first half of the twentieth century also laid down rigid patterns for the distribution of economic benefits. As economic productivity boomed in the mid-twentieth century, its fruits were distributed in patterns determined by the underlying allocations of land and labor controlled through segregation. In other words, the specific protection of an equal basic liberty attempted in the Jim Crow system established a basis for domination of some citizens by others across all three domains: social, political, and economic.[23]

Today, we would critique the case of segregation with the argument that, in fact, the Jim Crow system rested on only a false claim to protect a basic associational liberty. We would point out that in failing to protect the rights of African Americans, Mexican Americans, and Chinese Americans to move freely through society, the Jim Crow system was actually violating their rights of association while putatively protecting those of others. This is indeed the argument Rawls makes. Jim Crow may have been protecting the basic liberties of *some*, but it wasn't protecting *equal* basic liberty. One might therefore be tempted to say that in the era of Jim Crow, the only reason the patterns of domination sprang up in the social and economic realms was that *equal* basic liberties were not in fact protected. But this would be to miss another basic point about the equal basic liberties and their paradoxical potential to generate inegalitarian effects in both social and economic realms: Freedom to associate with those with whom we wish to associate simply is freedom to discriminate.[24] Freedom of association inevitably leads to social difference, and social difference has historically had a high likelihood of generating domination. Jim Crow rules were wrong *not only* because they exemplified a failure to protect freedom of association for all *but also* because they exemplified a case of protecting freedom of association in ways that undermined political equality. Jim Crow failed *not only* with regard to the requirement to protect negative liberties for all *but also* with regard to the requirement to protect positive liberties for all. The fundamental challenge of justice is to ascertain not only how to protect the equal basic liberties in ways that support political equality but, even more important, how to identify those modes of rights protection that will manifest themselves in emergent dynamics in the social and economic domains that are themselves supportive of political equality. Mine is a dynamic, not a static, picture of justice. I turn to that challenge now.

A fundamental expression of the right to free association is the right to marry whom one pleases. As people with a sense of affinity for one another pair up in marriages, they form the building block units of cultural homogeneity. Regardless of precisely how marriage markets are constituted in different historical and geographic contexts, they have typically generated distinguishable ethnic and cultural communities, and there is every reason to think that freedom of association is more likely to reinforce than to undermine that pattern. Scholars of social network theory have identified "homophily," the tendency of those who are like one another to flock together, as a basic building block of human social organization (Granovetter 1973). Even in an imagined world in which free association was protected not only from government intrusion but also from the limitations imposed by social sanction, there would still be every reason to think that homophily would drive the formation of distinguishable social groups.

And where there is social difference there can easily also be domination. Even without antipathy toward out-groups, members of social groups will often focus on gathering opportunities and resources for their own group, on the basis of nothing more than in-group preferences (Sidanius et al. 2008). Social differentiation, in other words, very often connects to opportunity hoarding and other efforts at resource control that can lead to the domination of some groups by others. At its most extreme, protection of free association can generate social differentiation that leads to caste societies, although these societies are marked by stiff social sanctions that in fact limit free association. The articulation of difference with domination in this fashion undermines a society's prospects for achieving political equality. Consequently, the goal of protecting political equality requires that we ask how we can have the social difference that flows from the protection of negative rights without also generating domination. How can we have difference without domination?

We know what difference *with* domination is. It is the situation in which patterns of social difference align such that some groups have active, or reserve, control over other groups. Difference without domination, therefore, identifies social patterning that does not eventuate in any group's having either direct or reserve control over another group, nor in any individual having direct or reserve control over another merely because of each party's social background. Difference without domination should be the principle guiding our choices about the basic structure, the laws and institutions that establish the basic rules of the game, for a society.

Protection of the equal basic liberties must be crafted in ways that ensure protection of those liberties not merely at some imaginary t_1 state of nature, when a society is founded, but also at $t_2, t_3, t_4,$ and so on, after social difference has developed settled patterns. Only such protections of the equal basic liberties can, in the end, count as protections. This is the point conveyed by figure 1 above. The idea is that human equality necessitates protections of the equal basic liberties, but these protections must themselves be crafted so as to align with the principle of difference without domination, if they are to succeed over time in protecting rather than undermining the equal basic liberties and political equality specifically. Protections of the equal basic liberties that are crafted in such a way as to fulfill the principle of achieving difference without domination in the social and economic domains should result in social equality and economic fairness and egalitarianism, cases I will make in the subsequent chapters. Here I will merely offer a preview.

What exactly is required of the principle of difference without domination in the social realm? How can we support social difference while disconnecting it from domination? The question is what is required of the basic structure, the fundamental political and social institutions, such that the social dynamics that emerge out of practices of free association do not articulate with hierarchy and domination and thereby undo the pathway to political equality?

The solution must lie in identifying features of the institutions of the basic structure that simultaneously protect free association and work against the development of phenomena like opportunity hoarding and group domination. These features of the institutions of the basic structure are those that permit and support difference, but without domination. We judge the institutions of the basic structure, then, for their likelihood of spurring difference without domination. I encapsulate the features of the basic structure that can make the relevant difference under a subsidiary ideal of "connected society" institutions.

Scholars of social capital distinguish among three kinds of social ties: bonding, bridging, and linking. Bonding ties are those (generally strong) connections that bind kin, close friends, and social similars to one another; bridging ties are those (generally weaker) ties that connect people across demographic cleavages (age, race, class, occupation, religion, and the like); finally, linking ties are the vertical connections between people at different levels of a status hierarchy, as in, for instance, the employment context (Granovetter 1973; Szreter and Woolcock 2004). As I will argue in chapter 4, an associational ecosystem that maximizes bridging ties should minimize the likelihood that social difference articulates with domination (Allen 2016a). Constructing an associational ecosystem that achieves this requires focusing on all of the policies that impact the use of land and space: transportation, housing, zoning, districting (including both for political representation and for education), public accommodations, and communications infrastructure (which affects spatiotemporal experiences). The question of how space and land use are organized affects whether the protection of the right to association will, over time, support or undermine the equal basic liberties, including among these the very right of association itself. In other words, more already existing policies may be directly germane to basic rights protection than we often realize. The standard of aspiring to achieve difference without domination does not necessarily generate a need for new policies or services. Instead, it requires a review of current policies across domains of social policy (transportation policy, housing policy, education policy, health policy, etc.) with a view to assessing how those current policies protect (or fail to protect) equal basic liberties. Where they fail either to protect equal basic liberties or to pass a strict scrutiny test for the achievement of difference without domination, then we have found places where we need to adjust our policies. Whereas many of our current policy domains are structured by a picture of justice that depends fundamentally on a focus on the distribution of material goods, I advocate an alternative approach to a policy review based instead on a picture of justice that depends fundamentally on political equality, or egalitarian empowerment.

A "connected society" is one where people can enjoy the bonds of solidarity and community but are equally engaged in the "bridging" work of bringing diverse communities into positive relations. It is one where people also individually desire and succeed at forming personally valuable relationships across boundaries of difference. By recognizing that we should choose strategies for protecting the equal basic liberties that also accord with the principle of difference without domination, we bring a heightened salience to policy areas that have long gone overlooked. The goal of acting in this policy space would be the cultivation of an associational ecosystem in which people do have the opportunity to choose their associates in order to realize their personal visions of the good life but also find themselves *routinely interacting* with those whom they have not, so to speak, chosen, and *routinely obliged to share power* in a variety of public contexts with these unchosen others.

If a connected society is the subsidiary ideal to be developed via application of the principle of difference without domination to the social realm, what accompanying subsidiary ideal captures the application of this principle to the economic realm? In the economic realm, the focus of policy-making generally falls not on land but on labor and capital. Thus, Rawls's difference principle—that any unequal distribution of material goods among members of a polity must in some sense redound to the benefit of the worst-off—is usually taken as a justification of redistributive tax policy. The expectation is that institutions that protect equal basic liberties will result in economies in which the rewards of productivity accrue differentially to the owners of capital, the managers, and the laborers. Such a result is acceptable, argues Rawls, but only as long as the benefits accruing to the owners and managers are in some fashion beneficial to the worst-off, as, for instance, when the managers' work raises the productivity of the whole economy and the standard of living for the worst-off, even as that group falls farther behind the owners and managers in income or wealth or both. In other words, Rawls acknowledges that in the economic realm, as in the social realm, we can assume that the protection of equal basic liberties will generate difference.[25] *Difference* is another word for "inequality," in a Rawlsian vocabulary, and with the difference principle Rawls provides us with a tool to steer away from illegitimate forms of inequality.

Yet if we ask instead the question of how we could build an economy that achieves difference without domination, we evaluate economic outcomes with a somewhat different lens. Patterns of material inequality are assessed with a view to whether they undermine the political empowerment of the citizenry. As we shall see in chapter 6, thinkers throughout the ages have considered an egalitarian economy, generating a strong middle class, a necessary foundation for the sustainability of constitutional democracy. This shift in focus—from questions simply of distribution to questions of the linkages between political economy and empowerment of the citizens—helps policy makers see not only the best-off and the worst-off but also everybody in between. Relatedly, some efforts to fulfill the requirements of the difference principle, by directing material benefit to the least well-off, may simultaneously erode the political capacity of the least well-off specifically, and the democratic citizenry generally, in cases where disempowering forms of dependency emerge. In such cases, the principle of difference without domination would suggest that we should find an alternative path to fulfillment of our material needs, one that does not sacrifice political liberties.

The application of the principle of difference without domination in the social realm led to a subsidiary ideal of a "connected society." In the economic realm, application of this overarching principle leads to a subsidiary ideal of an "empowering economy." As in the social realm, in the economic realm too, the standard of aspiring to achieve difference without domination does not necessarily generate a need for new domains of policy or services. Instead, it requires a review of current policies across domains of economic policy (e.g., labor policy, trade policy, the organization of the firm) with a view to assessing how those current policies protect (or fail to protect) equal basic liberties, positive as well as negative.[26] Where they fail to protect equal basic liberties or to pass a strict scrutiny test for the achievement of difference without domination, we find places where we need to adjust our policies. Whereas many of our current approaches to economic policy are structured by a picture of justice that focuses first and foremost on the distribution of material goods, I advocate an alternative approach to a policy review based instead on a picture of justice that depends fundamentally on political equality, or egalitarian empowerment. Again, use of a strict scrutiny approach with the difference without domination principle is of value here.

As we will see in chapter 6, when we apply this principle to the economic realm, four issues quickly emerge as salient: (1) the organization and operation of the firm and the experience of labor within it, and the necessity of building a world on the basis of "free labor"; (2) the impact of economic distribution on access to political voice and influence; (3) the relation between structures of production and the relative degree of inequality in pretax distributions of income; and (4) the question of whether the distributive shape of the contemporary economy itself relies on forms of decision-making that embed domination within them, for instance through technocratic decision-making that is excessively insulated from democratic accountability.

One other point must also be made about how the "difference without domination" principle affects consideration of economic justice. How we protect our equal basic liberties has an impact on economic outcomes not only directly, with regard to how firms operate or who wields power over economic decisions, but also indirectly, via our social structures. Recall, again, the example of segregation. That type of social structure itself eventuates in specific inegalitarian patterns in the distribution of material goods. If we seek economic egalitarianism, the application of the principle of difference without domination in the social realm is as important as in the economic realm. Particularly in conditions of pluralism, we can achieve an egalitarian economy that features difference without domination only if the underlying pluralistic social structure is also egalitarian. The emergence of a connected society in the social realm can be expected, in the inverse of the situation with segregation, to have more egalitarian impacts on patterns in the distribution of economic resources (see chap. 4).

The principle of difference without domination, considered with reference to immigration policy, gives us a further way of clarifying how social and economic realms are linked. In the US, the declining political power of labor—now broadly recognized as one of the main drivers of increasing income and wealth inequality in the late twentieth century—is itself a consequence of accepting incorporation into the labor force of approximately eleven million undocumented immigrants who have no rights to political participation (McCarty, Poole, and Rosenthal 2006). Their voices do not contribute to shaping policy, with plain results in the skewing of policy outcomes toward the interests of those who are financially better-off than they. A focus on political equality gives us more purchase on the challenges facing the pursuit of economic egalitarianism than does Rawls's difference principle. In addition, recognition of this linkage between the economy, political equality, and immigration will require that, along the way to fleshing out the ideals of a connected society and empowering economies, we also identify a subsidiary ideal to guide our thinking about membership in the polity and immigration. To this end, in chapter 5, I develop the subsidiary ideal of "polypolitanism," an ideal for enhancing political voice by activating the multiple memberships within political units that any given person will have.

Power-Sharing Liberalism

Mine is by no means the first effort to point out the entanglements, whether actual or potential, of liberal political philosophy with the problem of domination. Over the past three decades, critical race, settler-colonial, feminist, agonistic, and Marxist theories have all leveled challenges against liberal political philosophy on the grounds that its philosophical tradition is not accidentally but necessarily supportive of racial and patriarchal forms of domination. Some of these challenges focus on how liberal political systems have withheld rights from members of minority groups or others in a position of subordination. Some challenges have focused on how the social and economic differences that emerge from rights protection have come to articulate with domination over time. I agree with many of these critiques that liberalism as practiced in the eighteenth, nineteenth, and twentieth centuries accepted the continuation of domination. The difference between these other lines of criticism and my own comes in, however, with regard to the path taken once the problems are recognized.

Other critiques of the close connection between liberalism and patterns of domination have often resulted in efforts to set aside liberalism as such. My project instead is a reconstruction of a liberal theory—a theory of democracy, justice, and basic rights protection—on grounds incompatible with domination generally and racial domination specifically. The identification of the principle of *difference without domination* as a necessary entailment of the commitment to protect negative and positive liberties *simultaneously* and *for all* provides a new starting point for liberal political philosophy—one intended to enable a comprehensive reconstruction of liberal political philosophy on a ground of non-domination. "Difference without domination" is a more strenuously egalitarian principle than the Rawlsian "difference principle." It requires the sharing of power across all three domains—political, social, and economic. It also establishes a higher standard for our decisions about how we protect our equal basic liberties and identifies a larger swath of the policy landscape as pertinent to equal basic liberties. In seeking to establish a new foundation for liberalism that rules out domination, I introduce what might be called "power-sharing liberalism." Liberalism based on a principle of full inclusion and non-domination involves not just the protection of negative liberties for all but also the full protection of positive liberties, hence broad power sharing across political, social, and economic institutions.

Once we see the linkage between the social and economic realms, in relation to the application of the difference without domination principle on behalf of political equality, we can finally glimpse the true import of placing equal emphasis on public and private autonomy, on positive and negative liberties, on political equality and personal freedom. When the goal of a theory of justice is, above all, to protect private autonomy and the capacity of individuals to pursue the good life as they define it, questions of social structure are often seen as separate from the economy and politics. In Rawls's effort to single out private experience as the thing that justice ought especially to protect, he failed to attend to the necessary economic and political consequences of how our private, social spaces are structured on account of the operations of our public life.

Critics from Susan Okin to G. A. Cohen have pointed this out: Okin by emphasizing how Rawls disregarded issues of justice in the family, Cohen by arguing that Rawls failed to attend to the issues of justice inherent in our choices of jobs. The connections among the social, economic, and political realms are invisible only to actors whose private experiences have not generally been impinged upon by either the political or the economic realm—namely, those in the cultural or political majority or a position of economic privilege. In contrast, minoritarian viewpoints are defined by the permanent salience of the mutual entanglement of the political, the social, and the economic. Since politics is defined by pluralism—regardless of the empirical degree of social heterogeneity in any given polity—a complete theory of justice must incorporate the view from a minoritarian position. In the "veil of ignorance" thought experiment, Rawls's *Theory of Justice* not only defines specific situated perspectives—those of women, for instance, or racial minorities—out of the account of justice; it also defines a minoritarian perspective *as such* (i.e., *abstractly understood*)—that is, a perspective at odds with a majority perspective—out of his account of justice. The whole point of coming to consensus in the veil of ignorance is that at some fundamental level minoritarian perspectives are dissolved (Mills 1997). In contrast, a truly universal theory of justice will incorporate this minoritarian viewpoint and therefore start from an acknowledgment of the full and permanent entanglement of private and public autonomy, and from recognition of the intrinsic value of political equality, alongside personal freedom, just as W. E. B. Du Bois could see. The result is power-sharing liberalism.

While political scientists have elaborated a picture of a power-sharing politics in the consociational regimes of the Netherlands and Lebanon, that picture of power sharing has been group-based. Power is shared among religious or ethnic groups, and individual rights are constrained by group-based rights. Here in *Justice by Means of Democracy* I argue, in contrast, for power sharing as a concept that pertains to each and every individual in a democratic society. Power is shared broadly across individuals, regardless of social background. Power sharing flows from the protection of individual rights.

Difference without Domination: From Design Principles to Rules for Action

Before I turn to a fuller elaboration of the subsidiary ideals and their policy implications in the following chapters, it is worth reflecting again on how the pragmatist methodology provides a framework for making use of design principles. I return again to William James's idea that beliefs are rules for action. Our beliefs about justice translate into design principles for human social organization and behavior, and these in turn are operationalized in concrete laws and social norms. We can make this relationship between a design principle and legal rules concrete with regard to the principle of difference without domination by drawing on an example of a specific legal rule from a policy-making setting that implicitly adheres to this design principle. This rule has emerged from the realm of civil society through ongoing legal experimentalism in the policy domain of housing.

The US has a law called the Fair Housing Act that prohibits landlords from discriminating when they rent to tenants. That law has within it an exemption known as "Mrs. Murphy's exception." This is the rule that if you're, for instance, an Irish American woman named Mrs. Murphy, you have a building with four or fewer units, and you live in the building and want to rent only to other Irish Americans, your discrimination is permissible. The notion appears to be that the scale of Mrs. Murphy's enterprise is small enough to give us confidence that this kind of discrimination will not, in aggregate, result in systemic domination that hinders equal protection of the laws. Mrs. Murphy's exception accepts that the right of association generates difference and sets an outer boundary on where difference would begin to turn into domination—in a building of larger than four units. Here we see how the principle of difference without domination manifests in the form of a legal rule.

Interestingly, this sort of limit on the right to association, out of a principle of avoiding difference that attaches to domination, has emerged in other domains of law too, not because of design but as a principle emergent from practice. For instance, in small business law, businesses below a certain number of employees—the precise number varies in the US from state to state but tends to be in the range of sixteen to eighteen people—are exempt from nondiscrimination employment law. Or we could state it the other way around: the right of association, which spawns difference, can be protected up to the point at which it also spawns domination—here, in firms that exceed eighteen people in scale. I take this small business case exemption to discrimination law also to be an example of an implicit application of the principle of difference without domination. Our legislators and jurists appear to have made the judgment that the discrimination in these cases operates below a level that would produce systemic domination and that it results from the worthy protection of other basic rights, such as the right of association. These examples show how a design principle (difference without domination) can manifest in practices: as laws and norms.

The legal practitioners who devised these compromises were not working self-consciously with the principle of seeking to secure difference without domination. But now that we have articulated that principle, we can do just that. Pursuing justice by means of democracy requires ascertaining what specific applications—in the form of laws, rules, or norms—follow from our guiding design principles, including the principle of difference without domination, across the domains of political institutions, the economy, and civil society. The goal is to translate from the overarching design principles of the shared non-sacrificeability of negative and positive liberties, the five facets of political equality, and difference without domination to applications in the form of legal rules and social norms as specific as Mrs. Murphy's exception. To achieve this translation, we need to equip ourselves with subsidiary ideals for each of the three core domains of human life (political, economic, and social). Each subsidiary ideal is a domain-specific version of the guiding design principles. The subsidiary ideals then help us identify further domain-specific design principles that should be used to direct the strategic and tactical work of shaping legal rules and norms in the political, social, and economic realms. The tactics that will be found in particular places at particular times will be various. Thus, the overarching ideal of justice, the overarching design principle of difference without domination, and the domain-specific ideals will be universal, but they do not generate a single blueprint for institutions or human practices that might be derived abstractly in an a priori fashion or in an imagined original position. Instead, translated via design principles, these ideals are used to generate context-specific norms and rules that might realize the ideals in specific contexts of application. The moment of translation to context and the expectation that those translations will be various are necessary elements of understanding what is demanded by justice, on my account.[27] The rules for action of pragmatism, then, bridge universalizing theory with context-specific rules and norms through acts of translation.

The subsidiary ideal for each of the three domains describes the kind of world that would ideally exist in each domain, if our three domains of human life are to be able to function together to generate a virtuous circle sustaining difference without domination, political equality, positive and negative liberties, and therefore human flourishing and justice.[28] Tables 2 and 3 (p. 14) capture the overarching structure of the argument. The subsidiary ideals provide a foundation of principle from which flows the further work of organizing the powers of government and the structure of society and the economy.

As we have seen and as I will detail more fully in the chapters to come, justice by means of democracy is realized by pursuing our three design principles, including the principle of difference without domination. This effort will manifest as an orientation toward four subsidiary social ideals: in the political realm, an ideal of egalitarian participatory constitutional democracy; in the realm of civil society, an ideal of a connected society; in the realm of rules of political membership, an ideal of polypolitanism; and in the economic realm, an ideal of empowering economies. Table 3 (p. 14) provides an anticipatory look at where the argument is headed.

Our next job, taken chapter by chapter, is to spell out these subsidiary ideals and the domain-specific design principles that follow from them. They will, then, provide a framework that may be used by policy makers across a variety of specific domains of policy. Although the ideal for rules of membership in the polity is logically prior to the ideals for political, social, and economic domains, I will present each of the four subsidiary ideals in the order in which I came to understand them. The design principle of difference without domination is more immediately accessible to us in relation to our preexisting understandings of the realm of political institutions and civil society than in relation to the domains of membership in the polity and the economy. I have chosen, therefore, to order the chapters by articulating the subsidiary ideal for each domain in a sequence of increasing difficulty, or novelty. I start by exploring what difference without domination entails for political institutions and then turn to what it requires for the structure and functioning of civil society. Then I apply the principle to development of a subsidiary ideal for membership in any given democratic polity. Then I turn to how the principle should shape our understanding of a subsidiary ideal for the economic realm. The theory of justice I articulate here ultimately supports a political economy aligned with power-sharing liberalism. Like other liberalisms, this theory of justice starts from a protection of basic rights, but because it seeks to protect positive liberties as strenuously as negative liberties, this liberalism, and the political economy that flows from it, must constantly attend to the achievement of forms of social and economic relationship that support political equality. The insistence on attention to relationships and power drive a re-embedding of economic policy in social contexts. Chapter 6 will culminate our exploration by investigating how political economy would be reshaped once we understand justice as best pursued by means of democracy and what the full contours of a power-sharing liberalism would be. Finally, in chapter 7, I will take up the implications of the argument for how we understand civic agency and the civic life of individuals. We will by then have come full circle. Having started with the fact that our most recent paradigms of political economy have been upended by politics, we will have worked our way, starting from an underlying theory of justice, to a new framework of political economy from which to pose questions to economists, as well as a new understanding of the agency of ordinary people and why it matters.

PART II

Subsidiary Ideals of
Justice for Each Domain

3

The First Subsidiary Ideal

EGALITARIAN PARTICIPATORY CONSTITUTIONAL DEMOCRACY

Introduction

Justice, I have argued, is best pursued by means of democracy. Treating political liberties as a non-sacrificeable element of the basic liberties to be protected means seeking to achieve difference without domination across the three core domains of human society: political institutions, civil society, and the economy. Of course, those domains are fully integrated with one another; the challenge is to set rules for each, none of which undermines basic liberties in the others. Importantly, the rule-setting occurs both through political institutions and through the evolution of social norms and cultural understandings of horizons of value. The importance of emergent forms of social organization, however, should not obscure the fundamental role of political institutions in setting rules for both civil society generally and the economy specifically.[1] Political institutions deliver the law of association that gives civil society its structure; they also charter corporations and independent central banks, as well as establishing rules of membership and immigration that constitute the structure of labor markets. The responsibilities of political institutions are significant. How political institutions function is fundamental to the health of society, including its social and economic dimensions.

In order for political institutions to deliver on a conception of justice where the positive or political liberties are non-sacrificeable, they must be democratic; they must channel dissensus, or difference, without its being converted into domination. This chapter takes up our first subsidiary ideal: justice by means of democracy requires that in the political realm we create an *egalitarian participatory constitutional democracy*.

An egalitarian participatory constitutional democracy is not defined simply by majority vote. It is instead defined by mechanisms of participation—a tool kit that includes but is not limited to majority vote. This tool kit must give the citizenry final control over collective decision-making. Typically, the anchor of this popular control is the requirement that government decision makers must face elections wherein they gain or retain decision-making rights by winning a vote among eligible voters through majority or plurality rule, with a presumption that the franchise approaches universal adult suffrage among legal citizens.[2]

Many people's first instinct is to define democracy as a matter of making decisions by majority vote, but this is incorrect and raises the specter of the domination of minorities by majorities. In offering such a definition, people make a mistake of "synecdoche": they take a part to stand in for the whole. Majority vote is just one mechanism for operationalizing popular sovereignty. It is one among many mechanisms that might be used for ensuring both that the whole body of the citizenry is steering or setting the direction of the polity and that power has been equalized within the polity. Minority-protecting mechanisms—and we'll look at specific examples later on—are just as important as majority vote. This tool kit of mechanisms—both majoritarian and minority-protecting ones—must be refined and redesigned over time to respond to demographic changes that constantly impact the balance of power within the citizenry. In my definition of democracy, the *steering function of the people taken as a whole*—incorporating minorities as well as majorities in that steering—is the core element making democracy, democracy. In order to preserve over time the steering function of the people taken as a whole and to support dissensus without domination, a democracy will have within it mechanisms to undo efforts of subsets of the democratic population to develop monopolistic control over political institutions.

Democracy, then, consists first of institutions that give to the people as a whole—defined to include all permanent residents of the polity—a capacity to steer the direction of the polity. It consists also of institutions that counter and check the emergence of concentrations of power, whether of wealth holders, social majorities, social minorities, technocratic elites, or demagogues. More simply, a democracy exists when the people steer and when efforts to co-opt power from ordinary people can be blocked. In the vocabulary of the *Federalist Papers*, democracy succeeds when it both provides *energy* for the successful exercise of power based on popular sovereignty and delivers *republican safety* to ward off domination, that is, the co-optation of political institutions by interest groups or factions or the repersonalization of power by specific politicians.[3]

The design principles for egalitarian participatory constitutional democracy are (1) that power is depersonalized through governance processes that leave final decisions of accountability in the hands of the whole people; (2) that the depersonalization of power is also accomplished through mechanisms for checking and balancing different emergent sources of potentially monopolistic power; (3) that political institutions incorporate all permanent residents of the polity via open and accessible channels of participation in decision-making processes; and (4) that the mechanisms of governance deliver both energy and republican safety such that the will of the people can be discerned and implemented while basic liberties (both positive and negative) are consistently protected for all citizens. The last point requires that the people's power always exceed the power of the executive. Importantly, the people can maintain this power only by preserving healthy legislatures and norms of cooperation among themselves. In fragmentation, their power dissipates.

In what follows, I will provide a fuller explanation of these four design principles for egalitarian participatory constitutional democracy: (1) depersonalization through accountability mechanisms, (2) depersonalization through checking and balancing of countervailing powers,

(3) inclusion, and (4) energy and republican safety. These four design principles were not discovered simultaneously, and I present them in an order intended to make their historical sequence visible. Along the way, I will draw on examples from the US, and explications in the *Federalist Papers*, to show how the drafters of the US Constitution attempted to operationalize these principles and how they might be revisited now. The drafters of that instrument for organizing the powers of government knew that what they had designed would need redesign over time.[4] The solutions they developed in trying to fulfill the design principles of depersonalization, energy, and republican safety may not be the solutions we need now in new demographic circumstances. And they failed to include a principle of full inclusion in the basic design parameters for the institutions that they erected. Nonetheless, reference to the design challenges they sketched—and those they overlooked, such as inclusion—can clarify the kind of inquiry we should bring to reforming our political institutions in the present. Where our institutions do not deliver depersonalization, inclusion, energy, and republican safety, we have work to do. After I lay out the content of these design principles, which specify the subsidiary ideal of egalitarian participatory constitutional democracy, I will conclude with some brief reflections on what the idea that justice is best pursued by means of democracy means for dealing with nondemocratic states.

Depersonalizing Power

When the term "democracy" was first coined in ancient Greece, it stood in contrast to terms like "dynasty," "aristocracy," "oligarchy," and "monarchy." A "dynast" was someone who held power. A literal translation of that word is simply "powerholder." An aristocracy was a regime in which the "best" or "noblest" had control. An oligarchy was a form of political system in which a few people ("oligoi") ruled, and a monarchy was a system in which one person ruled. A democracy, in contrast, was one in which the "demos," the ordinary people or the mass, had power or strength and control ("kratos"), not the elites. The contrast drawn by the Greeks, from Herodotus to Aristotle, essentially focused on class divisions within society and the question of which class held sufficient control to steer the direction of the polity: the rich or the poor. Even in the Roman Republic, which aspired to be a mixed constitution balancing the interests of elite and ordinary citizens, the concept of the "public good" (or the res publica) incorporated the idea that the society had class divisions that required synthesis. Only with early modern philosophers like Thomas Hobbes, John Locke, and those who followed them in developing state of nature and social contract theories, did the idea of "the people" expand to incorporate all the members of the polity, conceived as participating together as a collective agent to steer the direction of the polity (Allen 2004, chap. 6).

Whether "the people" refers to the poorest and most numerous citizens and residents or to the entirety of a populace, democracy depersonalizes power. Its institutions make it impossible to attribute specific outcomes to specific individuals. This does not, however, mean that its operations must be impersonal. To the contrary, democracies depend on collective organizing and collective processes—from committees to assemblies—that require a high volume of personal, human interaction. But identifying where power finally resides in a democracy is and should be a challenge. In a successfully functioning democratic regime, it ceases to be possible to designate with an individual's name who finally holds the reins of power. This contrasts to monarchies, oligarchies, aristocracies, and autocracies. To build a democracy, designers of the political institutions that structure the polity must achieve this depersonalization of power. Indeed, the phrase "popular sovereignty" is just another way of naming this depersonalization.

The idea of the people understood not as the poor masses but as a "committee of the whole" for the polity delivered to our era the conception of popular sovereignty and depersonalized political power pithily captured in the second sentence of the Declaration of Independence. Here it is for a second time:

We hold these truths to be self-evident, that all men are created equal, that they are endowed by their Creator with certain unalienable Rights, that among these are Life, Liberty and the pursuit of Happiness,—That to secure these rights, Governments are instituted among Men, deriving their just powers from the consent of the governed,—That whenever any Form of Government becomes destructive of these ends, it is the Right of the People to alter or to abolish it, and to institute new Government, laying its foundation on such principles and organizing its powers in such form, as to them shall seem most likely to effect their Safety and Happiness.

This sentence provides us with a basic definition of constitutional democracy in which popular sovereignty and depersonalized power are secure. A synopsis might run as follows: The purpose of government is to secure basic rights. These include both negative and positive liberties, with the positive liberties evident in the requirement that final decisions about the direction of the polity always revert back to "the people" or the citizenry as a whole. The process of establishing and organizing a government depends on mechanisms that give the citizenry as a whole permanent steering authority ("consent"), in such a fashion as permits the people also to maintain functioning political institutions over time. Functioning political institutions are those capable of delivering "safety and happiness." In case governments become destructive of the end of securing rights, the mechanisms of constitutional democracy must equip the people with the capacity to achieve course corrections. Those mechanisms, in other words, must support both stability and adaptability. This sentence lays out the case for the pursuit of justice by means of democracy, arguing that popular sovereignty (or the depersonalization of power) is valuable not only for its own sake (qua "liberty") but also as a method by which the people can consistently steer over time toward the "safety and happiness" of the people as a whole. Democracy—that is, popular sovereignty—is not antithetical to justice but the best vehicle for delivering it. As either James Madison or Alexander Hamilton put it in *Federalist* 51, "Justice is the end of government. It is the end of civil society."

To understand how democracy depersonalizes power, we first have to understand the elements of power.[5] Leaving aside for the moment the administration of justice and focusing only on the legislative and executive functions of governance, the basic elements of political decision-making are as follows: (1) discovery or diagnosis of social circumstances that require correction or improvement via collective action; (2) decision about which principles should guide collective decisions and which modes of organizing the powers of government (policies and laws) should be employed; (3) development of specific prescriptions or proposed courses of action; (4) deliberation and decision on those possible pathways; (5) dissemination of decisions taken with regard to framing principles and recommendations for how to organize the powers of government; (6) implementation of those decisions; and (7) review of the effects of that implementation and a return to the beginning of the cycle, with the work of diagnosis and discovery. Those seven steps are the elements of governance in the domains of legislative and executive power. Steps 1–4 capture the responsibilities of the legislative power; steps 5 and 6 capture the formal responsibilities of the executive power. While the citizenry of ancient Athens gathered in the assembly to carry out steps 1–5 directly, they assigned steps 6 and 7 to officials sometimes selected by election and sometimes selected by sortition, or lottery (*Federalist* 51, 63; Lane 2020). They held these officials accountable at the ends of their terms of office through a procedure called the *euthuna*. All officials had to present their accounts—explain how in the course of their efforts to enact their duties they had spent the money allocated to them. Severe penalties awaited those who were found to have misused funds. The opportunity to scrutinize the accounts of officeholders gave the citizenry of Athens final authority over the direction of the city. The democratic citizens of ancient Athens held onto their power to steer their city through a blend of direct action in a "committee of the whole," their assembly on the Pnyx Hill, and also through mechanisms of representation and accountability for officeholders.

The institutional mechanisms of egalitarian participatory constitutional democracy must provide processes for all the elements of political decision-making needed for governance. The great discovery of the early modern period was that the mechanism of representation and accountability could be used across the whole of the governance process, without undercutting the placement of final authority in the hands of the people. All that was necessary to maintain power in the hands of the people was elections at a rate frequent enough that officeholders would always understand themselves to have to answer to popular opinion. Named officeholders would be held to account, so they would always hold power only in trust; it would belong to the people, who could recall it at relatively frequent fixed points. This arrangement, early modern philosophers recognized, would serve to depersonalize power and thereby establish popular sovereignty. In the *Federalist Papers*, Alexander Hamilton labels this design feature "due dependence" on popular will (*Federalist* 31, 70, 77).

The second discovery used to depersonalize power was the design principle of checks and balances. The necessary mechanisms of egalitarian participatory constitutional democracy include not only those through which "the people" as a whole might choose a direction for the polity but also mechanisms to achieve a balancing of powers as officeholders conduct their work. The American founders famously followed the French Enlightenment philosopher Charles-Louis de Secondat, Baron de La Brède et de Montesquieu, in designing the institutions of the federal government to divide legislative, executive, and judicial powers, and to establish mechanisms such that administrators and officeholders in those branches, servants of the people responsible for specific phases of political decision-making, might check and balance each other, thereby preventing any particular officeholder from accruing enough power to take over the whole system. The list of checking-and-balancing mechanisms they embedded in the Constitution itself to equalize the power held by different officeholders is extensive. Among them are the following provisions:

- No person can hold two offices at the same time (limits reach of potential bribery by appointment).

- No senator, representative, or other officeholder can be an elector in the Electoral College.
- No change can be made to presidential pay after an election.
- Presidential veto requires a two-thirds vote in Congress to overrule (qualified negative).
- Senatorial advice and consent is required for treaties (as force of resistance to personal temptations).
- Senatorial confirmation is required for many appointments.
- The House of Representatives has a set number of members who serve two-year terms; this creates a body that can combine adequate local knowledge with opportunity to learn about national conditions.
- States can determine the time, manner, and place of elections, but so can Congress, with the exception of the place of election of senators.
- During the period of the early republic, the census was connected to the states' tax burdens as well as to representation; this meant any incentive to inflate numbers to increase representation was counteracted by a desire not to have to contribute too much to the national budget: the mechanism generated counteracting incentives.
- Congress has the power of the purse, the "most compleat and effectual weapon with which any constitution can arm the immediate representatives of the people."
- Concurrence of opinion on legislation is required between the Senate and the House; this means that laws can be passed only when both a majority of the people (via representation in the House) and a majority of the states (via representation in the Senate) agree.
- Lawmakers are subject to their own laws.

But the practice of developing procedures that check and balance, and thereby equalize power, is not restricted to constitutional mechanisms. It is also an ordinary part of governance. For each of the seven steps of governance (diagnosis, values and powers clarification, pre-scription, deliberation and decision, dissemination, implementation, and review), there will usually be dissensus and contestation. The mechanisms for accomplishing each of these steps must be designed to balance the powers of competing interests and to block monopolization of power over the process by any given faction. Any number of mechanisms are needed to achieve a balance of powers and voices in these seven phases of governance. These include the use of delegation to committees, engagement of stakeholders, opportunities for public comment, deliberation, a diversity of techniques for structuring that deliberation, and a host of decision-making procedures, from lottery[6] to majority vote to supermajority vote to decision by consensus to delegation to a single, specific officeholder required to take advice from other officeholders or required not only to take their advice but also to win their consent ("advise and consent" procedures).[7] Balancing mechanisms such as these—in an infinite variety of combinations—are necessary to equalize voices and power in governance processes, and to achieve political institutions that meet the standard of difference without domination. In addition to structuring opportunities for an equality of voice and power, these mechanisms also provide the instruments by which democracy maximizes its epistemic power, integrating the knowledge resources of the population and melding it with the knowledge of experts and thereby achieving epistemic egalitarianism (e.g., *Federalist* 10, 53; cf. Ober 2008, 2017; Farrell and Shalizi 2015).

The founders of American constitutional democracy established as the intellectual foundation for the new enterprise the idea that "the people," encompassing the whole citizenry, should be the governing authority. Of course, their citizenry was itself limited and did not include all people. What they achieved, however, was a set of institutions to depersonalize power and give an actor called "the people," exclusionary though it was, the capacity to steer political decision-making. They achieved this assignment of power to "the people" via the combined mechanism of representation and routine elections and also through mechanisms to balance the powers of different officeholders.

The task of depersonalizing power did not end there, however. There was further work to be done to detach power from the interests of any particular section or faction within the country. Though they were focused on achieving power for "the people" as a whole, they did not neglect the ancient preoccupation with the division of any given population into classes based on economic interest, or other cleavages. They recognized both a division between the wealthy and propertied and everyone else and divisions among the interests of different parts of the economy—for instance, the agricultural and the commercial interests. They also recognized geographical or sectional interests. As early as 1776, they understood and had to take account of the conflict between the enslaving South and mercantile North, not to mention the distinct interests of each of the original thirteen states.[8] In making the case that legitimate political institutions would rest on depersonalizing mechanisms that make popular sovereignty real, they also designed their institutions to achieve a balancing of powers among the different kinds of demographically specific interests in the polity.

The framers designed mechanisms to balance rural and urban interests and those of rich and poor. The relevant power-balancing mechanisms included minority-protecting mechanisms. The purpose of the different modes of representation in the Senate and the House of Representatives was to give more weight to less-populous states in the Senate and to counterbalance that with more weight for the populous states in the House. That same principle flowed to the Electoral College, which is constituted with a number of electors that combines the number of each state's senators and representatives. The goal of this plan to balance rural and urban was to make it impossible to say that any one of these sections in particular held final authority in the polity. Each sectional interest would contribute to contests that would yield results that could not be fully claimed by any section in particular. No outcome would ever look exactly like what any party had initially proposed. Thus, all would share in co-ownership of the polity's political institutions and decisions.

The important point here is that for co-ownership, not only majoritarian but also minority-protecting mechanisms are necessary—both the Electoral College and the structure of the Senate are examples. But such mechanisms must be refined and redesigned over time in response to demographic changes that constantly impact the balance of power within the citizenry. If the minority-protecting mechanisms are too strong—as is currently the case with the Electoral College, which now overweights less-populous states—then an injustice is done to the majority. This has led many to call for the abolition of the Electoral College. But a better solution than to abolish an important minority-protecting mechanism would be both to increase the size of the House of Representatives and to allow electors to be appointed proportionally based on each candidate's share of the state's popular vote, rather than on a winner-take-all basis. This would reweight the minority-protecting mechanism such that a functional equilibrium would be preserved for the system as a whole, with reasonable degrees of protection afforded to both majorities and minorities.

If depersonalization of power was a process supported by the structure of institutions, it also was understood to require support from important norms of democratic governance. These mechanisms of depersonalization also incentivized movement toward norms of collaboration. When checks and balances fragment power, collaborating with others to form alliances is necessary, both to achieve influence and to get almost anything done. In the national government, the legislative and executive branches each need the other; in the original conception, this reliance was expected to spark mutual toleration and forbearance. Political scientists Daniel Ziblatt and Daniel Levitsky define the norms of mutual toleration and forbearance as, respectively, "the understanding that competing parties accept one another as legitimate rivals" and "the idea that politicians should exercise restraint in deploying their institutional prerogatives" (Levitsky and Ziblatt 2019, 8). Hamilton names this limit to the powers of officeholders and sectional interests, as well as the need to adhere to norms of collaboration, "due responsi-bility" (*Federalist* 70, 77). George Washington tries to argue this norm into existence across his letters to officeholders, for instance in this let-ter to Alexander Hamilton:

> Differences in political opinions are as unavoidable as, to a certain point, they may perhaps be necessary; but it is to be regretted, exceed-ingly, that subjects cannot be discussed with temper on the one hand, or decisions submitted to without having the motives which led to them, improperly implicated on the other: and this regret borders on chagrin when we find that Men of abilities—zealous patriots—having the same *general* objects in view, and the same upright intentions to prosecute them, will not exercise more charity in deciding on the opin-ions, & actions of one another. When matters get to such lengths, the natural inference is, that both sides have strained the Cords beyond their bearing—and that a middle course would be found the best, until experience shall have pointed out the right mode—or, which is not to be expected, because it is denied to mortals—there shall be some *infallible* rule by which we could *fore* judge events. (Washington 1792)

Here Washington articulates the norm that robust polarization itself should generate a decision rule of selecting the middle course. Robust polarization is evidence, in his view, that neither side has found the right answer to the collective problem at hand. Consequently, they should forbear from pressing their case to a breaking point and settle for the middle course. This is the norm of forbearance named by Levitsky and Ziblatt. It is the idea that checking and balancing of power should be understood not just as something designed into the structure of institu-tions but also as a moral norm. Officeholders should check themselves as well as being checked by the rules of the game.

"Due responsibility" forms a pair with "due dependence" to name the linked design principles that equalize power. Popular sovereignty, or the depersonalization of power, depends on both. First, there is the principle that the mechanisms that depersonalize power must nonetheless align with the possibility of holding individual officeholders to account for their actions within the system, for it is through the collective people's holding officeholders to account that final authority resides with the people broadly. There might seem to be a tension between designing a system to make it impossible to attribute outcomes to any particular individual and designing it so that holding officeholders accountable is the key to maintaining popular sovereignty. This is the tension voters are expected to resolve in every election. The people steers because officeholders recognize their due dependence on the people. Second, there is the principle that powers of various kinds must be checked and counterbalanced so that the final results from political processes can be attributed only to the whole system taken together. When checks and balances operate, both institutionally and via social norms, representatives enact the "due responsibility" that supports depersonalized, democratic power.

In the jury box, no one can overturn a jury's judgment of innocence. The jury is in this respect the authority of last resort. So too the collective democratic people must be the authority of last resort with regard to the question of the direction in which the polity as a whole should be steered by its administrators and officeholders. Just as it should be impossible to name the specific individuals who are the powerholders of last resort in a democracy, so too it should be impossible to say that one or another interest, or sectional faction, has come to be the final holder of power in the system. Aristotle's theory of justice required that political leaders know how to balance the principles of proportional equality and arithmetic equality and when to apply each one. The subsidiary ideal of egalitarian participatory constitutional democracy requires citizens and their representatives to understand when to design processes by which nameable individuals can be held to account and when to create countervailing powers that check and balance efforts to personalize power even though these countervailing powers can make it harder to hold specific people to account.[9] To affirm both that the final say on the direction of the polity resides with the voters and that no single person or faction is in a position to maintain monopolistic control over the voters' choices is to confirm that power has been depersonalized and citizens empowered.[10] Egalitarian participatory constitutional democracy delivers the opportunity for equality of voice through this depersonalization of power.

Inclusion, Part 1: Power Sharing

Of course, as I indicated above, the design of constitutional democracy at the American founding had flaws, among them, the definition of who might be a citizen in the sense of a participant in political decision-making. Thus far I have used the phrases "constitutional democracy" and "egalitarian participatory constitutional democracy" as if they were interchangeable. In the ideal of egalitarian participatory democracy that I am sketching here, they are in fact synonyms. Historically, however, they have not been. The early Americans set up a constitutional democracy in which some people could enslave others and in which the state as a whole could perpetrate genocide. Constitutional democracy did not become synonymous with egalitarian participatory constitutional democracy until the basic design principles of constitutional democracy were modified to include an expectation of universal suffrage, or full inclusion. This section identifies an error in the Declaration of Independence and builds on the contemporaneous criticism of Abigail Adams to articulate a second design principle for egalitarian participatory constitutional democracy: the principle of full inclusion.

The design principles used in the formation of the US Constitution may have worked to pull all the sections of the (exclusionary) citizenry into participation, and to balance their relative sources of power while also holding officeholders accountable, but the founders had an exclusionary (and more specifically, a patriarchal and racialist) conception of who was included in that citizenry. Indeed, the use of the Declaration of Independence to ground a contemporary account of the meaning and structure of an egalitarian participatory constitutional democracy provokes skepticism in contemporary audiences. Many people would respond to the question of whether the Declaration is relevant now with an emphatic "No!" Was not its lead drafter, Thomas Jefferson, an enslaver? Did the Declaration not invoke a principle of all "men" being equal, while women went unmentioned? Did it not underwrite genocide of Native Americans by castigating "merciless Indian savages"?

Let's take up these flaws. What about that enslaver, Thomas Jefferson? A few simple things should be said off the bat, as we work our way toward full understanding of the fundamental flaw in the design of the US Constitution. In the second sentence of the Declaration of Independence, which I quoted above, when Jefferson wrote that "all men are created equal," he did use the word "men" in a universalist way to mean "human being." We know this because his draft of the Declaration also included a passage criticizing King George for the trade in enslaved people. Jefferson lambasted the auctions where "MEN," which he wrote out in all caps, were bought and sold. Of course, auctioneers didn't traffic only adult males but also women and children, and Jefferson knew this full well. The "MEN" Jefferson wrote out in his version of the Declaration referred to all the human beings being bought and sold, regardless of gender or age. The word has the same meaning—"human beings"—in the phrase "all men are created equal."

What's more, Jefferson was the lead drafter of the Declaration, but he served on a committee otherwise populated by people with different views about enslavement, including both John Adams, from Massachusetts, and Benjamin Franklin, from Pennsylvania. John Adams had never enslaved people and thought enslavement was wrong. Benjamin Franklin had, earlier in his life, been an enslaver, but by the time of the drafting of the Declaration he had repudiated the practice and was working to end enslavement. Their antislavery views show up in the phrase, "life, liberty, and the pursuit of happiness." Indeed, we owe the word "happiness" to John Adams. The phrase would more conventionally have ended in the word "property," but by the spring of 1776 in the colonies, the defense of property rights had become closely linked to a defense of enslavement. As Adams showed in his April 1776 essay "Some Thoughts concerning Government," he developed an alternative vocabulary, one not linked to a defense of enslavement, for motivating a shared effort to build free self-government; he encapsulated that motivation in the word "happiness." Abolitionists soon adopted the Declaration's language and drew on it as part of an effort to bring an end to enslavement (Slauter 2011). By 1783, prior even to the end of the Revolution and the drafting of the Constitution, they had achieved success in Pennsylvania, Massachusetts, and Vermont.

Still, even if some of the key drafters of the Declaration genuinely thought that all human beings had basic rights, and even if they took that belief as a rule for action and brought an end to enslavement in three former colonies by 1783, nonetheless, they did erect in the Constitution a hierarchical form of power. Even if all had basic human rights, only some had access to power. What about that?

In the spring of 1776 Abigail Adams wrote to her husband John Adams to inquire about the progress of the revolution and the place of women in it; another politician, James Sullivan, wrote similarly to John to inquire about the place of people without property in the newly forming polity.[11] John Adams understood Sullivan to be inquiring about laborers both white and black. To both Abigail and James, Adams gave similar answers. He affirmed that the new polity would protect the rights of life and liberty of all. In other words, he asserted that the foundation of principle on which the new polity rested was meant to embrace everybody. But then he turned to the question of power, and its organization. Here, he acknowledged, he and his fellow politicians were not willing to give up what he called their "masculine system." They would insist that white men of property wield the levers of power but that they could do so in ways that would protect the rights of all.

Abigail's letter expressed skepticism of this view and cited the historical failure of husbands to exercise power appropriately in relation to wives. She warned that if the decision to lodge all the power in the hands only of men were to lead to the abuse of power, women would "foment a rebellion" seeking to end a world where women had "no voice or representation."

Abigail put her finger on exactly the mistake made by the founding generation. They believed that it was possible to recognize and secure rights for all even while putting power in the hands only of some. Abigail knew the truth: Unchecked power over others leads to abuse. Positive liberty is necessary for justice. Only with fully inclusive voice and power would political institutions ever be able to deliver on a foundation in principle committed to the basic human rights of all. Even in those early days, Abigail could identify how the foundation of principle would need reform. Alongside the principle of rights to life, liberty, and the pursuit of happiness, she insisted that all people also needed "voice and representation," a right to participate in wielding power through political institutions. Political institutions would have to rest on a principle of fully inclusive participation. All who reside permanently in a particular polity should have political voice within it; even those who reside temporarily should be protected by political voice, though their modes of participation and protection may take forms different from those available to permanent residents. (I discuss an ideal to capture this principle of membership in chapter 5.)

Martin Luther King Jr. also articulated this insight. In an important posthumous essay, "A Testament of Hope," he exhorts readers to lift their sights beyond the legal successes of the civil rights movement to a broader effort to bring about "changes in the structure of society." He writes:

> Justice for black people will not flow into society merely from court decisions nor from fountains of political oratory. Nor will a few token changes quell all the tempestuous yearnings of millions of disadvantaged black people. White America must recognize that justice for black people cannot be achieved without radical changes in the structure of our society. The comfortable, the entrenched, the privileged cannot continue to tremble at the prospect of change in the status quo. (1986b, 314)

Though King focused in several of his late writings on "the restructuring of the whole of American society," exegetes have mostly focused on what he had to say in other essays about restructuring of the economy away from capitalism. But in "A Testament of Hope" he focuses not on the economy but more broadly on a restructuring of civil society based on political equality. He writes: "Integration is meaningless without the sharing of power. When I speak of integration, I don't mean a romantic mixing of colors, I mean *a real sharing of power and responsibility*. We will eventually achieve this, but it is going to be much more difficult for us than for any other minority" (1986b, 317, emphasis added).

Where do co-residents of a polity share power and responsibility? First and foremost, in political institutions. A requirement of political equality is that all citizens have equal access to this decision-making apparatus. We are accustomed to arguing for such equal access in the context of voting rights protections. Just as important as the right to vote is the right to run for office. These are the two basic pillars of shared power and responsibility: voting and running for office. Ballot access— the set of procedures followed to get one's name on the ballot for a competitive election—is just as important as the ballot box. We need to bring the same attention to ballot access, and the same clarity of focus to it, as we routinely bring to the protection of voting rights. Ranked-choice voting and paths to primary ballots that are task-based rather than competitions are two reforms that would open up access to the ballot for potential candidates. Campaign finance reform is critical here too—and especially public financing strategies that even the playing field between incumbents and nonincumbents. The issues of pro bono provision of defense counsel for the indigent and right to counsel in cases of eviction are also relevant here. The question of precisely what institutional arrangements will most ensure egalitarian access to legislative, executive (including regulatory), and judicial decision-making processes at all levels of the government (federal, state, and local) is open to debate, but the ideal is clear: a pathway to pull the levers of power that is open to one should be, in fact as well as in principle, open to all, contingent on each individual's acquiring the legitimately established qualifications relevant to the use of that particular lever of power.

Yet, as I will explore in chapters 4, 5, and 6, the project of power sharing extends beyond political institutions to civil society and into the economy. Co-residents may share power in all the organizations—whether public or private, nonprofit or commercial—that constitute civil society. Egalitarian participatory constitutional democracy is an ideal for political institutions—a way of improving constitutional democracy—but it is also an ideal for the organizations of civil society. Design principles flow from this ideal. So far we have taken a look at accountability, checking and balancing, and inclusion. We have yet to tackle energy and republican safety. But as we equip ourselves with these design principles, we should keep in mind that they apply not only to how we continually reorganize the powers of government but also to how we design the mechanisms that guide civil society.

In the ideal, the equality provided by democracy is achieved through full participation of all sections of the citizenry in structures that produce balanced contests, so that no one in particular, and therefore everyone all together, is the author of the final steering decision for the polity. While decisions are depersonalized, the opportunity to participate should keep politics from being impersonal; it should engage, not alienate. Political voice should be available to all those affected by the decisions of the polity—albeit in different forms for those who are permanent residents, temporary residents, and nonresidents (again, see chapter 5). Only this sort of full inclusion can ensure forms of democracy that avoid abuse of power. Finally, the mechanisms function at their best when norms of cooperation across lines of disagreement and difference grease the turning gears of democratic process.

The ideal of egalitarian participatory constitutional democracy names a method of power sharing; it reflects a modification of the ideal of constitutional democracy to include the requirement of universal suffrage and universal participation in all the elements of governance. Importantly, this change does not mean that an ideal of equality was added to the picture of constitutional democracy. Constitutional democracy had historically always depended on the ideals of both equality and liberty; the founding generation defined the experience of citizenship focused on the creation and protection of positive liberty, or equal empowerment of the citizenry. What changed was a transition from an exclusive to an inclusive conception of the body of citizens. The success of egalitarian participatory constitutional democracy depends on the full inclusion in power sharing of those affected by the decisions made in the deliberative assemblies of political institutions. *The historical story of American constitutionalism is not about an evolution from liberty to equality but of a transition from an exclusive to an inclusive conception of who should have access to liberty and equality.*

Inclusion, Part 2: Aligning Natural and Actual Polities

The design principle of full inclusion has a further entailment: a need to clarify what counts as full inclusion from one decision-making context to the next. In resting on a design principle of fully inclusive participation, the ideal of egalitarian participatory constitutional democracy seeks to bring into alignment the category of those who are affected by the decisions of collective agents, or emergent social phenomena that impact identifiable networks of people (for instance, pollution), and the category of those who have voice in relation to those decisions, or the shaping of those phenomena. The effort to figure out who should be included in particular decision-making contexts can introduce considerations that transcend national boundaries. Consider, for instance, how we make decisions that impact climate change. Some of the broader global context involved in thinking about how people outside a nation are connected to decisions made in that nation will be taken up in chapter 5. But in this section, I focus just on the myriad contexts for decision-making that exist even within a single nation-state like the US to try to draw a fuller picture of what is entailed in the principle of full inclusion.

The economist Glen Weyl (2022b) offers a helpful distinction. He calls the networks of people who are affected by the same political decisions or social phenomena "natural polities." In contrast, he designates those people who participate in the political institutions generating the decisions as "actual polities." In the early US, for instance, women, enslaved people, and indigenous Americans were all a part of the "natural polity," but they did not have rights to participate in the "actual polity." Weyl (2022b) provides a list of situations where natural polities (NPs) and actual polities (APs) are out of alignment:

> Importantly, the failures of simple democracy when actual and natural polities diverge is one of the most persistent themes of political history. It is useful to divide historical cases into three buckets:
>
> 1. AP > NP: this is the case of minority or local group oppression, when the actual polity is much larger than the natural polity for an issue.
> 2. NP > AP: this is the case where important individuals are disenfranchised from the decision.[12]
> 3. NP ≠ AP: this the generic case when the natural polity cuts across the boundaries of the actual polity and is neither smaller nor larger; some members of the actual polity are in the natural polity, but not all, and there are members of the natural polity disenfranchised form the actual polity.

As examples of the first kind of failure, he cites the Rohingya genocide and the systematic underrepresentation and neglect in US cities of some communities by majority-elected city administrations. As examples of the second kind of failure, he cites anthropogenic climate change and migration and global inequality (I take up the latter example in chapter 5). And as examples of the final category, he cites control of international waterways and the US war on drugs. He writes thus about the final example:

> The brunt of the drug war has fallen not just against black and brown US citizens who have been incarcerated at literally record-setting levels, but on the tens of millions in Central and South America whose lives have been shattered by resulting violence. The NP here is the black and brown minorities of the United States plus the (sometimes minority, sometimes majority, depending on country) of Latin Americans

directly impacted by drug violence. Yet the AP of American citizens have consistently supported doubling down on policies destroying the lives of much of the NP. (Weyl 2022b)

A goal of governance under the ideal of egalitarian participatory democracy is to bring natural and actual polities into alignment, so that those who are affected by a political decision or emergent social phenomenon also have voice in relationship to it.[13] In other words, the principle of full inclusion in turn requires constant review of polity alignment; where there is nonalignment, a just government is obligated to bring the natural polity into alignment with an actual polity, through the development or evolution of governance mechanisms.

The original design of the US Constitution depended on just such an idea of the need to align natural and actual polities. "Federalism" was its name. As the delegates to the Constitutional Convention deliberated on the design of the new constitution, one of the topics they focused on was which functions should be assigned to a national government and which to a state government. The goal was to ensure alignment between governance and the population affected by the relevant process of governance. Defense of the country as a whole from military aggression would affect the whole population and should be handled at the level of national governance, they argued; the same was true for rules of trade. In contrast, security in local communities, as provided through policing, should be handled at the level of state governance; the same was true, they thought, for education, which depends for its success on effective and healthy links between schools, families, and communities.[14]

Reform in the direction of egalitarian participatory constitutional democracy has often required adjustments of the governance level at which a particular issue is addressed. The addition of the Fourteenth Amendment and contestations of the civil rights movement resulted in a transfer from states to federal government of the authority for ensuring basic provision of rights to all members of the polity (Gerken 2014, 2017, 2020). Similarly, the long-running debate about school funding and its dependence on property taxes is fundamentally a debate about whether natural and actual polities are well aligned with regard to educational policy. Efforts to shift funding responsibility for education to the level of the state rather than the municipality are in fact efforts to achieve alignment between natural and actual polities. The problem of justice in educational funding isn't best understood as one of distribution; it is instead a problem of governance (Hayward 2000). The question is whether the institutional mechanisms through which we govern education adequately protect the positive liberties of all citizens to steer collective decisions about the provision of education. This understanding helps highlight that the ideal of justice in education requires attending to issues of governance at all levels of a political system—not only the national but also the municipal, state, and regional levels. It also highlights the link between issues of positive liberty, governance, and justice with regard to material distribution.

The design principle of inclusion, fully understood, requires seeing all the contexts in which democratic governance is needed and ensuring that governance is developed at the right level to align natural and actual polities.

Energy and Republican Safety

Let's recap. The subsidiary ideal of egalitarian participatory constitutional democracy leads to a view that just political institutions will deliver depersonalized power through representation, accountability, balancing mechanisms that block the emergence of monopolies of power, and inclusion. The project of inclusion requires ensuring equal access to levers of power at all levels of a political system and constant vigilance and adjustment to achieve the alignment of natural and actual polities.[15] In being so constituted and functioning in this way, just political institutions secure positive liberty for members of the polity in formal or procedural terms. Institutions that function in accord with these specifications also deliver epistemic egalitarianism and maximize the epistemic power of democracy. We have one final design principle to outline for this ideal of democracy: the need to balance "energy" and "republican safety."

In addition to securing positive liberty in formal terms, an egalitarian participatory constitutional democracy must deliver positive liberty in substantive terms, via realization of the objectives for which people are exercising their positive liberty. When democracy succeeds, its institutions deliver substantive justice: to wit, the "safety and happiness" of the people, or the conditions for flourishing. They do this by providing "energy" and "republican safety," key terms in the *Federalist Papers*. That is, they permit the people as a whole to steer successfully and to accomplish its objectives: "energy." An energetic government is one that works. It is effective. As for delivering "republican safety," this entails maintaining the depersonalization of power over time and the protection of the basic liberties of the whole citizenry, via both "due dependence" and "due responsibility" as sketched above. An important element of republican safety is protection of minorities, such that the objectives accomplished by the people as a whole through its steering capacity never lead to the eradication of protection of negative and positive liberties for members of minority groups or factions. In chapter 2, I quoted W. E. B. Du Bois: "The power of the ballot we need in sheer self-defense—else what shall save us from a second slavery?" That political institutions should provide "republican safety" is another way of saying that they should achieve difference without domination through a durable commitment to positive liberties for all.

The principle that democratic institutions should deliver energy highlights the need to ensure that the depersonalization of power does not result in its dissipation and the collapse of "the people" via the inefficacy of their political institutions. And there is a danger lurking here: an elaborate system of checks and balances may bring decision-making processes to a halt. Too many veto points may prevent action, advantaging the status quo. The filibuster in the US Senate is an example of a balancing mechanism that has eviscerated the energy of the deliberative body, ensuring that little at all can get done. Just such a dissipation of energy is what the early American republic experienced under the Articles of

Confederation. Congress had ceased to be able to achieve a quorum; no legislation could move forward. Financial obligations could not be met.

Many observers have noted the relative conservatism of American political institutions that results from the constant contests among branches of the government and geographical subsections of the population. As mechanisms are designed to create countervailing power, so that no particular individual or group can develop monopolistic control of power, the conditions of efficacy appear to diminish. The goal of designing institutions that can deliver energy despite their reliance on the checking-and-balancing techniques of depersonalized power is intended to ensure that positive liberty—participation in a constitutional democracy—can deliver substantively for the people, permitting a full conversion of a discernment of the people's will into policies that are successfully implemented. Where the legislative branch is charged with the discernment of will and the setting of a direction for the people, the executive branch is charged with converting that into completed policy. The principle of energy is a requirement that the executive be just strong enough to bring the will of the people to fruition, thereby advancing the cause of substantive justice. Justice is substantively advanced by democracy to the degree and only to the degree that the people's direction-setting steering function has successfully operated on the basis of inclusive and equalizing processes. Proceduralism extended in this way to incorporate the requirements of non-domination becomes a vehicle for substantive justice. Democracy delivers justice, then, by means of achieving the capacity to implement policies devised through institutions that exemplify the five facets of political equality: non-domination, equal access to the institutions of power, epistemic egalitarianism, reciprocity, and co-ownership of political institutions. To achieve this, the mechanisms of due dependence and due responsibility, including checking-and-balancing mechanisms, require constant maintenance and adjustment over time. The arteries must be periodically unblocked.

Importantly, in delivering on justice, the executive must not be so strong as to endanger republican safety. In the case of the US, this feature of the design has been the most challenging. The aspiration that democracy should deliver justice—the safety and happiness of the people and general welfare—has led over time to a dramatic expansion of the powers of the executive in order that substantive goods might be realized—in particular, the good of security. Abraham Lincoln in the Civil War set in abeyance rights of habeas corpus. Franklin Roosevelt in World War II interned Japanese American citizens, and Harry Truman seized property. In the wake of September 11, the National Security Agency began the wholesale collection of American's telephone records, a massive violation of rights of privacy and free association. The arteries have often been unblocked through extension of the power of the executive.

Ironically, the Federalist designers of the founding generation saw the legislative branch as most likely to threaten both republican safety and energetic government. In various ways, they sought to guard against encroachment on the executive by the legislative branch. Their work succeeded beyond their wildest imaginings. The power of the executive branch has grown vigorously in the succeeding centuries. Since the nation's founding, Congress has overridden only 111 of 2,576 vetoes. Similarly, executive orders have become a prominent part of governance, replacing legislation, in part because Congress has been paralyzed in recent decades. Indeed, the expanded authority of the executive has, to some meaningful degree, repersonalized political power in the American case, making the question of who is president the first fact of our shared political lives.

Just this sort of repersonalization of power, in the figure of the president, was what the Anti-Federalists were most worried about at the time of the founding. They feared the introduction of the office of the presidency would lead to a resurgence of the monarchic government they had just overthrown. Here we must remember that Congress, not the president, was intended to lead and to give voice to the will of the people, filtering and synthesizing the national interest to set the national legislative agenda. Instead, Congress has become a reactive partner to partisan presidents, who get to set the agenda rather than executing the people's agenda as communicated by the legislature. The Anti-Federalists' worry, updated in light of the expansion of the presidency over two centuries, might be expressed thus: How can the principle of energy, and particularly energy in the executive, be squared with the preservation of positive liberty? While legal and political theorists have often litigated the question of how security should be balanced with civil liberties, they have typically treated this question as a matter of how to ensure protection of the negative liberties. Here we are pursuing a different question: How can the energy of a partisan presidency be made compatible with the preservation of positive liberty for all members of the polity?

The answer to the question lies in the health of the legislative branch. As we have seen, to achieve self-government a large society requires representation. The people as a whole forms its will through representatives who listen to their constituents, digest, contend and collaborate, achieve a synthesized agenda-setting vision, and report back to their constituencies to repeat the process, all the while participating in processes designed to achieve a balance of power among different segments of the citizenry.[16] In a representative democracy, the legislature is the only institution equipped to present a synthesized expression of "the will of the people." This is because the minority view is also present in the legislature. A unitary executive, such as the US presidency, is not designed to express the will of the people, and it cannot do so. It typically expresses the will of the electoral majority. For this reason, the presidency ought to be subservient to the legislature so that the president's work of executing the laws is constrained by the will of the people as a whole—minorities as well as majorities. Government by executive order guts the heart of the representative system. If we care to preserve democracy—to achieve a balance of republican safety and energy—we need to focus on achieving well-functioning national legislatures. All the features of depersonalization that we reviewed above are relevant to the well-functioning of national legislatures. In times and places where a national legislature is failing to achieve steering capacity within the system as a whole, the mechanisms driving its operations should be reviewed and revised where needed. In the current context of the US, we need to unblock the arteries not by expanding executive power but by modernizing Congress. Key reforms would include increasing the size of the House, transitioning to multimember districts and ranked-choice voting, and eradicating the filibuster.

Achieving a healthy legislature—where both due dependence and due responsibility are operable—is not, however, just a matter of redesigning institutions. It's also about the norms that reinforce due dependence and due responsibility. These are the norms that make processes with built-in forms of countervailing power workable: mutual toleration and forbearance, or, as it is put in the *Federalist Papers*, "a spirit of amity, and that mutual deference and concession which the peculiarity of our political situation rendered indispensable" (*Federalist 62*; cf. *Federalist 6*). The phenomenon that makes the democratic people most vulnerable to the erosion of its positive liberty by an energetic executive is factionalism. When the people, as embodied in Congress, is factionalized, it ceases to be able to operate its power, in a context where collaboration and compromise are necessary to get things done. That sclerosis leads to the expansion of executive power to maintain energy and dynamism. Consequently, securing republican safety requires not only modernization of the mechanisms by which Congress operates but also a shift of norms in Congress away from polarization.

George Washington, in his farewell address—the letter he wrote to the American people in 1796 after deciding not to run for a third presidential term—issued a warning about the dangers of factionalism: what happens when a nation forgets that it is one country, that its citizens and values and processes, whatever their inevitable disagreements, are indivisible.[17] Unity, he believed, had a moral dimension. It was also the best defense against bullying and tyranny, on the one hand, and gridlock, on the other. He wrote:

> The alternate domination of one faction over another, sharpened by the spirit of revenge, natural to party dissension, which in different ages and countries has perpetrated the most horrid enormities, is itself a

frightful despotism. But this leads at length to a more formal and permanent despotism. The disorders and miseries which result gradually incline he minds of men to seek security and repose in the absolute power of an individual; and sooner or later the chief of some prevailing faction, more able or more fortunate than his competitors, turns this disposition to the purposes of his own elevation on the ruins of public liberty.

Washington worried deeply about the prospects for the early American republic—and especially that factionalism might destroy it. *Faction*—an old word, but better than *tribalism*—captures the idea not just of political parties but of parties ready to fight existentially, as if unto death. Washington wrote of the "artificial and extraordinary force" of faction. In particular, he cited its capacity "to put in the place of the delegated will of the nation the will of a party, often a small but artful and enterprising minority of the community; and, according to the alternate triumphs of different parties, to make the public administration the mirror of the ill concerted and incongruous projects of faction, rather than the organ of consistent and wholesome plans digested by common councils and modified by mutual interests." In Washington's view, public liberty depended on a process of mutual consultation— adjusting the interests of various parties in relation to one another— with the aim of achieving "consistent and wholesome plans" that could provide stability of direction over the long haul. This is precisely the process of depersonalizing power sketched above. Our very political institutions, born of compromise and sketched in the Constitution, were this country's first plan. Washington believed that the business of government—of "public administration"—was to get important things done, that getting things done depended on compromise, that compromise was enabled by a commitment to unity, to a norm of mutual due dependence.

When Washington described public liberty as depending on the citizenry's ability to ward off the despotism of faction, he offered a profound insight: the precondition of democratic decision-making is unity.

If a political system that relies heavily on majority rule cannot keep minorities affixed to it through loyalty, then every fresh, durable minority faction that comes into being will bring with it the threat of breakup. A first secession will provide grounds for a second, and on and on; the polity will face a threat to its very existence. Undue concentrations of power sow division and factionalism. The creation of mechanisms of countervailing power is important for this reason also. But so too are the norms of forbearance and due dependence, as described above.

From antiquity through the formation of the American republic and beyond, those who have considered what is required to maintain free institutions—from Livy to Machiavelli to Washington to Lincoln—have repeated one lesson over and over again: *Choose unity.* Unity here refers to institutions that time after time yield singular, yet legitimate, decisions, even out of the great heterogeneity of a diverse people. No person can be named as the author of the final outcome. No final outcome looks exactly like what any individual contributed at the outset of the deliberation. The people's heterogeneity is perpetual, but so too must be the commitment nonetheless to deliver shared decisions, even from that heterogeneity. A commitment to unity—an unswerving insistence on unity despite difference—induces citizens to seek out ways of adapting their purposes so as to get something done. Because if unity is not negotiable, then there is no other choice. If you emphasize unity—and stipulate that it cannot be sacrificed—then it becomes a democratic tool. It encourages all sides to compromise. It is the opposite of executive decision-making fueled by the self-interest or anger of one part of the electorate. Compromise is what allows us to stay together in the space we share. The goal is not unanimity; that is neither achievable nor desirable. Compromise entails embracing not the outlook that winners make policy and losers go home[18] but, rather, the view that the winners deserve a leadership role in steering the conversation toward the "wholesome plans" that Washington spoke of. Winners get to chair the committees and set the agenda, but losers are still on the committee. The Old English root of the word *whole* means "healthy." That is what we seek—to be a healthy people. We fight over words like *patriotism, solidarity, loyalty.* Yet there is a word that defines our relationship. Abraham Lincoln knew what it was. The word is *union.* In a political sense, the word points to something concrete. It means talking honestly, fighting fairly, and planning together.

The historical examples from US history in which ideologically opposed segments of the white population found ways to compromise at the expense of minorities—for instance, with the end of Reconstruction and the erection of Jim Crow—do not count as examples of unity. The choice of unity requires a commitment to solutions that secure permanent protection of basic liberties, both positive and negative, for everyone, including racial minorities. Again, minority-protecting mechanisms must be part of the basic tool kit defining democracy. Choosing unity, then, and preserving republican safety, even in the face of an excessively energetic executive, requires not merely constantly rebuilding norms of mutual toleration and forbearance but also perpetually adhering to a norm of universal suffrage and full inclusion across the full breadth of our political institutions. These norms have been called the guardrails of democracy (Levitsky and Ziblatt 2019), but they aren't built once, to stand on their own. They instead are the product of constant, intentional cultivation. Republican safety cannot in the end be secured by institutional mechanisms alone; it will turn out to depend also on our practices of citizenship, the subject of chapter 7.

In sum, a healthy democracy depends on a virtuous cycle in which well-functioning political institutions generate positive incentives for healthy participation and a healthy political culture reinforces positive participation in the organizations of civil society and those institutions. If we expect ourselves to commit now to constitutional democracy and to build twenty-first-century commitments to one another, moving beyond past legacies of injustice and conflict, we must also build ourselves inclusive and successful political institutions and social norms worthy of our commitment.

We have now completed our sketch of the subsidiary ideal of egalitarian participatory constitutional democracy. This democracy protects negative and positive liberties and achieves power sharing and equal empowerment, in contexts of universal suffrage and access to participation in the diversity of avenues of governance. This it does with mechanisms of accountability, countervailing power, and inclusion as well as with norms to support a balance between energy and republican safety.

Justice by Means of Democracy and Political Institutions in Nondemocratic Regimes

A rightly constructed theory of justice will start from the premise that political equality is non-sacrificeable. The route to justice, then, is through, and only through, democracy. Benevolent autocracies may be able to achieve material well-being for their populations, but by definition they will never achieve the basis for full human flourishing, and so will never achieve full justice (Sen 1999a,1999b). Yet despite my best arguments on behalf of justice as I understand it, there will be those who choose another path and eschew democracy. I recognize this as an inevitable fact of the world.

Modifying John Rawls's schema in *Law of Peoples*, I expect a world with the types of regime listed in Table 5. In my argument, only the top two categories of regime type are on the path toward justice. They become homologous if the constitutional democracy embraces inclusion in full. The third and fourth categories of regime (the two kinds of autocracy) may be considered decent enough insofar as they achieve some rudimentary level of rights protection. The foreign policy of a democracy would presumably take into account the status of the different regime types in deciding on the nature of particular engagements with any given regime. But the principle that justice is best achieved by means of democracy does not lead to the conclusion that democracies should intervene on behalf of regime change in other societies. Indeed, it would be a violation of the principles defining this account of how to achieve justice through democracy to force others to be free.

With regard to leaders and citizens who repudiate democracy, the view that justice is best pursued by means of democracy demands an orientation like that articulated by Michael Walzer in a 2008 essay, "On

TABLE 5 Diversity of the world's regime types: Twenty-first-century frame

	Regime category	Basic material security	Negative liberties/ rights	Positive liberties/ rights	Social rights	Social equality/ nondiscrimination
Well-ordered regimes	Egalitarian participatory constitutional democracy	Y	Y	Y	Y	Y
	Constitutional democracy	Y	Y	Y	Y	?
	Rights-protecting autocratic regimes	Y	Y	N	Y	?
	Material-well-being-protecting authoritarian/ autocratic regimes	Y	N	N	Y	?
Outlaw regimes	Non-decent, rights-violating regimes	N	N	N	N	N

Source: Allen (2021).

Promoting Democracy." In general, any given citizen of a democracy might justly choose to offer aid and comfort by peaceful means to those within the nondemocratic polity who seek by peaceful means to build democracy. This is the only normatively acceptable path to achieving justice by means of democracy in countries other than one's own.

4

The Second Subsidiary Ideal

A CONNECTED SOCIETY

Difference without Domination and Social Policy

Justice by means of democracy requires the design of political institutions for power sharing. Yet the project of power sharing extends beyond political institutions to civil society and into the economy. Co-residents may share power in all the organizations—public and private, nonprofit and commercial—that constitute civil society. Egalitarian participatory constitutional democracy is a subsidiary ideal for political institutions, yes, but egalitarian participatory democracy more generally is also a subsidiary ideal for the organizations of civil society. The design principles of accountability, checking and balancing, and inclusion apply not only to how we continually reorganize the powers of government but also to how we design mechanisms of civil society. The question in front of us now is how to apply the principle of difference without domination to the social realm.

Let me recapitulate. As I argued in chapter 2, of all the possible strands of equality, it is political equality, and, with it, democracy, that we ought to take as the starting point for a theory of justice. The concept of democracy that I have in mind originates in a basic recognition of human moral equality. That equality flows from the nonnegotiable need of all people for both private and public autonomy for flourishing.

The moment you begin to protect public autonomy, which is to say, participation rights and empowerment, you have also begun necessarily to protect private autonomy, because public autonomy requires rights of expression and thought. While the positive liberties supporting public autonomy may have been historically prior to the private liberties, there is no conceptual priority between the two sets of liberties. They are not merely co-original and co-equal but, more importantly, co-constituting. Democracy is a project justified by the pursuit of human flourishing. As such, it begins with the protection of positive and negative liberties with a view to securing egalitarian empowerment for all people in the polity. I identified five facets of egalitarian empowerment and argued that the work of designing political institutions must attend to fostering all five. These are non-domination, equal access to the instruments of social decision-making, epistemic egalitarianism, reciprocity, and co-ownership of the assets represented by political institutions.

Yet at that point a challenging paradox emerged: Protection of the basic liberties—for instance, the right to association—is likely to generate social differences that might easily come to be attached to patterns of domination. Even without out-group antipathy, social groups may practice opportunity hoarding, and from that fact alone, structures of domination can emerge out of a social context that began with the recognition of all participants as free and equal members of society.[1] Recognition of this paradox led me to articulate a principle, "difference without domination," as the key to cultivating a social realm that does not undermine the project of political equality. In other words, "difference without domination" captures our normative goal for the cultivation of a social domain that is positively reinforcing of political equality. The goal of the justice project, as I'm defining it, is to protect the basic liberties and constitute the basic structure of society in such a way as to protect the emergence of difference—which is an expression of freedom—while also blocking the conversion of that difference into domination. Note, then, that on the basis of a theory of justice that treats positive liberties and political equality as non-sacrificeable, what we seek as a core democratic aspiration in the social realm is not the traditional target of social cohesion but, rather, egalitarianism defined as difference without domination. As we shall see, egalitarianism is attained through the vibrancy of network effects in a society, and those network effects can provide a source of resiliency for the social fabric and can and should replace the patriarchal and hierarchical bonding relations of a traditionalist picture of social cohesion.

This chapter takes up our second subsidiary ideal: justice by means of democracy requires that in the social realm we create a *connected society*.

A connected society is one in which citizens have ample opportunities for both bonding and bridging relationships. Bonding relationships are ties to those who are our social similars; bridging ties link us to social dissimilars.[2] Healthy bonding relationships will be those that also support the formation of bridging ties, and a connected society will be one where the rules that structure the emergent ecosystem of associations in civil society maximize the likelihood that bridging ties will form.

From Difference without Domination to Social Connectedness

What exactly is required of the design principle of difference without domination in the social realm? How can we support social difference while disconnecting it from domination? The question is what is required of the basic structure, the fundamental political and social institutions, such that the social dynamics that emerge out of practices of free association do not articulate with hierarchy and domination and thereby undo the pathway to political equality. The answer I offer is that we need policy frameworks that help us achieve a "connected society" and "social connectedness." This subsidiary ideal is in turn defined by two key design principles: (1) that institutions should be organized to maximize the formation of bridging ties, and (2) that cultural habits should be promoted that help individuals flourish in enacting social connectedness. Let me explain this ideal of a connected society in somewhat more detail.

As I pointed out in chapter 2, scholars of social capital distinguish among three kinds of social ties: bonding, bridging, and linking. Bonding ties are those (generally strong) connections that bind kin, close friends, and social similars; bridging ties are those (generally weaker) ties that connect people across demographic cleavages (age, race, class, occupation, religion, and the like); finally, linking ties are the vertical connections between people at different levels of a status hierarchy, as in, for instance, the employment context (Granovetter 1973; Szreter and Woolcock 2004). Bridging ties are the hardest ones to come by. Bonding ties take care of themselves, really. They start with the family and radiate out. But bridging ties are a matter of social structure. Schools, the military, political bodies—these have typically been the institutions that bring people from different backgrounds together. A connected society is one that maximizes active—in the sense of alive and engaged—bridging ties. This generally takes the work of institutions. To say that we need to maximize bridging ties is not, however, to say that we can ignore bonding ties. For the sake of healthy psychological development, all people need bonding relationships (Bromberg 2011; Honneth 1992). Bonding builds a sense of security and of trust, supports for self-confidence that can, in the right contexts, undergird success. The question, we will see, is how to cultivate the kinds of bonding relationships that also facilitate bridging relationships.

Importantly, there is good reason to expect that more connected societies—those that emphasize bridging ties—will be more egalitarian along multiple dimensions: health outcomes, educational outcomes, economic outcomes (e.g., Ober 2008; Szreter and Woolcock 2004). These empirical facts are the basis for my development of the connected society ideal. Consider the impact of connectedness on labor markets. Research has shown, for instance, that the majority of people who get a new job through information passed through a social network have acquired that information not from a close connection but from a distant one (Granovetter 1973). In other words, bridging ties spread economic opportunity rather than letting it pool in insular subcommunities within a polity. This makes sense. One's closest connections share too much of one's world to be likely to introduce new information. We all know this intuitively. Whenever we're trying to help a friend who has been single or unmarried too long, we scratch our heads to think of a further removed social connection who might connect our friend to a whole new pool of possibilities. Perhaps that seems like a trivial example. But the most important egalitarian impacts of social connectivity flow from bridging ties and their impact on the diffusion of knowledge. Scholars working in the domain of network theory routinely invoke the epistemic benefits of bridging ties to explain why so many economic, political, educational, and health benefits flow from them.[3] To the degree that a society achieves greater levels of connectedness, and more equally empowers its members in economic, educational, and health domains, it builds the foundation of political equality.

Perhaps one of the most profound examples of a failure at the level of associational life in a democracy is the case of racial segregation in the US. This time I do not refer to a historical phenomenon, for instance, the relics of the mid-twentieth century. Racial segregation continues to have a significant impact on American life in the present and has been pretty conclusively shown to be at the root of racial inequality along all dimensions: educational inequalities in terms of achievement gaps between white and African American students; inequality in distribution of wealth; inequality in terms of employment mobility; and inequality in terms of health (Loury 1977, 2002; Anderson 2010; Rothstein 2013). Modern segregation is different from the mid-twentieth-century kind. Both suburbs and middle- and upper-class urban areas are more ethnically mixed than they were thirty years ago. But socioeconomic segregation matters more now. Poor African Americans and Latinx individuals are more likely now, in contrast to three decades ago, to face hypersegregation—along dimensions of both class and race.

A study of segregation by a group of economists shows that social network effects have a great impact on the distribution of goods and resources, such that segregation can be a driver of group inequality, even in hypothetical, quantitative models where groups begin with equivalent skill sets and opportunities (Bowles, Loury, and Sethi 2014).

Why does segregation have such profound effects? Common sense points to an explanation, which research has confirmed. All you have to do is think about what flows through social networks. At the most basic level, a human social network is like a web of streams and rivulets through which language flows. As language flows, it carries with it knowledge and skills. That knowledge can be of the sort we recognize in schools: knowledge about the world or history or politics or literature. Or it can be of a practical kind: Which jobs are about to come open because someone is retiring? Where is a new factory about to be built, bringing new opportunities to an area? This sort of information also flows with language along social networks.

Any individual has access to just as much knowledge, skill, and opportunity as his or her social network contains. And since knowledge, skill, and opportunity are power, isolation in itself reduces resources of fundamental importance to egalitarian empowerment (Anderson 2010). Language itself is one of the easiest markers to use in assessing how relatively well connected or fragmented any political community is (Lareau 2011).

Now I need to underscore that the point I am making here is not about race or ethnicity. It is about social experience for all people. Everyone is benefited by a rich social network and harmed by a relatively isolated or resource-impoverished social network (Lareau 2011). The American case of racial segregation just happens to be an extreme example of a basic phenomenon that crosses all contexts, times, and places. More egalitarian societies, scholars have shown, are generally more connected societies, and connectivity is equalizing (Ober 2008; Szreter and Woolcock 2004).

Achieving a connected society does not require that individuals shed cultural specificity. Instead, it requires that we scrutinize how institutions build social connections with a view to ensuring that there are multiple, overlapping pathways connecting the full range of communities in a country to one another. A connected society is one in which people can enjoy the bonds of solidarity and community but are equally engaged in the "bridging" work of bringing diverse communities into positive relations; in it, people also themselves individually desire and succeed at forming personally valuable relationships across boundaries of difference. Importantly, in a connected society, the boundaries among communities of solidarity are fluid, and the shape of those communities can be expected to change over time. By continuously maximizing bridging ties, a connected society ensures steadily shifting social boundaries; some bridging ties will, over time, become bonding ties. And as what were once bridging ties become bonding ties, the quest to build bridging ties must migrate to new lines of difference and division.

Achieving difference without domination in the social realm, and as a support for political equality, requires, on the one hand, policy and institutions and, on the other, habits and practices. Achieving such an ideal therefore requires both a revised framework for policy-making and a project of cultural transformation. This brings us back to the two design principles connected to the subsidiary ideal of a connected society: (1) institutions should be organized to maximize the formation of bridging ties, and (2) cultural habits should be promoted that help individuals flourish in enacting social connectedness. I'll turn to both of these dimensions—institutional policy and cultural work—and their design principles in a moment, but first let me situate the ideal of social connectedness within contemporary debates.

Beyond Assimilation and Multiculturalism

I am offering up a subsidiary ideal of "social connectedness" as a route to social egalitarianism, and I argue that this is itself in turn a support for political equality in conditions of diversity. In doing so, I am intervening in a long-running debate about the incorporation of immigrants and minorities. The poles of this debate have been defined by concepts of "assimilation" on the one hand and "multiculturalism" on the other. I offer "social connectedness" and "the connected society" as an alternative that overcomes the difficulties of each of the other two positions. The ideal of "social connectedness" depends on a shift away from the conceptualizations of both human identity and social groups used in these earlier paradigms.[4]

In the US in the twentieth century, our thinking about democratic social relations was governed first by ideals of assimilation and integration and then by a competing ideal of multiculturalism. Although these earlier ideals have long been discredited in scholarly circles, they easily re-emerge in lay conversations as individuals working inside particular organizations grapple with the topic of how to scaffold social relations in conditions of diversity. Hence, it is worth being clear about their content and consequences.

First, for assimilation, I'll use the US case again to work through these concepts, though the concepts do apply more broadly. In the late nineteenth and early twentieth centuries, a "common schools" movement spread across the US, broadening the reach of public schooling and, by 1918, achieving compulsory education in all forty-eight states then in the union (Katz 1976; see also Goldin and Katz 2008). The purpose of this movement was not, as we might now imagine, to increase the population's level of educational attainment but to spread Americanization in the face of staggeringly high rates of immigration. The image of the "melting pot"—an America in which ethnic differences would be smelted and fused into an identifiably "American" synthesis—dates to 1908, when it expressed a powerful ideal of assimilation (Schlesinger 1992, 32–33). As formal systems of Jim Crow segregation were dismantled in the 1950s and '60s, the goal of achieving healthy social relations took on the added dimension of the need to integrate across race lines. These two ideas—assimilation and integration—defined discussions of social relations from early in the twentieth century through the early phase of the civil rights movement. The authority of these ideals waned in the late twentieth century, but even as late as 1992, the eminent historian Arthur Schlesinger Jr. could still organize his analysis of the prospects for US social life around them, and his treatment provides a good example of the core problem with these ideals. He wrote: "Assimilation and integration constitute a two-way street. Those who want to join America must be received and welcomed by those who already think they own America" (Schlesinger 1992, 19).[5]

Although Schlesinger argued for a "two-way street," he in fact described a one-way transaction in which one group assimilates into a dominant culture and the second group has only to embrace the idea of that assimilation (Parham 2012). As many have said, the assimiliationist ideal converts majority cultural norms and styles into the standard to which all others, whatever their cultural background, must adhere. To the degree that members of minority groups assimilate to the cultural forms of the majority group, the cultural resources of their original traditions disappear. For instance, one expression of the assimilationist ideal experienced by one late-twentieth-century immigrant to the US—and reinforced even by medical advice—was the view that immigrant children should actively suppress their mother tongues in order to maximize their performance in English.[6]

The novelist Ralph Ellison articulated a counterideal in his 1952 National Book Award–winning novel, *Invisible Man*:

> Whence all this passion to conformity anyway?—diversity is the word. Let man keep his many parts and you'll have no tyrant states. Why, if they follow this conformity business they'll end up forcing me, an invisible man, to become white, which is not a color but the lack of one. But seriously, and without snobbery, think of what the world would lose if that should happen. America is woven of many strands; I would recognize them and let it so remain. (Ellison [1952] 1980, 557)

In place of the melting pot, Ellison evoked an image of the US as a woven tapestry, with richly intricate patterns of difference.

As a novelist, Ellison did not convert his embrace of diversity into formal policy proposals, but those who worked in his wake—drawing on any number of intellectual, artistic, and activist traditions that had made points similar to his—developed a politics of multiculturalism. Canada was a leading site, thanks to the work of the 1960s' Royal Commission on Bilingualism and Biculturalism;[7] and the Canadian philosopher Charles Taylor provided the groundbreaking philosophical expression of this ideal in his 1994 book *Multiculturalism: Examining the Politics of Recognition* (Taylor 1992).[8]

Yet the multicultural ideal, too, has come under critique, from both right and left. Some voices, primarily but not exclusively on the right, feared that multicultural policies were antithetical to social cohesion, generating instead—to quote Schlesinger again—"fragmentation, resegregation, and tribalization" (Schlesinger 1992, 17–18).[9] On the left, cultural critic Homi Bhabha argued that the multiculturalist view dangerously essentializes culture, as if there were fixed boundaries between cultural groups, and, for each of us, an unchanging individual identity tethered to the cultural tradition into which each was born (Bhabha 1994). Bhabha made the case that cultural life is instead characterized by hybridity, or a constant evolution in how each of us represents our identity, fashioning that identity, as we do, in contexts of contestation, out of whatever materials are to hand, which may themselves have disparate historical and cultural sources (Bhabha 2011).

Bhabha's arguments have been extended through the work of feminists like Iris Young and Kimberlé Crenshaw, who have argued for the importance of "seriality" and "intersectionality" to the identity of any given individual (Young 1994). Let me take myself as an example. I happen to be a black, mixed-race, professional woman who is a mother of two and also a lover of poetry. Each of these roles comes into greater salience in different contexts. When someone invokes the responsibilities of mothers, I stand as one in a long series of mothers who've been called to attention by social and cultural cues. This is true of all my roles, which we might also say (modifying Young's terminology) that I inhabit serially, one after another, in an unending sequence that is unpredictable in its ordering. Additionally, the intersections of these different roles can be complicated: my identities as a professional and as a mother are often in conflict.

These approaches to the topic of personal identity underscore a challenge for any effort to think about democratic social relations in conditions of diversity. Our selection of an approach has significant consequences for what we presume about individual identity. The assimilationist approach assumes that we can shed traditions in which we've been raised without doing damage to ourselves. The multicultural approach does not provide adequate space for self-identifications and for engagement in culture as hybrid and contested. Each approach is therefore autonomy-constraining and thereby connects difference to domination. The assimilationist and multicultural frameworks, then, provide inadequate bases for pursuing human flourishing. Any approach to democratic social relations that hopes to displace these two paradigms must do a better job of recognizing that both tradition and adaptation matter for personal identity and, on the basis of this recognition, provide a framework for supporting individuals' psychological, as well as their social, flourishing.

If one accepts the fluidity, hybridity, and intersectionality of identity, and the changing contextual salience of the various components of a person's identity, then the conceptualization of social groups must also shift. The concept of a social group with fixed boundaries that in some sense predates politics can no longer be the central object of social scientific analysis. The groupings that have a meaningful impact on the political process shift and adjust over time, and those adjustments may even result from active political and social cultivation. For instance, an assembly of national legislators may be viewed through the lens of the members' gender and sexual identities, and the social groups represented in that assembly will be mapped one way. Or that same assembly of legislators may be viewed alternatively in terms of socioeconomic status or ethnicity, and the groupings and alliances of interest may be mapped another way. The same is true for national populations. Where and how groups form through alliances around particular interest positions and where and how marriage markets develop and generate kinship networks are contingent matters, emergent from a variety of social practices (Alexander and Christia 2011; Singh and Hau 2016; Hanchard 2018). The ideals of social connectedness and a connected society rest on the hybrid, fluid, intersectional conceptions of identity and also on a complementary view of social groups not as fixed a priori but as emergent from our political and institutional choices, and changeable (Allen and Somanathan 2020).

To recognize that social groupings are endogenous rather than exogenous sociopolitical phenomena does not require a full redirection to methodological individualism, and to a starting point assumption that the individual is the only relevant unit of analysis. Scholars can instead focus on relationality—where and how different kinds of social ties form. The foundations for such study have been laid down in network theory, starting with the foundational work of Mark Granovetter and, more recently, dramatically extended by scholars like Matthew Jackson. As I have already indicated, the work of sociologists and political scientists who have focused on social capital and on bonding, bridging, and linking ties is also relevant here, as is the work of neoinstitutionalists, who scrutinize the emergence and solidification of institutions in part by looking at how those institutions entrench social ties. Similarly, historians have traced how alliances and solidarities adjust around linguistic shifts that tie to evolving patterns of interest identification and formation (Hattam and Lowndes 2007).

A focus on where and how social ties form, where and how they are deployed by political actors, and where and how they provide the context for the formation of the identities of individuals orients social scientific scholarship toward the meso level of human experience, the practices that mediate between the micro level of individual action and the macro level of structural phenomena and aggregate and emergent patterns (Loury 2020). The focus on social networks and their effects provides a framework for diagnosing when social difference does or does not generate domination. One task of a connected society is constantly to seek to thwart, redress, or mitigate those kinds of network formation that articulate with domination. Contemporary efforts at antiracism similarly often seek to undo such patterns of domination. The connected society ideal, however, stretches also in a positive direction to articulate the kinds of bonds and bridges we should proactively seek to form with one another. The principle of difference without domination sets the parameters for work of social policy as we seek to enable the emergence of a connected society. The project of building a connected society works, in the first instance, at the meso level, seeking to understand the institutional choices that will generate a pattern of maximal bridging at the structural level, and at the micro level, seeking to provide individuals opportunities for rewarding social ties of both the bridging and the bonding variety.

With this context in place, we can now turn to the subsidiary ideal of a connected society and its design principles more directly.

Building a Connected Society: An Institutional Design Principle

As we have seen, the ideal of assimilation pursues social cohesion while sacrificing individuals' particular needs for connections to their communities of origin. The ideal of multiculturalism valorizes connections to those communities of origin at the expense of both a reasonable account of identity and the valuable fluidity of social bonds. In contrast, an ideal of "social connectedness" and of a "connected society" is autonomy-preserving (Allen 2013). As I have argued above, an associational ecology that maximizes bridging ties should bring egalitarian effects and, therefore, should minimize the likelihood that social difference articulates with domination.[10] I have, then, articulated a principle of social organization. The question is how to convert this principle into institutional form. This is where the design principles come in: an institutional design principle and a cultural design principle.

With regard to the first principle, institutions should be organized to maximize the formation of bridging ties. As I argued initially in chapter 2, constructing an associational ecosystem that can support a connected society first of all requires focusing on all of the policies that impact the use of land and space: transportation, housing, zoning, districting (including for both political representation and education), public accommodations, and communications infrastructure. More policies may be directly germane to basic rights protection than we often realize, and the standard of aspiring to achieve difference without domination requires us not so much to layer additional policies on top of the protection of equal basic liberties but, rather, to revisit the spectrum of possibilities for how equal basic liberties are protected in the first place. We need a principle of strict scrutiny. In other words, as we protect the basic liberties, we should choose modes of protecting them that align with the five facets of political equality discussed in chapter 2. Doing so requires study of policy domains not typically associated with basic rights protection.

In the US some conventional policies are relevant here. Mixed-income housing is important, as are other policies that seek to roll back, or undo, the effects of "exclusionary zoning, persistent red lining, selective withdrawal of public services, the segregation of low-income public housing, 'stop and frisk' policing concentrated in minority areas, school funding tied to property values and the political fragmentation of metropolitan areas" (Sampson 2013; see also Rothstein 2015). Revised approaches to federalism and the overlapping structure of legislative districts could support an expanded education for citizens in the interest positions of others, as well as more equitable distribution of power to minorities and dissenters (Gerken 2014). Elsewhere, I have argued that in the context of US college admissions, we could increase the degree of bridging ties on college campuses, particularly elite campuses, by placing more emphasis on geographic diversity at the level of zip codes (Allen 2014a).[11] Similarly, many rural areas of the US lack adequate transportation connections to link them efficiently to one another and to multiple major urban hubs. High-speed rail projects would provide great advances for social connectedness. The constant application of a design principle of social connectedness—defined as maximizing the rate of formation of bridging ties—to institutional design and design of the built environment should transform the relational context out of which groups and social patterning emerge.

Second, deploying the institutional design principle of supporting bridging relationships to design an associational ecosystem that can support a connected society requires focusing on labor policies and all of the policies that impact mobility and cross-class interactions. For instance, Berkeley professor David Kirp pointed to the value of mixing rich and poor kids in preschool, and other scholars have shown the values of socioeconomic mixing in educational contexts at all levels (Kirp 2014). Michael Reich and Ken Jacobs, also at Berkeley, argued for local minimum wages where wage policies cover work performed in the area in order to tie wages to local living standards. This localism lifts wages without reducing jobs and refocuses employers on their obligations to people across class lines within their own communities (Reich and Jacobs 2014). This small set of examples is meant to be illustrative, not exhaustive, and simply to assist in making imaginable the points of intersection between the design principle of connectedness for the institutions of civil society and policy choices

The pursuit of political equality and the concomitant effort to achieve difference without domination and social connectedness themselves necessarily bring in substantive standards in relation to economic policy. By reorienting a theory of justice to protect positive and negative liberties equally, we bring into visibility policy areas that have been largely obscured by twentieth-century liberalism's incessant focus on taxation and redistribution—areas like housing, transportation, and labor. An underlying point of this book is that projects of justice require understanding the feedback loops and interactions among the political, social, and economic domains. Importantly, institutions we design to support protection of the basic liberties through social connectedness will change the underlying demographic facts of the system, which themselves will be changed by the institutions. The demographic contexts and the institutions are mutually co-constituting, and to avoid the emergence of difference with domination will require perpetual work of redesign. The goal, however, is to ensure that dynamic social systems are constantly oriented toward the correct principles.

Building a Connected Society: A Cultural Design Principle

Pursuing the subsidiary civil society ideal of social connectedness and a world in which no group dominates any other cannot be accomplished through institutional design alone—even with the accompanying recognition that institutional design must itself be dynamic. There is just as much work to be done on the cultural front. The basic institutional design—in the areas of both land and labor—provides the backdrop against which civil society organizations form. Civil society organizations that grow out of a sociopolitical world in which the basic structure already supports a high rate of formation of bridging ties are more likely themselves to replicate principles of connectedness in their own approaches to membership policies and participation. Achieving a richness of potential for bridging ties in the membership of the organizations and institutions that populate US civil society is as much a matter of achieving a more broadly egalitarian social structure as it is of the choices that particular institutions make. Yet the mere opportunity for social connectedness in the membership of organizations of civil society is insufficient to achieve a connected society. Even if our policy frameworks help us build more institutions that require, enable, or nudge us toward bridging ties, leveraging those ties for positive social outcomes will depend on our having a deeper and richer understanding of the ethical practice of social bridging and the art and science of connected forms of social association. This brings us to our second design principle: cultural habits should be promoted that help individuals flourish in enacting social connectedness.

Just how much work is to be done can best be seen by revisiting some of the arguments in the "social capital" literature. Over the last two decades, the idea of "social capital" has played an important role in debates about democracy, diversity, and healthy or failing social relations. The scholarly literature encompasses multiple, and even conflicting, definitions of this term (Bourdieu 1986; Coleman 1988; Putnam 1993, 2000), but work by Robert Putnam, particularly in his best-selling book *Bowling Alone*, has come to define the landscape and shape policy terrain. In Putnam's formulations, "social capital" refers to the resources that individuals develop through their social networks, and the private and public payoffs that those networks bring. We gain jobs through social networks, but also well-being and happiness. These are private goods. As to public goods, our communities benefit from our social networks through their production of generalized trust, mutual support, cooperation, and institutional effectiveness (Putnam 2000, 21–22). In Putnam's analyses, social capital is simply what arises from certain kinds of interaction: volunteering, participating in political campaigns, attending block parties and neighborhood picnics, and joining service and leadership clubs like the Jaycees and Rotary Club.

By virtue of focusing on declining participation in such clubs in the 1970s and 1980s, Putnam traces a decline in "social capital" in the US over the second half of the twentieth century. Notably, Putnam's research identifies social capital as emerging deterministically from certain facts on the ground, in particular, demographic homogeneity. He also argues that, conversely, diversity inherently erodes social capital, as in his influential 2006 Johan Skytte Prize Lecture (Putnam 2007). In that lecture, Putnam made the case that there is a necessary "trade-off between diversity and community" that can, at best, be "ameliorated" (Putnam 2007, 164). His proposed technique for ameliorating the trade-off between diversity and community is to reduce the salience of identity in people's lives.

In contrast to Putnam's empirical studies of what appear in his data to be erosions of social capital in diverse neighborhoods, complexity theorists and social psychologists have studied diversity in teams, both formally and empirically, and have come to the countervailing conclusion that diversity can and ought to strengthen the epistemological capacity of groups, but that achieving this depends on the group's developing successful modes of interaction (Page 2007; Maloney and Zellmer-Bruhn 2006; Saxenian 2006; Homan et al. 2008).[12] In other words, social capital and epistemological success in team contexts are not things that emerge, organically, from demographic facts themselves. Participants on a diverse team, or in a diverse community, must have a body of knowledge—as well as skills and capacities—pertaining to social interaction, if they are to succeed at generating social capital from their opportunities for social interaction.

This conclusion helps us see an important lacuna in Putnam's argument. Our interactions with others in both structured activities (clubs, political parties, and so forth) and unstructured informal interactions are not unmediated, "natural," or somehow "essential" activities (Ferguson 2012). Instead, we bring to them expectations, capacities, competencies, skills, and knowledge (or the lack thereof) that generate the phenomena that emerge from our interactions: perhaps trust, perhaps distrust; perhaps a commitment to mutual benefit; perhaps an agreement to disagree and drift apart (Homan et al. 2008, 1204–22). Structured activities—for instance, club membership—can help set expectations for participants and educate them in the competencies, skills, and knowledge that lead to interactions that generate "social capital" (Homan et al. 2008; Maloney and Zellmer-Bruhn 2006). Even informal, ostensibly "unstructured" interactions are mediated by protocols of engagement disseminated by local and national cultures. In this regard, the activities that Putnam sees as the source of social capital are perhaps better understood as clusters of rituals, rules, and protocols that mediate interaction in ways that do (or do not) generate "social capital." Once one sees those structured and unstructured social interactions in this way, one realizes that they can be broken down into (a) the interactional contexts into which they invite participants, (b) the particular capacities they demand of participants, and (c) the capacities, skills, and knowledge they cultivate in participants.[13] Seen in this light, specific activities like clubs, political parties, and recurring bridge games, are no longer necessary to the production of social capital. Instead, what is necessary is capacities, knowledge, and skills that enable people to actualize the potential value of social relationships.

Another point follows from this recognition that "social capital" emerges not from any given activity itself but instead from capacities, skills, and knowledge applied to interaction in the contexts of particular activities. The capacities, skills, and knowledge activated by any given structured activity guide participants in interaction that will successfully generate social capital *in that particular social context* (Maloney and Zellmer-Bruhn 2006). That is, if the relevant social organization has a very homogeneous membership (for instance, if all members are women of a certain race and class), then the body of knowledge captured and conveyed through the activity of participation in that organization will be very specific to the production of social capital in that sort of demographic and cultural context. What follows from this is the idea that capacities, skills, and knowledge relevant to producing the interactions that are most likely to generate social capital must vary with the social contexts in which they are supposed to operate. A further thought is that when bodies of knowledge that were developed in one social context are applied to a new social context, one should expect them to fail because of the mismatch.[14]

This helps explain an intriguing fact hidden beneath Putnam's data in *Bowling Alone*. Putnam mentions the US judicial system only once in that book, when he makes a reference to the Supreme Court's 1896 decision in *Plessy v. Ferguson,* which affirmed racial segregation in transportation as legally valid. Putnam's failure to attend to the legal context of his data is a considerable lacuna. In the period from 1954 to 1985, the period in which Putnam traces a major decline in participation in thirty-two face-to-face chapter-based associations, the US legal system, at the level of the states, Congress, and the Supreme Court, rewrote the law of association, with very direct impacts on precisely the private clubs that Putnam analyzed. Most important were the legal changes and court decisions that made illegal the gender-exclusive membership policies of organizations like the Jaycee's and Rotary Club. Until the 1970s, those organizations had been all male. In the 1980s, the courts required them to use inclusive membership policies, and women began to enter. Importantly, those court cases followed developments at the state level that had moved in this direction, and those in turn had followed shifts in citizen values away from gender-exclusive organizational forms. Not all of Putnam's thirty-two organizations were equally exposed to the legal changes, however; some were not affected by them because of protections for religious organizations or because their members were children. Whereas the median decline in membership for the whole set of thirty-two organizations over the period from 1970 to 1997 was 58 percent, the five organizations that were gender segregated but legally protected because of religion or the status of their members as children saw declines ranging only from 5 to 18 percent.[15] What Putnam diagnosed as a decline in social capital is, I believe, better understood as organizational erosion that emerged from nonalignment between old forms of social knowledge and changed institutional and organizational forms. The older gender-exclusive clubs were operated by forms of social knowledge that were also nondemocratic. As organizational forms have changed toward inclusion, they have created a demand for social knowledge that can support their democratic and egalitarian operations.[16] Whether new social capital emerges depends on whether we forge a new alignment between organizational design and the social and cultural knowledge that can sustain inclusive organizations. Can we build the bodies of knowledge needed to operate inclusive and democratic social organizations?

In other words, the organizations that suffered in the US in the middle of the twentieth century were those whose historical cultures of interaction no longer aligned with the new principles of membership they had either chosen or been required to adopt. Diversity itself is not "the problem" when something like "social cohesion" seems to be falling away. The problem lies, rather, in a mismatch between historical cultures for interaction and new organizational designs that require new forms of social knowledge for their successful operation.

If we begin to deploy policy frameworks that increase the frequency of the formation of bridging ties and move us toward a connected society, we will need to support that policy work with cultural work that develops the interactional habits and practices to support success for all at actualizing the potential for value in bridging relationships. How can this be done? Let's take universities as an example. Across the US over the past fifty years, universities have changed their practices for recruiting and admitting students to achieve diverse and inclusive student bodies. The mission of those universities has not, however, changed. In the broadest terms, they all continue to pursue academic excellence. They therefore have the job of developing principles for campus practices and a campus culture that can enable a diverse community of learners and educators to form relationships that can sustain the pursuit of academic excellence (Allen, Fung, Weenick, et al. 2018).

Enabling those learners and educators to form those relationships requires cultivating in all of them the capacities, skills, and bodies of knowledge necessary to generate social capital in contexts of demographic diversity. The relevant capacities, skills, and knowledge are not merely technical or informational but also include ethical content, as I've discussed in *Talking to Strangers*. They include knowledge not only about one-to-one interactions, or even group dynamics, but also about the material conditions that impact interaction, for instance, whether we have individual bathrooms or group gender-assigned bathrooms; whether a podium can be lowered to the height of shorter speakers or will always obscure their faces, and so on. In the next section, I offer more detail about the sort of interactional norms, capacities, skills, and knowledge that we need to cultivate for institutions and organizations aspiring to support social connectedness.

Capacities, Skills, and Knowledge for Social Connectedness

A "connected society" may be one that maximizes bridging ties, but bridging ties do not arise merely by virtue of assembling a group of people characterized by demographic diversity in a single location. Bridging ties emerge when individuals are able to interact successfully across boundaries of difference. They emerge when people are able to convert a social relationship that is initially costly—in that it starts without a preexisting supply of shared tacit social understandings—into one that brings mutual benefit. What are the cultural habits that can help individuals flourish in enacting social connectedness?

I argued above that our social interactions with others are mediated by capacities, skills, and bodies of knowledge, which we can draw on to produce social capital in the specific contexts to which those capacities, skills, and bodies of knowledge pertain. To build a connected society, then, we need to identify the capacities, skills, and bodies of knowledge that constitute an "art of bridging," an art of forming productive social relationships across boundaries of difference. Certain categories of professional routinely build valuable bridging ties: translators, interpreters, mediators, patient advocates, community organizers engaged with diverse populations, and members of global business teams (Maloney and Zellmer-Bruhn 2006; Homan et al. 2008). Each of these groups of professionals has a tacit body of knowledge that might be tapped to flesh out the content of the art of bridging that requires cultivation, in order for egalitarian social relations to arise in conditions of diversity.

We can see the relevant bodies of knowledge emerging. In a context where school district leaders seek to support a diverse cohort of educator colleagues in working well together in contexts of diversity, they introduce meeting protocols such as this:

- Listen for understanding.
- Share the airtime.
- Stay present and engaged.
- Focus on students.
- Experience discomfort.
- Expect and accept non-closure.[17]

In a college classroom, the norm of "listening for understanding" can be reinforced by asking students to repeat back what they have heard another student say to confirm correct understanding before they turn to sharing their own response or perspective. And being present and engaged is a norm that can be supported by requiring each student who speaks in response to another to use the name of the other, to show that they are present and engaged to the others in the conversation.

I have observed emergent practices of "social connectedness" in the context of my own service on policy commissions seeking to develop policy recommendations in highly controversial areas—from inclusion and belonging on a university campus to democracy reform to civic education (Allen, Fung, Weenick, et al. 2018; Allen, Heintz, Liu, et al. 2020; Educating for American Democracy 2021). Across the three leadership commissions on which I served, shared practices emerged for pursuing cooperative interaction toward decision-making in contexts of great diversity. Here I will share three particularly important features, all of which can be understood to meet the design principle of supporting the cultural habits that can help individuals flourish in enacting social connectedness.

All three commissions decided to use at least a three-person group of chairs as the leadership team. The view was that a minimum of three cochairs was necessary for sufficient diversity of perspective within the leadership cohort itself. This three-person structure required all of the cochairs to learn new leaderships practices as they sought to lead together. Practices that grew stronger over the course of the work included ensuring that all three chairs had equal airtime in the team's agenda-setting meetings; that all three chairs were comfortable articulating when they felt uncomfortable about a direction being pursued and that the others were responsive to that discomfort and sought to find solutions for it; that all three chairs were comfortable with no individual chair claiming credit for any particular dimension of the work and with consistently directing credit to the commission as a whole.

A second key choice made by all three commissions was to establish a membership larger than those of past commissions of a similar kind, in order to ensure, again, that there would be enough diversity in the group—demographic, cultural, ideological, professional, and experiential. And once groups are larger than they might have been in another era—forty people instead of twenty in one case, or three hundred instead of fifty—then there is a need for innovation in meeting protocols and technologies to ensure effective collaboration, opportunities for voice, and deliberation. Techniques include real intentionality around when to use committee-of-the-whole processes and when to use breakout groups; the use of real-time polling and survey questions to help make visible the knowledge and perspectives in the room; and explicit discussion about norms for group decision-making, including when the approach will require coming to consensus and when it will require a majority vote.

A third key feature of all three commissions was beginning the work with an effort to identify some shared values and purposes that all could sign on to unanimously. Over the course of long processes of significant and often heated debate, those original shared values became a North

Star for the deliberations. But the time spent discussing them at the beginning of the commission process also provided an opportunity to forge mutual understanding and to build relationships before the groups turned to making concrete and nitty-gritty choices with real trade-offs. All three of these features of the policy commissions supported effective bridging relationships, and out of the work of bridging, bonding also grew.

Indeed, to say that we need an art of bridging is not at all to say that we can ignore the art of bonding (Bromberg 2011; Honneth 1992). Let me introduce some data in order to flesh out the subtle ways that bonding and bridging ties interact. A comprehensive 2008 study of student social life at the University of California, Los Angeles, published by Russell Sage as *The Diversity Challenge*, provides significant insight into this question. The study traces in-group and out-group friendships for the four major ethnic groups on the UCLA campus (black, Latinx, Asian, and white), as well as participation in ethnic organizations. Students who came to campus having already had greater than average out-group contact continued in that direction, forming out-group friendships at far higher rates. Students of all ethnicities whose precollegiate experience had, in contrast, tended toward in-group bias (that is, more positive feelings toward one's own group), anxiety about intercultural competence, and perceptions of discrimination were more likely to develop an extensively in-group friendship set. Yet the results of this proclivity for in-group bonding were different for different groups. On the negative side, this bonding further increased in-group bias for all groups, as well as also increasing perceptions of discrimination and interactional anxiety. Also on the negative side, for Latinx students at UCLA during the time of the study, those in-group bonding relationships led to lower motivation, attachment, and commitment, all of which negatively impact academic success. Yet for the Asian and black students in the study, these bonding experiences led to higher commitment to academics, and in addition, for black students, they led to greater attachment to the university and higher academic motivation, all clearly good outcomes.

These data dramatically illustrate that not all bonding is the same and that there is much work to be done to understand (1) the mechanisms that generate bonding's positive effects, (2) the mechanisms that generate its negative (antibridging) effects, and (3) the mechanisms by which bonding itself might serve to teach people how to bridge rather than be insular.

The question of how we bond is deeply entangled with the question of whether we are able to bridge (Bromberg 2011). The critical question for a democratic society is how we can bond with those who are like us so as to help us bridge even with those who differ from us. In order for any method of bonding—for instance, that which begins from social homogeneity or that which begins from interest affinity—to support our capacity to bridge, the very experience of bonding must cultivate receptivity toward the potential of participation in our bonding group by social dissimilars. For now, I will call this "cosmopolitan bonding." (In chapter 5, I will relabel this form of bonding "polypolitan.") The question of just what sorts of styles and methods of social bonding can be cosmopolitan in this way is a difficult one, which I will not address here.[18] It will suffice for our purposes simply to mark out the terrain by identifying this, too, as a core component of the capacities, skills, and knowledge necessary to build a connected society.

The important message, then, is this: everybody needs opportunities both to bond and to bridge, and everybody therefore needs arts of both bonding and bridging. We also, importantly, need to learn ways of bonding that enable us to bridge. We need to give more attention to understanding and cultivating these two intertwined arts.

But here we come to an impasse. If our families and our therapists help us learn how to bond, who helps us learn how to bridge (Eng and Han 2000)? There remains much research to be done—by sociologists, psychologists, anthropologists, historians, and philosophers—to deepen our understanding of the art of bridging, in order that we may more effectively cultivate it. For instance, we need research that translates the insights developed in the literature on business management (about diverse teams and intercultural competence) and interpreter studies and multilingualism (about communication) to a wider array of social contexts (schools, colleges, training programs, associations, political institutions, workplaces generally, neighborhoods, and so on). The work in the management literature rests on a foundation of social psychology, a foundation which ought to be updated with reference to the literature on stereotype threat. Moreover, the skills, capacities, and bodies of knowledge that make it possible to take advantage of diversity appear to be related to personality factors. In addition to social psychologists, we need to engage researchers whose focus is individual psychology on the question of how to scaffold forms of personality development that can support acquisition of the art of bridging. And, last, we need to connect all these conversations to educational research. In order to maximize educational achievement, we need above all to learn how to train teachers to succeed in pedagogic relationships that operate in conditions of diversity (Jeffries 2022).

By directing our attention toward an art of bridging, the ideal of social connectedness helps make imaginable the forms of human development necessary for cultivating egalitarian climates inside our institutions and maximizing the benefit we draw from diversity. I must also underscore in closing, however, that new cultures of interaction are not themselves enough to achieve a connected society, if we do not also adopt a policy framework that increases the rate at which bridging ties can form. In other words, the cultural framework for social connectedness that I propose here requires, as its necessary partner, a policy framework for a connected society.

Conclusion

The US is living through a major demographic transition that will surely upend its earlier approaches to thinking about identity, community, and social relations.[19] The question of whether in, say, fifty years, Americans will live in an egalitarian country where no group is in the majority and where such inequalities that persist do not track ethnic or racial lines depends on choices made now.[20] If citizens of the US make the wrong choices, they may find that a black/nonblack binary has reasserted itself and that racial privilege is as strong as ever. Something similar might be said about Europe—grappling as it is with a conjunction of low birthrates in the native population, a refugee crisis, internal European migration, and the question of the future of Europe. Demography is not destiny, but decisions a citizenry makes about demography will be. For all of the challenges presented by contemporary demographic turbulence, the best hope for converting new diversity into durable and healthy, albeit heterogeneous, free societies, I argue, is to reinvigorate the core egalitarian commitments of democracy and to focus policy efforts on projects of participation and egalitarian empowerment. A justice framework that begins from the pursuit of and protection of political equality and that employs the guiding principle of difference without domination can provide a way to navigate these social complexities (Allen 2014b). We often forget that institutional and cultural work go hand in hand. We often want to know what laws we ought to change in order to achieve justice. Yet law does and should have limits, and beyond those limits, the responsibility to achieve our goals falls on our own shoulders.

In closing this chapter, I want to make one final point. This argument about embracing a subsidiary ideal for the social domain of social connectedness, as a part of reinvigorating democratic commitments to political equality, has consequences for what we understand "the people," that is, the "democratic people" of any given polity, to be. Just as social groups emerge according to the opportunities and constraints established by the basic structure of the society, and by the interactional work done by members of the polity, so too "the people" itself emerges from the protocols and practices of interaction. As new members of the polity are incorporated in participatory processes, whether in civil society organizations or political institutions, the content contributed to the collective conversation about what the people should do will change. As that content changes, and as the people make new decisions about the directions of their collective conversation, the people will continuously make itself always something somewhat new, including in cultural terms.

This idea is a relatively easy one for people in the US and other settler societies to accept because ours have always been cultures in the making, as our rapid demographic shifts transform the pattern of voices contributing to the shared activity of our decision-making. Given the histories of Europe's countries, where moments of settler formation, such as the Norman conquest, lie much further in the past, the idea is less easily assimilated in European political discourse. But the idea is important nonetheless. To embrace democracy, political equality, and a connected society as core elements of justice is also to relinquish the idea that we can delineate the cultural shape of a specific democratic people a priori or once and for all.

As I have said, my vision is that of a pragmatist wherein the project of democracy is to fill preexisting forms and, as we fill them, to change them and be changed—to paraphrase the poet Frank Bidart's response to Jorge Luis Borges's short text "Borges and I" (Bidart's poem, too, was called "Borges and I"). The empowerment that comes from democracy makes acceptance of this open-ended, ongoing process worth it.

5

The Third Subsidiary Ideal

POLYPOLITANISM

Introduction: Review and Preview

Thus far, I have argued that a rightly constructed theory of justice will start from the premise that political equality is non-sacrificeable. The route to justice, our overarching ideal, is through and only through democracy. Benevolent autocracies may be able to achieve material well-being for their people, but by definition they will never achieve the basis for full human flourishing. Therefore, they will never achieve full justice (Sen 1999a, 1999b).

In chapter 2, I argued that justice, rightly understood, is grounded in political equality and the institutions that undergird it. In chapter 3, I addressed the relation between a non-sacrificeable principle of political equality, the principle of difference without domination, and political institutions and sketched a subsidiary ideal of egalitarian participatory constitutional democracy. In chapter 4, I addressed the relation between those same principles and social policy and sketched a subsidiary ideal of a connected society. Across all three of these chapters, I argued that within the polity, a theory of justice that treats political equality as non-sacrificeable recognizes human moral equality in full and seeks to build political institutions, structure social policy, cultivate economies, and enable inclusive cultural work that activate a full sharing of power and responsibility.[1] The protection of freedom will ensure that difference emerges, but the pursuit of justice requires continually working to ensure that the forms of difference that do emerge—whether in the social or economic realm—do not articulate with the domination of some by others, or of any individual over other individuals. To eschew domination is not to renounce hierarchy. Rather, legitimate hierarchies avoid an arbitrary or rights-violating exercise of power (Pettit 2014; Rogers 2020). Similarly, a connected society does not renounce in-group bonding relationships but does work to support forms of in-group bonding that also cultivate openness to connections across lines of social division. In chapter 4, I called the relevant kinds of relationships "cosmopolitan bonding" relationships. Now, to characterize justice in the social realm, I am going to replace that idea of cosmopolitanism with a new subsidiary ideal: "polypolitanism."

By polypolitanism, I have in mind the idea that any one of us might have affiliations with multiple political communities and many political roles, and that we need to form connections with any particular political community in ways that open us up to the possibility of embracing many other, nonoverlapping affiliations, both for ourselves and for others. Cosmopolitanism asks us to look past our membership in a nation-state to our membership in the global community. We are to imagine connecting with any and every human being from anywhere on the planet. In contrast, polypolitanism orients us toward the need to support one another in embracing multiple, nonoverlapping organizational and political affiliations. It asks us to look to other forms of membership, alongside our membership in the nation-state, and to learn to navigate the experience of social diversity that comes from being a member of multiple, nonoverlapping political and social networks. Like cosmopolitanism, the concept of polypolitanism softens nation-states as conceptual boundaries for ethics and politics, but it doesn't dissolve social groupings altogether. It instead asks us to conceive of the world as a set of layered social networks, among which nation-states have a special prominence.[2] In a world understood thus, we all have multiple memberships that we need to learn to navigate successfully.

Ideally, those multiple memberships combine to support our empowerment. A connected society is supported by polypolitan, rather than
cosmopolitan, bonding relationships.[3]

To bring the subsidiary ideal of polypolitanism fully into view, it
will be necessary to begin the journey from society to economy. Polypolitanism emerges as a necessary subsidiary ideal at exactly the point
where the social and economic domains intersect—when we have to
set the terms of political membership and immigration. After all, the
rules of membership structure labor markets. This chapter explores the
intersection of political economy and immigration policy in order to
bring the ideal of polypolitanism into view.

Difference without Domination: From Politics to Society to Economy and Back to Society

If the design principle of difference without domination yields a subsidiary ideal of egalitarian participatory constitutional democracy for the
political realm and an ideal of a connected society for the social realm,
what sort of subsidiary ideal does it yield for the economic realm? We
have to explore what approach to political economy could embody the
principle of difference without domination and be built upon a theory
of justice that treats political equality as non-sacrificeable. The answer is
pretty straightforward. The ideal for political economy, on this account
of justice, is to build empowering economies, economies that empower
the citizenry to succeed as civic participants. This quickly turns out to
have a social question at its base—who are the members of society for
whom empowerment is relevant in the first place? Before we can dive
fully into the question of political economy, we have to take up a second
question about the social domain: how should political membership be
defined to accord with difference without domination?

The idea that a just economy empowers citizens is not new. Both
Aristotle and the founders of the United States thought that a "middling" or "middle-class" economy was the necessary foundation for a
polity of free and equal citizens. Similarly, nineteenth-century American

president Abraham Lincoln believed that the economy of a republic had to rest on "free labor" in order for citizens to remain free from domination and fully empowered. In contrast to Aristotle and the first generation of American founders, however, Lincoln also connected the idea of an empowering economy to that of a nonexploitative economy. "As I would not be a slave," he wrote, "so I would not be a master. This expresses my idea of democracy. Whatever differs from this, to the extent of the difference, is not democracy."[4] Ultimately, for him, the need to rest the republic on an empowering economy required the eradication of enslavement, so that the empowerment of some would not rest on expropriation from others. The effort to end enslavement attempted a fundamental reorientation of the American political economy—for all the twists and turns of the strategies and tactics with which Lincoln pursued it and for all the unevenness of the effort's results (Foner 2011; Witt 2012). Lincoln sought to make a commitment to labor relations without domination or exploitation a precompetitive matter—that is, a matter not governed by the marketplace but baked into the background rules of the marketplace as established by political institutions. For the subsidiary ideal of an "empowering economy," the goal is to ascertain how to build an empowering, nonexploitative economy. Exploitation is the act of profiting from vulnerabilities that characterize those in the weaker position in a relationship of domination. An economy will be nonexploitative, in other words, when it is also free from relations of domination.

As we begin to consider how to secure an empowering economy free from domination and exploitation, it soon becomes clear that the most urgent question concerns immigration—in other words, a social question. The question of who gets to be a citizen, and in which polity, is, I will argue, the first economic question. Ascertaining how to build nonexploitative and empowering economies for a citizenry of political equals turns out to require, as its first building block, a just immigration policy (cf. Carens 2010, 2013; Miller 2016; Meissner 2019; Salam 2018; Shachar 2009, 2020; Song 2018). Consequently, before we can fully engage the development of a subsidiary ideal for the economy, we need one more subsidiary ideal for the social realm: an ideal for political membership. Polypolitanism is the relevant ideal. This ideal will in turn generate design principles for an approach to immigration policy that is compatible with the principle of difference without domination.

To make the content of polypolitanism clear, I will first explain how the ideal of an empowering economy in a domestic nation-state context interacts with questions of membership. Then I will explore the relationship of the global economy to the world's rules for political membership. As we consider what that relationship can teach us about the puzzles to be solved in building empowering and nonexploitative economies, we will uncover design principles for membership.

Along the way, I will pause to consider one recent proposal for adjusting global immigration and membership rules At first blush, the Visas between Individuals Program (VIP), proffered by legal theorist Eric Posner and economist Glen Weyl in their book *Radical Markets*, might seem to align with the principles that I will articulate. Their idea for adjusting membership rules has as its goal the achievement of global distributive justice. Yet, as we will see, pursuit of this goal does not automatically bring cultivation of empowering economies. Indeed, a close look at the VIP proposal usefully clarifies the logical consequences that flow from the normative frameworks that currently dominate policy-making—in particular, the commonplace utilitarian and distributive justice views that fail to recognize the non-sacrificeability of political equality. Although Posner and Weyl have now repudiated their proposal, review and analysis of it still helps clarify the conceptual choices in front of us. In contrast to the VIP proposal, I will seek an approach to political membership that aligns with the principle of difference without domination.

This inquiry will bring into view both the ideal of polypolitanism and the complete set of design principles needed to operationalize it. As I have said, polypolitanism is the idea that any one of us might have affiliations with multiple political communities and many political roles. Whether we have access to political equality is not a unitary question but, rather, a question of how our memberships accumulate and interact. Recognizing this allows us to reconceptualize political membership and will help us fully come to see the ideal of polypolitanism. Having fully unearthed the ideal and its related design principles, I will then provide some examples of immigration policies that might instantiate them.

Where Society and Economy Meet: The Role for a Subsidiary Ideal of Political Membership in a Theory of Justice

Immigration policy is fundamentally about questions of membership. Who gets to belong to a particular society? Most importantly, who gets to be a citizen? Who gets access to this vaunted political equality that, I am arguing, is the foundation for full justice? Issues of migration, immigration, and naturalization are clearly political questions. Beyond that, they might seem at first glance to be social, not economic questions. But this is incorrect.

Rather counterintuitively, membership policies have no impact on the design principles for a connected society that I sketched in the previous chapter. There, I argued that a social policy that accords with the principle of difference without domination will focus on building a society that supports in-group relationships with openness to connections across lines of social division and on designing private and public institutions to maximize the formation of bridging ties. These principles pertain regardless of the democracy's membership policies. Whether the society's members are native born or immigrants, speakers of a dominant or a minority language, and in what proportions, the design principles of a connected society will be the same. Their implementation will change with the demographic facts on the ground, but the design principles themselves will not. The nature of the social differences with the potential to fragment a society and that need to be overcome will vary from context to context, but even relatively homogenous societies have fallen into civil war. And even relatively homogenous societies are healthier if they are more connected. Similarly, one or another migration and membership policy will put varying kinds of pressure on the institutions of a connected society, but in each case, the connected society ideal establishes a goal to maximize bridging relationships and to support the kinds of bonding relationships that can reinforce bridging. There may be interesting questions to consider about the rate of social dynamism that can be sustained, given particular institutional configurations of bonding and bridging relationships.[5] But those are empirical questions. Variations in membership policy don't change, or undermine, the theoretical fundamentals of the connected society ideal.

The same cannot be said of the economic realm. The question of what sorts of membership policies we choose will constrain the possible set of political economies and whether we can find our way to an empowering economy at all. As we turn from the application of the principle of difference without domination in the social realm to its application in the economic realm, the question of membership in the polity—of who has visiting, residential, and/or national political rights—becomes distinctively salient. The question of who gets to be a member of which polity and on which terms is, perhaps, the first economic fact. Since property rights, for instance, are anchored by the legal regimes of particular political communities, membership in a specific political community (or lack thereof) even precedes property. The allocation of membership within particular national polities is one of the building blocks of the global economy and therefore of the economy of any particular polity. Questions of just approaches to migration, immigration, and membership are a necessary way station on the path to envisioning a just political economy.

Envisioning a political economy that aligns with the principle of difference without domination intersects issues of membership in three ways. First, previous efforts to build empowering and egalitarian economies have often not only failed to align with the principle of difference without domination but have proactively used domination as a tool to support the construction of an empowering economy for a privileged group of people classed as citizens. Second, in our current world, the opportunity to migrate presents would-be migrants with a meaningful chance to improve their own economic and social prospects, but the asymmetry between the human right to freedom of movement, as articulated in the Universal Declaration of Human Rights, and the absence of a right to be received in any particular place (except in the case of refugees) sets up potential conditions for exploitation. Third, the world's membership and migration policies structure the world's labor market and therefore structure the potential of both global and national economies for growth, efficient operation, and equitable distribution of the gains of productivity. Not only migrants themselves but also receiving societies stand to benefit materially from labor mobility (even if some specific members of the receiving societies might lose out). In other words, the material bases of an empowering economy are affected by the world's membership and migration policies. If we are to maximize the power of the global economy to deliver to the world's peoples the material bases for civic agency, we need approaches to membership that make it possible for the workers of the world to move. Yet the coupling of the material benefits of migration to both migrants and receiving societies with the asymmetry between rights to move and rights to be received further entrenches the vulnerability of would-be migrants to exploitation. By organizing the world's labor market, the world's membership policies not only structure the potential of both global and national economies for growth, efficient operation, and equitable distribution of the gains of productivity; they also establish patterns of power and vulnerability for the world's populations.

How, historically, has the goal of an economy that empowers a body of citizen equals been linked through membership policies to the problem of exploitation? How do frameworks of membership structure the economy and patterns of power and vulnerability? Answering these two questions will lead to parameters for an empowering economy that accords with the principle of difference without domination. The answers will also clarify how thoroughly the economy is embedded in society.

Why Membership Matters: Empowering Economies and the Historical Problem of Exploitation

As I said above, political economies directed toward the empowerment of the citizenry are not new. Both Aristotle and the founders of the

United States thought that a "middling" or "middle-class" economy was the necessary foundation for a polity of free and equal citizens. In ultimately seeking to end enslavement, Lincoln pursued an empowering economy that also ruled out the most extreme forms of domination in labor relations and made a commitment to "free labor" a precompetitive feature of market societies. Importantly, in deciding to fight enslavement, Lincoln sought to replace the founding generation's model for a political economy of empowerment. The founders of the early American republic had sought to ground political equality in economic egalitarianism (Mandell 2020). For instance, the Georgia land lottery gave land out to white men, widows, and orphans in equal-sized plots via a lottery (Allen 2016b). Yet the land lottery was, of course, not open to the enslaved population. Even more fundamental, the land being given away had been expropriated from Native Americans. In other words, an empowering economic egalitarianism was created only by virtue of designating a subset of people as existing outside the circle of political inclusion.[6] Indigenous Americans had access to none of the tools that economist Albert Hirschman has identified as independently or in aggregate providing both freedom and a well-functioning economy: exit, voice, and influence through loyalty (Hirschman 1970).[7]

Historically, societies committed to political equality have typically relied on exploitation of those outside the penumbra of protection. This is a philosophical as well as moral error that requires correction. The correction we need is the one Lincoln offered, namely, the recognition that democracy should be defined by the following moral orientation: "As I would not be a slave, so I would not be a master." The goal is to avoid the moral failure exhibited in the Georgia land lottery. A twenty-first-century effort to ground a theory of justice in the nonsacrificeability of political equality within a polity must show how an economic order can be constructed that supports a domestic project of political equality without making the exclusion of others from access to political equality a necessary condition of its own success. This is the twenty-first-century equivalent to the nineteenth-century injunction to imagine an economy without slavery.

Why should we care whether a domestic project of protecting political equality and of securing an empowering economy exploits the lack of access of others to political equality? Our own pursuit of political equality rests on recognizing its value to human flourishing generally. This general applicability is why we should respect political equality's importance for those outside our polity as well as for those within it. Such respect does not necessitate bringing about political equality for others. We can't wave a magic wand and transform every person on the globe into a citizen in a well-functioning democracy. Indeed, not only can we not do so; we should not do so. Political equality is not something that some can create for others; democratic agency must be made by its own agents for themselves. Forcing others to be free, for instance at the tip of a spear, would violate the principles defining how to achieve justice by means of democracy. How to structure membership in national polities to support the project of justice is more complicated than the democratizing invasions of various imperial armies (including those of the US) have seemed to suggest. *Instead, respect for the value of political equality to human beings generally entails refusing to take advantage of the vulnerabilities that accrue to those who do not have access to political voice and influence.*

The membership policies of the world's countries create vulnerabilities by differentially distributing political equality. Some countries offer political equality to some residents but not others; some countries offer political equality to only a very few residents. Some people have access to voice and influence because of the membership status into which they were born; millions are stateless and have no access to voice and influence at all. Of course, economic inequalities within any given country also affect who has genuine access to voice and influence. Yet membership policies are prior even to this. Membership policies across the globe will affect the degree of vulnerability we are morally obliged to avoid taking advantage of. As citizens of democracies seek to build empowering economies, our work is less likely to slip into injustice to the degree that vulnerabilities of others stemming from the lack of access to political equality are minimized. We ought therefore to seek this minimization, simply in order to protect ourselves. Our moral question is this: how can we avoid treating other parts of the globe as the founders of the United States treated indigenous Americans?

Before we can explore how to build empowering and nonexploitative economies, then, we need to ascertain how to build membership policies for the globe's states that simultaneously, and in relation to each other, maximize the potential of labor to move, for the migrants' own sake as well as for the sake of the economies of receiving societies, while minimizing the vulnerability of the world's populations to exclusion from political equality. Here, then, are preliminary versions of the design principles for a just system of membership for the world's states and for a just political economy focused on the development of economies that are simultaneously empowering and nonexploitative:

1. The global membership system should maximize the freedom of labor to move . . .
2. . . . while minimizing the vulnerability of the world's populations to exclusion from political equality.

If we are to develop a political economy that accords with the above criteria, we will need to probe in greater depth how frameworks of membership structure the economy and patterns of power and vulnerability.

How Membership Structures the Economy

The world has never seen an economy disembedded from social relations, nor is such a thing imaginable (Polanyi [1944] 2001). The world's global economy is embedded not only in the political systems of particular nation-states but also in a global system structured above all by rules about membership, migration, and immigration. Those rules of membership typically flow from underlying paradigms for belonging: the two dominant ones have been nationalism and cosmopolitanism.

In *Radical Markets*, Posner and Weyl offer a very helpful review of the intertwining history of capitalism and migration from the eighteenth century to the present; through their review we can also see the intertwining histories of nationalist and cosmopolitan concepts of membership.

In the late eighteenth century the protectionist mercantilism of the early modern European sovereigns gave way to policies of free international trade advocated by thinkers like Jeremy Bentham, Adam Smith, and David Hume. These political philosophers argued that free exchange across borders—of goods, capital, and credit—would maximize the total welfare delivered by an economy to the citizens of any given nation.

Importantly, migration was not a focus of the work of the eighteenth-century free marketeers, largely because migration just did not matter that much at that point in time. Despite the age of exploration, and the significant movements of people driven by the transatlantic enslavement trade, "persistent differences in mass living standards across countries were unknown until the late nineteenth century" (Posner and Weyl 2018, 133). As Posner and Weyl put it, in the late eighteenth and early nineteenth century, the most extreme gaps in prosperity, as between China and the United Kingdom, "were only a factor of 3," while by the 1950s the gap had reached a factor of 10. They combine several historical data sets on global inequality and show a remarkable transformation in the period between 1820 and 2011. Most importantly, they find that income inequality across countries "increased from about 7% in 1820 to about 70% in 1980"; since 1980, the degree of inequality has shrunk somewhat, thanks to growth in China and India, but it is still at about 50 percent. At the same time, average within-country income inequality has held relatively steady, and even shown a slight decline. That decline reflects both increases of inequality in wealthy countries and decreases of inequality in developing countries. The combination of the dramatic increase in between-country inequality and the modest decrease in within-country inequality means that on the whole, global inequality is far greater now than it was in the early nineteenth century. In other words, people's standard of living varies significantly with the accident of where they were born. The consequence of these economic facts is, as Posner and Weyl argue, that the world of Bentham, Smith, and Hume was one "in which migration did most people little good" while "ours is one in which migration can be a primary route to well-being and prosperity for most people in the world."

Whereas the early theorists of capital argued for the free movement of goods and capital, they made no equivalent case for the free movement of people. This was not because they were against such free movement but simply because migration was not relevant to maximizing the efficiency of the globe's economy in the late eighteenth century. The intervening centuries have changed that. And in parallel, the globe's countries have also become more controlling of migration. Migration was relatively unrestricted until the early twentieth century. Then the wealthy countries of the world began to close their doors to migrants, doing so just when migration had begun to matter for maximizing the capacity of the global economy to deliver welfare to all the world's peoples (Posner and Weyl 2018, 137). Over the course of the twentieth century, and into the early twenty-first century, as the globe marched forward, breaking down residual forms of trade protectionism and mercantilist economic policy, capital was set free to flow across the globe in the direction of its maximally efficient allocation. For the most part, labor was not similarly enabled to travel. People with higher levels of education have been able to move freely, but less well-educated workers have not shared that same mobility.

Where experiments have been made, as in the European Union, which permits free movement of the citizens of member states within EU boundaries, the asymmetrical flows of people from poorer countries, such as Poland, to wealthier ones, such as the United Kingdom, generated backlash to the necessarily ensuing cultural hybridization (including, ultimately, Brexit). In other words, the EU experiment reveals that different kinds of friction attach to the movement of people versus capital. The frictions are not a matter of interest rates or the availability of viable investment vehicles. Instead, they consist of matters of language, culture, and religion—the bases for collaboration. The well-functioning of human societies depends not merely on individuals' competencies and resources but also on communities' success at forming healthy patterns of interaction. The successful movement of people requires cultural connection and integration. Consequently, the frictions attached to the movement of labor need to be addressed as part of thinking about how to maximize the productive potential of the world's labor markets. Yet the resistance to the free movement of ordinary workers, often flowing from those frictions, means that the gains from freely moving capital go largely to the owners of capital, and the growth of a globalizing world has been captured by wealthy elites rather than being "widely shared" (Posner and Weyl 2018, 140).

In addition to pointing out that methods of globalization have freed goods and capital to flow to where they can be put to their best use without having similarly freed labor and that these methods have consequently resulted in unequal gains in the global economy, Posner and Weyl also underscore the consensus among economists that nearly all of the benefit to be had from liberalizing trade and capital flows has already accrued. At this point, the single component of the global economy with the biggest potential for positive impact on the distribution of wealth and the material bases for welfare around the world is migration policy. In short, membership policies—in the form of restrictive immigration policies in the early part of the twentieth century; European experimentation with liberalization of membership in the late twentieth century; and European retrenchment in the twenty-first century—are currently one of the most important constitutive elements for adjustments to the functioning of the world's economy. (Energy flows might be another.) Since no national economy can now operate without attention to its place within a global economy, the question of what just and empowering economic policy at home might be depends on each country's approach to migration and membership, and the world's resulting aggregate framework.

This story of restrictive immigration policies, experimentation with openness, and retrenchment reflects an underlying dialectical argument between nationalist and cosmopolitan concepts of membership.

The former dominates the current structure of the global economy, but both are relevant to understanding its operations.

Thanks to the Treaty of Versailles, and its articulation of principles of national self-determination, later reinforced through the United Nations, a concept of a culturally unified people that determines a life-form for itself shapes common contemporary expectations for membership. The nationalist concept of membership is therefore frequently "ethnonationalist." Immigration poses a challenge by definition because it very often entails the arrival within national borders of people without a historic or cultural connection to "the people" who constitute the polity at issue. The settler societies—the United States, Australia, and Canada—have always been the exception to this model. In these countries immigrants overwhelmed indigenous populations and obliterated any stable concept of an indigenous cultural basis for membership. While these countries have themselves seen episodic efforts to establish a cultural basis for membership—and the US is living through such an effort now—the thoroughgoing hybridity of the population makes this an impossible task. Nonetheless, these countries, too, have sought significant immigration restrictions, reinforcing by practice, if not by ideology, the dominant pattern in the globe of nationalist, and even ethnonationalist, models of membership. Importantly, these nationalist models of membership restrict the capacity of the globe's political economy to maximize material welfare for all the peoples of the earth. The protection of the nationalist ideal depends on relegating some populations around the globe to deeper forms of poverty than is, strictly speaking, economically necessary. With restrictive membership policies, the effort to pursue an empowering economy in any developed country means that the benefits of internal egalitarianism rest on exploitation of peoples outside the borders of the country, much as was the case when the economic egalitarianism of the early American republic rested on the exploitation of native peoples.

The clear relationship between membership policies and political economy has also generated arguments for cosmopolitanism—the other end of the conceptual spectrum. According to the arguments of cosmopolitans, the gains to distributive justice to be had from allowing the free movement of peoples mean that all the countries of the world should have open borders. With labor able to move freely, the globe's economy would generate maximally fertile conditions for material welfare, and the wealth produced would be distributed in a maximally egalitarian fashion. This is a utopian picture of the relationship between membership policies and economic policy. It treats the phenomenon of human movement as on par with the movement of capital, as if people and capital could move with equivalent degrees of frictionlessness. But the cosmopolitan vision for how to maximize distributive justice founders on the unwillingness of populations in any given society to admit any and every person to membership in their society simply as arriving migrants see fit. Nor is this unwillingness altogether reprehensible. Social connectedness reduces the transaction costs within an economy and itself contributes to productivity. If we increase the movement of labor for the sake of economic growth, we should avoid doing so in ways that simultaneously undermine growth by increasing the friction of within-economy transactions. The cosmopolitan ideal founders because it fails to address the frictions that necessarily attend the movement of peoples and that introduce additional transaction costs to the functioning of an economy.

The nationalist model of membership entails members of wealthy countries securing their material good via exploitation and at the expense of those in other countries. The cosmopolitan model of membership entails members of poorer sending countries improving their material well-being at the expense of the viability of the political and social institutions of wealthier receiving countries. The flaws of the nationalist model lead us to ask what membership policies might support a domestic egalitarian empowering economy without relying on the domination and exploitation of those not included within the penumbra of political membership. The flaws of the cosmopolitan model lead us to ask how to minimize the specific kinds of friction that attend the movement of people.[8] The former correction requires finding a path to free movement of labor coupled with access to political voice; the latter correction requires finding methods for reducing the frictions attendant on movement. We can modestly revise our design principles for political membership to support a just political economy, one that cultivates economies that are simultaneously empowering and nonexploitative:

> The global membership system should maximize the freedom of labor to move by means of a framework that

> 1. minimizes the vulnerability of the world's populations to exclusion from political equality, and
> 2. reduces the frictions attendant on migration.

The first prong corrects nationalist and ethnonationalist approaches to immigration and membership; the second, corrects cosmopolitanism.

From Distributive Justice to Political Equality as First Principle

But we haven't quite gotten where we need to get yet. The membership design principles stated above do not yet align with the principle of difference without domination. We can see this by reviewing a recent policy proposal that aligns with the principles sketched above but that nonetheless would establish conditions of domination for migrants. I have in mind a proposal put forth by Posner and Weyl called the Visas between Individuals Program (VIP). Although the authors have now repudiated the program, it provides a useful touchstone for evaluating the design principles we are developing.

The VIP proposal is a market-based policy designed to minimize the frictions of migration by aligning the incentives of migrants and native-born citizens through market transactions in the interest of securing global distributive justice.[9] The objective of this proposal is to spur global economic growth in ways that more equitably distribute the material benefits of growth across the world's populations.

Under the VIP, citizens of wealthy countries would be permitted to sponsor as immigrants workers of their choice from elsewhere in the world, much as companies now sponsor highly skilled workers. Any individual citizen would be able to sponsor one worker at a time, so each citizen might sponsor either a "rotating cast of temporary guest workers" or "one permanent migrant over a lifetime" (Posner and Weyl 2018, 150).[10] Sponsorship would include securing housing, health care, and employment for the migrant and committing to pay the migrant a specific wage. The migrant could work directly for the sponsor and receive the agreed-upon wage, or the sponsor could find the migrant other employment at a higher wage and pocket the difference. For this to work, under the VIP, migrants would be permitted to work for less than the country's minimum wage, though all other worker protection laws and regulations would apply. Sponsors would themselves be civilly liable should the migrant they are sponsoring commit a crime of any kind or abscond from their designated residence. Nor would migrants automatically receive any commitment to permanent residence in the receiving country. The VIP proposal optimistically conjures a scene in which, after a period of enhanced earnings in the receiving country, migrants want to go home and use these earnings to help reboot the economies of their home countries.[11]

The goal of the VIP proposal was to turn migration into something that benefits a receiving country's native citizens as well as the migrants. Under current migration programs, a native-born, low-skilled worker in a wealthy country might find themselves displaced by a migrant willing to work for less, but under the VIP, the native-born worker could sponsor that same migrant and receive remuneration as the agent for the immigrant workers who take their place. By turning migration into something that can economically benefit non-elites in the native population, the VIP was designed to take the sting out of the cultural impact of the arrival of people who speak different languages, eat different foods, worship different gods, and sing different songs. Nationalism and cosmopolitanism are reconciled, or such is the aspiration, in the cause of global distributive justice.

In originally presenting the VIP policy idea, Posner and Weyl acknowledged that their program might seem objectionable, on the grounds that it was like a program of indentured servitude. They sought to ward off this objection by asserting that "migrants would be free to leave at any time" (Posner and Weyl 2018, 153) and that the program was analogous to the current US programs by which companies bring in highly skilled workers and families bring in au pairs from other countries. But in fact, this assertion does not help the case. Someone earning below minimum wage would probably not be in a position to travel back to their home country and would in most cases be at the mercy of their sponsor if they wished to secure exit.[12] In addition, an important requirement of the current US programs in which corporations sponsor highly skilled workers is that these workers be paid at the prevailing wage. The VIP proposal explicitly depends on abandoning such a requirement. And programs for au pairs have recently come under great scrutiny because they are rife with exploitation.[13] Indeed, another analogous practice of migrant sponsorship—namely, sex trafficking—emblematizes all that is wrong with the VIP proposal. While it is true that the VIP policy does not include sponsorship of migrants to perform illegal work, the other features of the program bear important similarities to sex trafficking. The migrants would be dependent on their sponsors for any access to their rights; and their economic power within the receiving country would be limited in ways that would undermine any meaningful access to exit or voice. The VIP proposal rests on an account of how the economy of the world would be better-off, in this model, with increased productivity and gains shared between citizens in wealthy and poorer countries. But the migrant workers would be vulnerable to exploitation to such a degree that we should expect that gains projected to accrue to them would probably be captured by sponsors and others in the receiving country. Since the migrants' gains would be at the mercy of the good-faith behavior of their sponsors, they would be exposed to the arbitrary power of their sponsors day in and day out, and so would be subjected to domination. In addition to the likely capture of their material gains by those in a position to dominate them, we have to add into the balance the psychological and social costs to the migrants of an ongoing experience of domination. The productivity gains expected from this mode of free movement of labor would be undercut by the hindrances to productivity introduced by domination.

This is not to say that indentured servants have never flourished. Surely some did or currently do in those parts of the world where indentured servitude still operates. But any broad economic gains that arose in the seventeenth and eighteenth centuries from indentured servitude are unlikely to have been distributed equally or equitably.[14] Moreover, the monetary gains that might be achieved through this approach to productivity growth would be offset by the psychological and social costs of domination, which are real and measurable, as demonstrated by Richard Wilkinson and Kate Pickett in *The Spirit Level: Why Greater Equality Makes Societies Stronger*. The VIP policy is not a solution to the question of how to organize membership in the world's polities with a view to promoting empowering economies in accord with the principle of difference without domination and a standard of justice. It does, however, help bring into focus how market mechanisms can help reduce the relevant kinds of frictions and transaction costs associated with the free movement of labor.

Posner and Weyl called their program the Visas between Individuals Program. We might call it, more loosely, a free-market approach to membership. In their model, the boundaries of membership would adjust wherever a free-market transaction led to a stable relationship between a sponsor and a migrant. The boundaries of polities—and of who was inside each of them, whether as a citizen or not—would continually shift as market forces moved labor around the world. Yet just as the nationalist and cosmopolitan views are each compromised by a form of exploitation, Posner and Weyl's model, too, is so compromised, by the exposure of migrants to domination by sponsors (cf. Kopplin 2017). Their proposal attempts to free labor to move (counter to the nationalist paradigm) while also reducing the frictions of movement (counter to the cosmopolitan paradigm). In that regard, it accords with the design principles articulated in the previous section. And their model helpfully identifies the dynamics of a global labor market and free-market transactions as elements of a system of membership that might guide us toward nonexploitative economies. But they failed to adjust their model to protect against the domination of migrants. This brings to the surface the consequences of attending only to the material benefits of immigration, via a focus on distributive justice, without also attending to protections for political equality.

Taking what is positive, and seeking to avoid what is negative in the VIP proposal, we can make another adjustment to our design principles for approaches to political membership that might build empowering economies in accord with the principle of difference without domination:

> The global membership system should maximize the freedom of labor to move by means of a framework that
>
> 1. creates incentives for host citizens to welcome migrants and support migrant integration, and thereby avoids an increase to transaction costs in the receiving economy, and
> 2. ensures that migrants have access to political equality within receiving countries.

Now we have worked our way to a set of design principles for a global membership system that accords with a theory of justice that treats political equality as non-sacrificeable. The next question is how to articulate an ideal for political membership that could serve as a conceptual anchor for these design principles.

Polypolitanism: An Ideal of Membership to Support Justice by Means of Democracy

A viable membership policy, I suggest, will be one that provides migrants access to the protections of political equality while simultaneously maximizing the value of the liberalization of labor markets. That is, any liberalization of labor markets must be constrained by the requirements that migrating laborers have access to political equality and that the receiving country be able to integrate immigrants. How might that be done?

I have been arguing that the set of just polities that can sustain human well-being includes only those forms of political arrangement that provide access to political empowerment in relation to polity-level decision-making. This might seem to lead to the requirement that every resident in a polity have access to citizenship rights to provide that access to political empowerment. Indeed, historian of political thought Richard Tuck argues for just this position, questioning the value of liberalized immigration policies (Tuck 2019). Yet against this position, I will argue that the range of political arrangements that can protect political empowerment (or "active citizenship," in Tuck's vocabulary) is broader than is typically recognized. While provision of citizenship to residents in a polity is the fundamental means of providing access to political empowerment, it is not the only means. Here is where we run into, and must adjust, the rigidity of our expectations with regard to membership policies. Our cultural horizons have been trained for so long on a nationalist framework that we can scarcely imagine political equality outside the context of national political institutions. The invocation of access to political equality leads us immediately to think that what must be meant is that those to whom that equality will be provided will be voting in national elections. My goal in what follows will be to sketch some of the other routes available to protections for political equality.

With but the smallest step back from the nationalist view, and shift of focus, we can readily see that each of us who lives in a developed democracy possesses multiple political memberships. We are political members of our towns, of our states or federal subunits, and of the national polity. If we are members of a labor union, we also have access to political equality through that solidaristic structure. If we are employees at a corporation, under current US law, that corporation can function as a "person" in political discourse and presumably does so on our behalf. If we are a member of a political party, we have access to political equality through that organization. We might remind ourselves that at an earlier point in American politics it was common that some people could vote in city elections but not in state or national elections. Takoma Park, Maryland, currently gives municipal voting rights to noncitizens who do not have the right to vote in national elections. Recently, New York City has reintroduced the concept of providing voting rights to noncitizen residents. If we could broadly recover an orientation to the many kinds of membership that provide access to political voice and influence, and so to political equality, we would have more tools for building fresh paradigms for immigration. Those of us who are members of developed democratic nation-states do not need to think of ourselves as either nationalists or cosmopolitans. We might instead think of ourselves as "polypolitans"—people who are members of several polities simultaneously. As polypolitans, we have multiple avenues for accessing political power and protecting our interests. The odds are that most polypolitans use many fewer of the resources of political power than are available to them. Polypolitanism also provides resources for giving migrants access to political voice.

Polypolitanism is not a new phenomenon; it has perdured alongside democracy since the origins of popular rule. Ancient Athens found polypolitanism a great challenge, as it periodically had to tamp down the emergence of power channeled through tribal affiliations rather than through the political institutions of the city. Indeed, polypolitanism can bring instability when political affiliations at different levels come into conflict. The US Civil War is a good example. National and regional affiliations and forms of membership came into conflict. Moments of crisis have often revealed that people function in the world in "polypolitan" ways; the crisis emerges when they have to choose between their loyalties to different political institutions and therefore to different avenues for voice. Yet despite the dangers of reminding people that they have access to several political memberships, those multiple membership roles may provide an important institutional opportunity as we try to re-envision just politics and economies in the twenty-first century.

Now we can elaborate for a final time on the design principles for a just system of membership for the world's states. This time I seek to incorporate how an ideal of polypolitanism for the social realm could undergird a system of global membership supportive of justice by means of democracy:

A polypolitan global membership system would maximize the freedom of labor to move by means of a framework that

1. creates incentives for host citizens in nation-states to welcome migrants and migrant integration, and thereby avoids an increase to transaction costs in the receiving economy, and
2. draws on the resources of layered polity memberships, multiple affiliations, and multiple pathways to voice to ensure that migrants have access to political equality within receiving countries.

Polypolitan Policy

One possible policy approach to political membership that would meet these criteria would adopt the sponsorship model proposed in the VIP framework but would align it more closely to the policy design in which corporations sponsor highly skilled migrants. The modified program would not place the power of sponsorship in the hands of individuals. Instead, it would place it in the hands of corporate bodies capable of and responsible for providing voice and influence, and therefore political equality, to those who are their members. By "corporate bodies," I do not simply mean for-profit or commercial corporations; I mean, rather, all the organizations of civil society. In particular, cities, states (understood as subunits of the national polity), labor unions, faith organizations, and other civil society organizations could serve as sponsors for migrants for roles in which migrants would be paid a prevailing wage, in exchange for a fee migrants would pay to their sponsors. Indeed, Canada has successfully operated precisely such a program for refugee admissions for four decades. The proposal here is to expand that model to migration generally. The number of available sponsorships could be calibrated annually in relation to the size of the receiving country's population, with the goal perhaps of hitting a target of admissions of 1 percent of the existing population annually.[15] Sponsored slots could be divided between permanent residents and temporary workers, so long as there was also a policy for opening the possibility of permanent residency to qualifying temporary workers after a set time period. Permanent residency should include a path toward full citizenship, also. Sponsors would benefit financially;[16] the fees paid to sponsors could support a market in sponsorship, just as fees paid to the providers of study abroad programs support a market in study abroad programs. Sponsorships of this kind would accelerate migrant integration—by making the sponsoring organizations responsible for that integration. Sponsoring organizations would also be responsible for their role in protecting the rights of migrants and giving voice to them via routine auditing by an Office of Civil and Political Rights, the office that would approve organizations to be sponsors in the first place. Sponsorship approaches to migration would permit greater intentionality around migration policy, including greater responsiveness to specific labor market needs and attention to regional economic variation as regional sponsors took responsibility for clarifying and presenting their specific needs.

The proposal is in effect an updated and formalized variant of an informal nineteenth-century approach to supporting labor migration: the use of transnational worker's mutual aid associations. In the nineteenth century, as laborers were migrating from agricultural to urban areas, and also from one part of the globe to another, they commonly formed mutual aid associations: organizations like the Oddfellows, Masonic lodges of various varieties, the Knights Templar and Knights of Columbus, and many others.[17] Civil society associations of these kinds formed—in advance of the development of the liberal welfare state—to secure health care, unemployment insurance, and retirement resources for the unprotected workers of the nineteenth century. Because these organizations were cross-regional and even transnational, they could support the movement of laborers to markets where opportunity was greater, as well as facilitate their integration upon arrival. In addition, these organizations often provided voice for the politically voiceless. As an example, the Prince Hall Masons, formed in the late eighteenth century in Boston, provided political power to disenfranchised African Americans. The Prince Hall Masons achieved their formal organizational status through affiliation with a network of Scottish Masonic lodges—securing voice for themselves that was not available within US political institutions. With solidaristic efforts through the Prince Hall Masonic lodge, these African American laborers were able to pursue the abolition of slavery in Massachusetts (achieved by 1783), to contemplate removing themselves to Africa (a question of late eighteenth-century labor mobility), and to develop resources to deliver education to the children of their community. The emergence of the welfare state and the institutionalized provision of social rights led to the waning of associations of this kind. But we might now encourage their regrowth in support of a sponsorship model for immigration.

Indeed, the Canadian model has inspired the growth of new associations of this kind. Where once they formed primarily to secure something like social rights for workers, now they might instead operate to deliver voice, to protect civil rights, and to provide representation in political processes, in that sense delivering political rights. With the opportunity for migrants to secure protection through political voice in solidaristic societies, developed economies could set a pace for the rate of admission of migrants into full national citizenship that avoids cultural backlash, while also avoiding the injustice of a caste system where some members of the polity are permanently disenfranchised. Just as native-born citizens pass through stages of membership and participation, so too might migrants. Rather than being simply without political voice, they might—as polypolitans—begin their lives as civic participants in their receiving societies by means of access to political voice through avenues other than national political institutions. They might begin with participation in solidaristic civil society organizations. Nor should we forget, of course, that some migrants will have access to political voice through the political institutions of their sending country. Receiving countries ought also to ensure that the embassies and consulates of sending countries are appropriately empowered to provide voice to migrants from their countries.

The Canadian model for the private sponsorship of refugees is widely recognized as a success; the question, then, is whether we can indeed extend such a model to migration generally and, as we do so, offer migrants a "polypolitan" path to political equality that includes participation in and representation through solidaristic civil society organizations.

Conclusion

Because any economy interacts with the political system in which it operates, it can be tempting to think that particular economic goals ought to be achieved by means of adjustments to the underlying political regime. In some cases, this instinct may be correct. The end of the communist political structures of the former Soviet bloc, for instance, was very much in the interest of the economic well-being of the populations living under Soviet jurisdiction and could be achieved only by means of adjustment of political structures. Yet the economic benefit was not the reason for seeking an adjustment in the direction of democratic politics. The choice of a polity form rests not on economic foundations but on broader conceptions of human well-being. Consequently, the question of which polity forms can sustain human well-being should be answered before asking which economic systems to adopt. The complete set of polity forms that can sustain human well-being across all of its dimensions establishes limits on possible structures for a just political economy.

Connected societies live up to the principle of supporting difference without domination and in so doing lay the groundwork for empowering economies. Connected societies can be pursued on a nationalist or cosmopolitan model, but to achieve not only a social universe but also a political economy that lives up to the principle of difference without domination, we instead have to transition to a polypolitan model. For market economies, the requirements of a just polity establish what sorts of commitments should be precompetitive—for instance, a commitment to the protection of positive and negative liberties and a commitment to free, nonexploitative labor. These precompetitive commitments will be most flexibly fulfilled through a polypolitan approach to membership.

This subsidiary ideal of polypolitanism makes salient that any individual can simultaneously have political memberships in more than one political community. We should analyze access to political empowerment by recognizing the possibility that individuals may hold multiple and diverse kinds of memberships in a diversity of polities. The aggregate of the memberships they possess should result in their political empowerment in relation to the polity-level decision-making that affects them. This look at how any given person aggregates membership and pathways of access to political empowerment provides versatility for how we think about immigration, migration, borders, and the global movement of labor. This versatility helpfully embeds protection for political empowerment and political equality in the foundations of any just political economy. It also maximizes the set of polity forms available to support empowering economic well-being across the globe.

Some economists have been tempted into advocating for caste systems in their effort to achieve a maximally egalitarian distribution of the fruits of productivity. In so doing, they have sought to answer the questions prompted by political philosophy. The reigning paradigm raised this question: "How can we distribute the fruits of the world's productivity in the way that benefits the least well-off?" Though *Radical Markets* may already have been repudiated by its authors, Posner and Weyl simply answered the question that had been posed to them by philosophers. They responded that we can achieve global justice by giving up on political equality. In this answer, they were in good company. John Rawls, too, sometimes argued that political equality should be sacrificed in order to seek improvement of material conditions. In other words, Posner and Weyl gave the right answer to the question that has been put to economists by philosophers for the past three decades—a question about distributive justice that implicitly took political equality off the table, which economists answered by taking it off explicitly. We get this kind of answer—proposing fresh establishment of a caste system—*because* we philosophers have already taken political equality out of the equation that we are asking economists to solve. We stopped conveying its importance to them. Can we, then, develop a different political economy if we put a different question on the table? If we ask for a political economy structured by a commitment to political equality, will we get one?[18]

With an overarching ideal of justice by means of democracy, a guiding design principle of difference without domination, and the subsidiary ideals of egalitarian participatory constitutional democracy, a connected society, and polypolitanism, I believe that we have our initial conceptual tools for laying out an ideal of empowering economies and the design principles that can guide their construction.

6

The Fourth Subsidiary Ideal

EMPOWERING ECONOMIES

Introduction

Over the course of the first five chapters, readers may well have developed some nagging questions about the argument that we should prioritize political equality in a theory of justice. For instance, this question has surely arisen: "But don't people need material supports for the political equality you have in mind?" And "How can you have social connectedness or *social* equality when great *material* inequality exists and power differences flow from that inequality?" In other words, my argument's consistent focus on the theme of political equality may seem willfully avoidant, as if I were simply disregarding some of the hardest problems currently facing the citizens of developed democracies and their representatives—namely, problems of political economy. After all, our politics are beset by the consequences of significant increases in income and wealth inequality within the borders of any given developed democracy. Moreover, in the US, other kinds of entrenched inequality—for instance, structural racism—seem to render the prospect of a truly connected society remote.

I have held off from a discussion of political economy in order to discipline us to think about forms of equality other than the material, and to restore economic questions to a secondary place within the structure of human aspiration and theories of justice. This strategy borrows from the philosophical perspective of Hannah Arendt. I propose to view economic questions as critical to laying a foundation for political equality and human freedom, but not as ends in themselves. Whereas political equality and human freedom are intrinsically valuable, economic justice is an instrumental objective, in my account. We seek economic justice—or, I would say, economic egalitarianism—in order to secure political equality and human freedom. We can find our way to the necessary political economy only if we discipline ourselves to ask questions about the economy secondarily to clarifying for ourselves the content of political equality. This we have done in the first five chapters, so now we are ready for those questions of political economy.

As a reminder, the goal of developing a political economy compatible with the principle of difference without domination is to support political equality. This means the goal of political economy, on this account of justice, is to build empowering economies, economies that empower the citizenry broadly to succeed as civic participants. Let me further specify the ideal of an "empowering economy." An empowering economy provides the material bases of empowerment. To paraphrase George Marshall in his announcement of the post–World War II Marshall Plan, we need an economy that works—that delivers growth and productivity and stable transactions and prices (the opposite of Venezuela)—"so as to permit the emergence of political and social conditions in which *free institutions* can exist" (emphasis added). On my definition, free institutions (chapters 3 and 4) will incorporate the principle of full inclusion. Consequently, the goal is not only a dynamic but also an inclusive economy—where all are empowered. There is no room for domination in this economy. But how is this achieved?

Four design principles are key. First, an empowering economy organizes the productive structure of the economy in accordance with the principle of difference without domination; this means focusing on building an economy around free labor and democracy-supporting firms and aiming for a good-jobs economy. Second, an empowering economy supports investments in bridging relationships that cut across cleavages that otherwise emerge as a result of market competition or social competition; this commitment orients policy toward productive collaborations among the public sector, market organizations, and nonprofit concerns (including universities), avoiding domination by any one of those sectors.[1] Third, an empowering economy depends on democratic steering of the economy—through fiscal policy, public-goods investment, chartering authority over monetary policy, and rule-making—rather than on unchecked delegation to technocrats. Experts should be valued advisers but should not themselves rule. Fourth, an empowering economy rests on charters and rules that protect equal basic liberties, both positive and negative, both directly and indirectly.

An empowering economy protects equal basic liberties directly through securing the rights to property, private contract, and association as well as rights of political participation and political equality. It protects the basic liberties indirectly by choosing methods for securing those rights that steer the economy overall in directions that reinforce difference without domination in the political and social spheres. In other words, neither the productive structure nor the distributive framework of the economy should erode basic liberties or access to political equality. Taken as a whole, this goal of a dynamic and inclusive economy and these design principles constitute an ideal of a market-based economy whose rules and charters shape emergent social patterns in egalitarian directions and whose operations also benefit from those social patterns. *This is a power-sharing liberalism where a virtuous and mutual cycle of reinforcement has been set up among the political institutions of an egalitarian participatory constitutional democracy, the social institutions of a connected society, and market structures of the empowering economy.* The goal of this chapter is to specify further the design principles entailed by this ideal of an empowering economy, and also to specify the concrete policy choices that flow from them. The aspiration for this framework is to equip economists with the right questions to answer to support a flourishing democracy. I seek a paradigm change:

a final section on the place of education in economic policy will help drive home the nature of that paradigm change.

As the eighteenth-century jurist and philosopher Cesare Beccaria put it: "In every human society, there is an effort continually tending to confer on one part the height of power and happiness, and to reduce the other to the extreme of weakness and misery. The intent of good laws is to oppose this effort and to diffuse their influence universally and equally." I agree. Here let me offer a brief example of the role of law in constituting the framework for political economy. I draw on the figure of one of the founders of the American political order, Thomas Jefferson. He is famous not merely as the drafter of the Declaration of Independence, the first secretary of state, and the third president; he was also responsible for bringing an end in the infant United States to primogeniture laws of inheritance where property passes to the firstborn son. He understood this legal structure to secure Europe's system of large, aristocratic landed estates. He believed that preserving political equality required organizing land and capital in ways that worked against the concentrated accumulation of wealth by a small elite. He sought the fragmentation of large estates into a network of midsize properties. This was to secure the famous middling-class economy that Aristotle, like both Jefferson and Marshall, thought was necessary for a stable polity capable of securing conditions for human flourishing and the emergence of free institutions.

Land, labor, and capital should be organized by a legal framework that protects basic rights of contract, property, and association as well as positive rights of participation. As a matter of their ordinary, day-to-day workings, political institutions, even those of the most laissez-faire variety, establish the legal frameworks that organize land, labor, and capital. To identify arrangements for land, labor, and capital as part of the basic structure of society and to propose attending to these domains as a matter of basic right is not to propose new areas of intervention. It is, rather, to propose that we deploy already existing structures of intervention—in the form of the law—in directions that protect equal basic rights and political equality.

A Paradigm Change: Social Connectedness, the "Relational Turn," and Empowering Economies

Before turning to the specifics of an empowering economy and its related design principles, I want to pause to underscore that the overarching principle of difference without domination changes the focus of economic analysis from transactions to social relations. This is a fundamental paradigm change. Here I am channeling the work of economist Glenn Loury, who begins a recent essay with an image of an economist who developed a tantra-like mantra to fend off the nightmare that the discipline of economics cannot explain or address racial inequality: "Relations before transactions; relations before transactions; relations before transactions. . . ." (Loury 2020). Loury's imagined economist chants this, trying to free himself from his discipline's insistent focus on transactions.

Loury uses this mantra to initiate a "relational turn" within the discipline of economics. When he scrutinizes the landscape of any society for inequalities, he begins by assuming that the explanation for the relevant inequality lies not in a series of exchanges or transactions but in an underlying structure of relationality that is itself generating the relevant, inegalitarian transactions. This is what it means to recognize the economy as embedded in society. Working with a colleague, Rajiv Sethi, on issues of crime and punishment, Loury makes the argument that stereotypes themselves can help generate harmful social equilibria capable of explaining disparities in criminality, sentencing, and incarceration. For Loury, when we see a nonrandom distribution of people in organizations and institutions, that observation is the starting point for an inquiry. We have a reason to ask, "What nonrandom process has led to this result?" The mere fact that a nonrandom process has led to a result—say, the percentage of national prizewinning poets from Poetry Lover Land is out of proportion to the percentage of the national population that lives in Poetry Lover Land—does not in itself delegitimize that result. One first has to know whether the nonrandom process that resulted in the failure of this distribution of national prizewinning poets to mirror the demographics of the national population is itself legitimate or illegitimate. To distinguish between legitimate and illegitimate social and institutional processes, we employ a principle of non-domination as an analytic tool. Legitimate social processes are those that, even if they lead to disparate outcomes, are free of domination. To address problems of material and social inequality, then, one must focus not merely on transactional approaches to distribution—the question of whether the transaction of the prize selection process functioned appropriately and without discrimination—but on achieving healthy processes and practices for the distribution of the opportunities that led to participation in the contest in the first place. Are these processes and practices characterized by non-domination? While the overrepresentation of people from Poetry Lover Land on the stage at poetry prize ceremonies may not be a cause for concern, the underrepresentation of women in the sciences will be. The former is unlikely to result from relational structures of domination; the latter, quite likely to do so.[2]

The principle of difference without domination, then, shifts our attention from transactions to relations. This shift of focus helps make visible a core problem with Rawls's difference principle. As I have noted, Rawls's difference principle lies at the heart of a great deal of contemporary policy-making in liberal democracies. Rawls wrote that social and economic inequalities must satisfy the condition that they be to the greatest benefit of the least-advantaged members of society.[3] This principle has been used almost exclusively to address questions of how the talented, who excel professionally, should be compensated, and how the rewards of a growth economy driven by those talented professionals should be distributed, and, even more importantly, redistributed. In other words, *the focus is wholly transactional* and oriented toward private compensation contracts and public social-welfare contracts. The point of Loury's mantra—"relations before transactions"—is that contemporary economics, like Rawlsian liberalism, overlooks the question of the structure of social relationships that lie beneath an economy and generate patterns of opportunity, modes of production, and emergent patterns of first-order distribution prior to any taxation-based redistribution (see also Okin 1991; Cohen 2009). The neoliberal economy—with increasing rates of return directed toward the holders of capital and the possessors of high levels of education—produces a skewed distribution, and the Rawlsian principle (or an extension of it, like guaranteed basic income) provides a way of remediating or mitigating that skew through redistribution. But the Rawlsian principle does not provide a means to address the underlying structures of relationality that generate the highly skewed distributions in the first place (and the same is true for a universal basic income).

In contrast, Loury asks us to shift our gaze to the underlying relational organization of the economy. As it turns out, by focusing in chapter 4 on the ideal of a connected society, we have already initiated the work of building a new framework for political economy. If we seek economic egalitarianism, the application of the principle of difference without domination in the social realm is the place to start. Particularly in conditions of pluralism, we can achieve an egalitarian economy that secures difference without domination only if the underlying pluralistic social structure is also egalitarian. The emergence of a connected society, in the social realm, can be expected to have egalitarian impacts on patterns in the distribution of economic resources, in the inverse of the situation of segregation (see chap. 4).

Yet we can go beyond the ideal of a connected society. We might, Loury suggested, undertake a more comprehensive effort to identify and reform the laws structuring the forms of relationality undergirding any given economy. And that is the job of this chapter. The next step is to convert the language of relationality and non-domination into the vocabulary of economic policy. The three policy domains of economics are preproduction, production, and postproduction. As economists Dani Rodrik and Stefanie Stantcheva put it (2021, 1–2), "Pre-production policies determine the endowments that people bring to the market, such as education and skills, financial capital, social networks and social capital. Production-stage policies are those that directly shape the employment, investment, and innovation decisions

TABLE 6 Types of egalitarian economic policy

		At what stage of the economy does policy intervene?		
		Preproduction	Production	Postproduction
What kind of inequality do we care about?	Bottom	• Endowment polices (health, education) • Universal basic income	• Minimum wage • Job guarantee	• Transfers (e.g., EITC) • Full-employment macro policies
	Middle	• Public spending on higher education	• Good-jobs policies • Industrial relations and labor laws • Sectoral wage boards • Trade agreements • Innovation policies	• Safety nets • Social insurance policies
	Top	• Inheritance/ estate taxes	• Regulation • Antitrust	• Wealth taxes

Source: Closing presentation by Dani Rodrik, Harvard University, at the conference "Combating Inequality: Rethinking Policies to Reduce Inequality in Advanced Economies," Peterson Institute for International Economics, October 17–18, 2019.

of firms." In contrast, postproduction policies "are ex post policies, that transfer income and wealth once they have been realized (e.g., redistributive transfers, progressive taxation, and social insurance). They reshape inequalities after the economic decisions regarding employment, investments, or innovations have been made." The kinds of egalitarian policy available in each domain are listed in Table 6.

As in the social realm, in the economic realm, too, the standard of aspiring to achieve difference without domination does not necessarily generate a need for new domains of policy or services. Instead, it requires a review of current policies across preproductive, productive, and postproductive domains of the economy (investments in education, labor policy, trade policy, the organization of the firm, etc.) with a view to assessing how those current policies protect (or fail to protect) equal basic liberties. Where they fail to protect equal basic liberties or to pass a strict scrutiny test for the achievement of difference without domination, then we have found places where we need to adjust our policies.

The answer to how we can achieve an empowering economy, focusing on the relational above the transactional, emerges quickly: the most important relational aspects of the economy, in contrast to its transactional elements, reside in the domain of production. Indeed, when we apply the principle of strict scrutiny for difference *with* domination to the economic realm, we find that the most salient issues concern the domain of production: reduced labor mobility and job lock, problematic immigration policies, practices of domination that have developed inside firms, and the emergence of market concentrations, particularly in the technology sector. In addition, we will quickly see that democratic steering of the economy has been undermined across all three domains (preproduction, production, and postproduction) by the acquisition of political power by wealthy elites (Gilens 2012),[4] by technocratic independence, and by the technocratic orientation toward transactional rather than relational questions.

To clarify the nature of these challenges, and solutions to them, we will focus on three of the design principles for an empowering economy: (1) free labor, democracy-supporting firms, and a good-jobs economy; (2) investment in bridging relationships; and (3) democratic steering of the economy. With regard to the fourth design principle that I named at the start—direct rights protection—I am taking as given throughout this chapter that any policy that will align with justice by means of democracy will affirm direct protection of negative and positive liberties. Those protections are precompetitive matters, and so I assume them in what follows. The focus for the rest of this chapter will be on how the first three design principles for an empowering economy can help develop a political economy that not only directly but also indirectly supports positive and negative basic liberties—and on how, taken together, these add up to a paradigm change.

The First Design Principle: Free Labor, Democracy-Supporting Firms, and a Good-Jobs Economy

Building an empowering economy starts with a commitment to free labor, which we can update for the twenty-first century as a commitment to building a good-jobs economy. Focusing on overall GDP is not enough to measure whether we are building an inclusive and dynamic economy that connects all to opportunity and security and thereby provides a foundation for political empowerment. In addition to measuring the overall output of the economy, we also need to track how well we are doing at creating good jobs and at ensuring that they are available across society. A good job enables a middle-class existence, by a region's standards, with enough income for housing, food, transportation, education, and other family expenses, as well as some saving. More broadly, good jobs provide workers with clear career paths, possibilities of self-development, flexibility, responsibility, fulfillment, and time and stability to support civic participation (Rodrik and Sabel 2022; Allen, Gerard, Cerny, et al. 2021–22).

But *the very first principle of a good-jobs economy is free labor*. This means ending enslavement—a problem that still exists worldwide, including in the US (Caruana et al. 2021)—and ending wage theft. After non-slavery, the next core requirement of free labor is labor mobility, the idea that workers need to be able to move to where opportunities are (Posner and Weyl 2018; Caruana et al. 2021). A striking feature of the contemporary American economy is the reversal of historical trends of high mobility. In the period from 1947 to 1970, roughly 20 percent of Americans a year changed residence. A steady decline began in 1971, and in 2018, for the first time since 1947, fewer than 10 percent of Americans moved (United States Census 2019). Strikingly, the length and impact of the Great Recession of 2008 were not significantly resolved through mobility, as had been the case in previous economic downturns (Katz

2010). While the housing crisis of that period and underwater mortgages were among the drivers of this mobility decline, they are not the only causes. The decline has been steady since the early 1970s, with the exception of an increase for one year in the mid-1980s. Broader issues of housing costs in high-opportunity areas, transportation challenges, and job lock occasioned by our fragmented and nonportable health care system (the modern-day version of serfdom) have also contributed.[5]

Achieving free labor requires ensuring that workers are able to exit unsatisfactory work environments and move to alternatives (Hirschman 1970). If free labor is to be a reality, housing, transportation, and related policy areas must be organized to support the mobility of workers. There are answers to each of these problems—often cultivated at the level of city or state. Minneapolis is changing its zoning laws to permit greater density of housing and break the monopoly of the rich over residences near employment. Massachusetts is changing zoning to support density near transit. Mortgage insurance would be another mechanism to free people from currently existing housing traps. By maintaining the individual mandate for health insurance, Massachusetts continues to sustain a market that makes insurance both affordable and adequate with regard to the provision of care, including insurance independent of any employer. One can take a leap and quit a job in Massachusetts without having to forgo access to medical care. Policies that increase mobility end serfdom and affect the macroeconomy for the better. We need to develop a bundle of policies that invest in people, that break up the monopolies over opportunity held by a few, and that undo the housing and (in the US) health care traps that keep people locked in place.[6]

Mobility on its own, however, is not enough. In chapter 5, I argued that the principle of free labor requires supporting labor mobility with access to political voice. Workers who move without acquiring political voice find easily themselves dominated. The fact that the US has approximately eleven million undocumented residents with no formal pathway to political voice has eroded the working-class component of the electorate and public discourse. Many have observed the erosion of labor's bargaining power over the past fifty years. The inability of a meaningful subset of the population to participate in the election of representatives who might take up labor issues has been a contributory factor, as political scientists Christopher Hare and Keith Poole (2014) argue. Even more striking, they make the case that the absence of noncitizen workers from the pool of potential voters has contributed to polarization:

> The steady growth in income inequality and changes in immigration trends in the United States over the last half century also have implications for political polarization. Poorer citizens routinely exhibit lower levels of political participation, and the influx of immigrants who are low-income workers and/or non-citizens has further increased the proportion of non-voters at the bottom end of the income distribution. In effect, this has shifted the position of the median income voter upward along the income distribution and, thus, the active electorate is less supportive than the mass public of government spending on redistributive social welfare policies. This helps explain how the Republican Party has been able to move steadily rightward over the last 40 years without major electoral consequences, whereas Democrats have not been able to move further left than where the party was in the 1960s. (417)

Hare and Poole's argument suggests that we should think of the problem of polarization as, in part, reflecting a decline in political competitiveness as the range of opinion within the electorate shrinks through exclusion and the erosion of fully inclusive political equality. The health of democracy requires full inclusion (as I discussed in chapter 3). Now it turns out that the health of the economy does too. The protection of labor—and pursuit of the principle of free labor—depends on the access of workers to political voice. This ultimately requires a revised approach to immigration, as discussed in chapter 5.

The policy proposal I examined in chapter 5 was for a sponsorship model of immigration, an expanded version of what Canada currently employs. The sponsorship model would secure political voice for migrants in the wealthy developed democracies that received them. But that picture of immigration policy requires one further detail. The effort to ensure that labor is free requires democracies that are receiving countries to invest in the conditions that enable free labor in the sending countries. Even foreign policy can be a matter of political economy. Securing free labor in wealthy countries may require supporting the development of the conditions for free labor in sending countries, lest we find ourselves building our own prosperity on extraction from others, for instance on the labor of workers who lack access to political voice in unstable societies. For instance, in the US the question might be how to help stabilize functioning legal regimes in Central and South America. The goal is not to build democratic political institutions in other counties but merely, through investments in economies and a healthy civil society, to foster the conditions in which such institutions can exist—à la Marshall Plan.

In addition to securing both exit (via mobility) and voice for workers, and in order to realize in concrete form the design principle of a political economy built on free labor, a just political economy will give workers a meaningful opportunity for "loyalty" inside the firm. In Albert Hirschman's classic interpretation of social contract theory and its economic implications, the power that comes to members of an organization from "voice," specifically, can be exercised either on the outside (through protest or litigation, for instance) or on the inside. The latter occurs when the relevant organization functions to ensure that members are heard when they propose reforms or improvements and therefore that they have good reason to be "loyal." The idea that a healthy economy requires voice internally for members of organizations such as firms aligns with a theory of justice guided by an overarching principle of difference without domination. A key element of realizing free labor will be ensuring democratization of the firm itself. This brings us to the need for democracy-supporting firms, a second key component of a good-jobs economy.

DEMOCRACY-SUPPORTING FIRMS

I am not the first political philosopher to seek to address topics of political economy from within an account of justice that takes public autonomy, political equality, or democracy as its starting point. Both Elizabeth Anderson and Carol Gould have already advanced this line of argument. They, too, argue for democratization of the firm.

Elizabeth Anderson famously opened up this line of work with her 1999 essay, "What Is the Point of Equality?" That essay, like this book, develops a critique of Rawls's *Theory of Justice* for its failure adequately to recognize and protect political equality. Over time, Anderson has expanded her analysis of equality into a theory of freedom, focusing on achieving a conjunction of negative freedom, positive freedom, and republican freedom—in her vocabulary, a combination of freedom from interference, freedom to participate, and freedom from domination. In her 2015 Tanner Lectures, "Liberty, Equality, and Private Government," Anderson argues for applying this theory of freedom to the organization of the capitalist firm and provides a framework for reconstituting labor rights. In the US, she argues, "the boundary of the firm is defined as the point at which markets [and market freedoms] end and authoritarian centralized planning and direction begin" (Anderson 2017, 39). She continues: "Why do we not recognize such a pervasive part of our social landscape for what it is? Should we not subject these forms of government to at least as much critical scrutiny as we pay to the democratic state?" (40). Anderson argues that justice requires us to ensure that the vertical or linking relationships within organizations, like firms or other units of economic activity, are not characterized by domination. Relevant issues can range from compensation, workplace governance, and firm ownership to matters like assignment of hours and access to time for bathroom breaks. The assignment of hours is particularly important from the point of view of whether workers can participate in civil society and political life versus having all their time consumed by the need to secure basic necessities or dominated by the arbitrariness of how hours are assigned, with the result that they cannot plan for other activities (cf. Rose 2016). Anderson concludes by arguing for legal reform in support of worker freedom and worker participation in firm governance, holding up the German model of codetermination as one successful example.

Carol Gould also applies a theory of justice that starts from an argument for the good of democracy to political economy, arguing for, in her ideal framework, worker ownership and self-management of firms and, as second-best, participatory and democratic management (Gould 2016; see also Gould 2004, 2009, 2014; cf. Hacker 2011; Polanyi [1944] 2001). In other words, as developed by Anderson and Gould, an important step toward a political economy of empowering economies and achievement of free labor would be to reintroduce principles of human freedom to the legal structures used to frame employer-laborer relations and firm management. Changes such as these would help firms evolve in a democracy-supporting direction.

The arguments of both Anderson and Gould contain two particularly valuable ideas. First, they restore the possibility for the redevelopment of freedom and social equality inside the workplace, including even in workplaces with the necessary hierarchies of a division of labor. They advance the cause of difference without domination by identifying instruments that can be used to structure labor contracts so that the forms of differentiation that emerge in a capitalist economy do not articulate with domination. Second, and even more important, at the core of their economic argument is a shift of focus from transactions to relations. Their question is not, in the first instance, what wage structure or CEO compensation structure should obtain in a firm, but what structure of relations should obtain. The implicit presumption is that democracy-enhancing relationality inside the firm will drive transactions, too, in democracy-enhancing directions. Again, the German example provides some evidence in support of that hypothesis: worker ownership is linked to lower levels of CEO pay.

In *Capital in the Twenty-First Century*, French economist Thomas Piketty (2014) pursues a historical investigation of causes of income and wealth inequality. Part of his argument is much like that in the rest of the economics literature, namely, that skills-biased technological change has driven a wage premium on skill that has produced distributive inequality. Yet income growth at the highest end accruing to what he calls "supermanagers" reflects social acceptance of skyhigh executive pay. In his argument, such social norms constitute and reinforce a political ideology endorsing "hypermeritocracy." Reining in income inequality therefore requires social and political change—that is, a change in the values driving firm behavior.

In the interest of spurring such a change in values, Harvard Business School professor Rebecca Henderson argues for the need to encourage the emergence of "purpose-driven" firms.[7] Her colleague Malcolm Salter argues that firms should, can, and sometimes do extend their sense of purpose beyond shareholder value maximization and profit maximization to what he calls "reciprocal justice." He makes these arguments as part of an effort to revive "stakeholder capitalism," in contrast to "shareholder" capitalism. Whereas shareholder capitalism orients all attention and transactional energy toward the owners of capital and profit, "stakeholder capitalism" takes its sense of purpose from the consequences of commercial operations not only for shareholders but also for labor, communities, and polities. Salter (2017, 2; cf. Salter 2022) writes:

> In its most plain form, reciprocal justice is achieved when the standard of "fairness" or "fair return" governs relationships (or transactions) among various parties comprising the enterprise. *By direct implication,* legitimate corporate purpose according to the principle of reciprocal justice should reflect a fair balancing of interests of parties comprising the enterprise and affected by the enterprise, recognizing that each of these parties have different minimum thresholds of "fair returns" and fair treatment necessary to keep them as participants in, and supporters of, the enterprise. For employees that minimum is typically defined by the value of wages and benefits; for shareholders that minimum may be defined by their required rate of return on investment considering the riskiness of that investment; for the community affected by the enterprise the accounting may be less quantitative but no less critical.

The new and increasingly frequent requirements that business enterprises produce environmental impact statements as part of justifying an investment provides an example of how innovative forms of accounting can help redirect capitalist behavior. Henderson has developed approaches to performance measurement to support evolution of firms in this direction. She argues that "reimagining capitalism requires embracing the idea that while firms must be profitable if they are to thrive, their purpose must be not only to make money but also to build prosperity and freedom in the context of a livable planet and a healthy society" (Henderson 2020, 36). She makes the case that firms of "authentic purpose" can indeed outperform firms focused only on profit maximization. Moreover, they outperform for a very specific reason—one having to do with relationality. They are better positioned to implement what she calls "high road organizational structures." Henderson (2020, 9; see also Henderson 2022, 196–97) writes:

> Authentic purpose must by definition be expensive since authenticity requires putting the purpose of the firm ahead of profits some significant fraction of the time. This would seem to imply that genuinely purpose driven firms would be routinely less profitable than their more conventional competitors, and thus that they would be much less likely to survive—suggesting that those firms who claim to be purpose driven must be largely greenwashing. But if authentically purpose driven firms are much better positioned to implement high road organizational structures—and if these structures are actually more productive then there's good reason to believe that purpose driven firms cannot only survive but thrive whilst routinely sacrificing profits in the service of purpose. . . . In the US, for example, on average the most productive plants in any given industry make almost twice as much output with the same measured inputs as the least productive. . . . These differences are strongly correlated with differences in the adoption of high performance management practices—differences in the degree to which firms pay a great deal of attention to skills development, implement incentive systems that use much more than simple quantitative metrics to measure performance, use self-directed teams to manage work and create widespread opportunities for distributed communication and problem solving (Bloom & Van Reenan, 2007, 2010, 2011, Bloom et al., 2019, Jon, Ichniowski and Shaw, 2002; Ichniowski and Shaw, 1999).

An authentic purpose-driven firm, then, will see its primary responsibility as being, to paraphrase Henderson, to the health of the social, institutional, and natural systems on which it relies. In a society organized around the principles of "justice by means of democracy," this would entail evolving firms in a democracy-supporting way. This involves elements of non-domination internal to the firm—for instance, the use of "self-directed teams" and "distributed communication." Henderson's theory of the purpose-driven firm makes the case that such firms will also be more productive, thereby contributing to a productive economy able to deliver the material bases of support for a democracy.

Democracy-supporting firms of this kind are a highly attractive prospect. What, then, would it take to achieve the evolution of firms in this direction? As Salter sees it, in the US some industries have indeed come to adopt a "more reciprocally just conception of institutional purpose" and capacities to negotiate across complex fields of interest that include the interests of the democratic community at large. The motivation has often been political. He writes (Salter 2017, 4; cf Salter 2022):

> Some industries (automotive, civil aircraft, textile, semiconductor, telecommunications, healthcare, just to name a few) have been forced by economic and political circumstances to adopt at various stages in their history a more reciprocally just conception of institutional purpose and governance than that adopted by strict followers of shareholder capitalism. These circumstances include a range of factors that (a) require fair exchanges of value among multiple contracting parties comprising and affecting the firm for the firm to continue operating and (b) where the opportunities and benefits of intimidation and predation are low.

The first factor on Salter's list, generating a more reciprocally just conception of institutional purpose, is the "political salience of the industry." He continues (4–5):

> Of all these factors, political salience seems to play a key role triggering dynamic reciprocity. While the direct effects of the remaining factors

deserve further inspection, what prior research in the industries referenced above indicates (Salter & Dunlop, 1989) is that in politically salient industries, firms tend to be (and are required to be) more politically attuned. Such firms therefore tend to view themselves as entities that have participants with both overlapping and competing claims on its resources. Thus, in addition to shareholders (and bondholders), customers, employees at all levels, and members of the community affected by the firm's business policies all represent legitimate interests that need to be negotiated and mediated in the context of the organization's purposes and industry dynamics.

Achieving free labor, via democracy-supporting firms, will turn out to require the engagement of a democratic citizenry. This underscores the need for democratic steering of the economy. I'll return to that design principle of democratic steering in the next section, but there is still a bit more to say about what it takes to achieve a good-jobs economy.

SUPPLYING GOOD JOBS

The ideal of an empowering economy is realized first through focus on free labor and democracy-supporting firms, both key elements of production and productivity. But the success of the free-labor principle also depends on an adequate supply of "good jobs" to provide the material bases of empowerment. Here I draw on a framework developed by Dani Rodrik and political scientist and legal scholar Charles Sabel. They write:

> The definition of "good job" is necessarily slippery. We have in mind in the first instance stable, formal-sector employment that comes with core labor protections such as safe working conditions, collective bargaining rights, and regulations against arbitrary dismissal. A good job enables at least a middle-class existence, by a region's standards, with enough income for housing, food, transportation, education, and other family expenses, as well as some saving. More broadly,

good jobs provide workers with clear career paths, possibilities of self-development, flexibility, responsibility, and fulfillment. The depth and range of such characteristics may depend on context: the prevailing levels of productivity and economic development, costs of living, prevailing income gaps, and so on. We expect each community to set its own standards and aspirations, which will evolve over time. (Rodrik and Sabel 2022, 62)

Importantly, economic policy as currently formulated—with a focus on monetary-policy-driven capital growth and redistribution—has left us with a real economy that innovates with and assimilates technology unevenly, "bottlenecking" opportunity in urban areas and leaving rural areas with lower productivity contexts. Rodrik and Sabel (2022, 65) write: "We do not view this simply as a problem of inequality and exclusion, but also as a problem of gross economic inefficiency—a case of operating deep inside the production possibility frontier." The question is what approach to economic policy can integrate a population fully into technology-driven opportunities. Rodrik and Sabel suggest that whereas GDP has been the metric of economic success for the past generation, a better metric would be the number of good jobs generated year over year. Success at generating jobs of the kind they have in mind would pull the real economy back in the direction of a middle-class economy, thereby securing the material base for justice by means of democracy.

But how can we achieve that supply of good jobs? Free labor cannot now rest on expropriation and exploitation, as it did in the nineteenth century with the Georgia Land Lottery and the Homestead Act (Caruana et al. 2021). Here is where Rodrik and Sabel make their most significant contribution: their answer is, in effect, that good jobs will come from democratization of decision-making around economic investment and experimentation. They argue for public-private partnerships, involving the full range of stakeholders, to make decisions in participatory regulatory processes about how firms might best invest in good jobs. They draw on preexisting governance models for decision-making in conditions of uncertainty, in particular the cases of fostering advanced technologies (as in DARPA, a federal government program that invests in defense technologies) and crafting environmental regulations (Rodrik and Sabel's example uses the case of Irish dairy farming). In these domains, private-public partnerships support active project management, collaborative review, adjustment of milestones, peer assessment of local problems, and "new forms of collaboration with networks of extension experts." Techniques of these kinds might be used, they argue, with place-based specificity, to help firms produce more good jobs and evolve their own firm practices in directions supportive of free labor. In short, the goal is participation-based regulatory processes in conditions of uncertainty. Firms' development of capacity to participate in these rule-making processes would be another dimension of their evolution toward increased democracy support. Rodrik and Sabel (2022, 80) write:

> The concept of "good job," like clean water, is imprecise and needs to be operationalized in a way that is both evolving and context-dependent. Reasonable, attainable targets for good-job creation must remain provisional, to be revised under new information. . . . Achieving the targets depends on decisions on investment, technological choice, and business organization, the consequences of which are unknowable ex ante. Governance under uncertainty takes as its starting point the provisionality of ends and means and the need for disciplined review and revision. . . . .Fostering good jobs depends at least as much on solving highly idiosyncratic, place-specific problems: failures of coordination between local firms and training institutions; between firms and their (potential) supply-chain partners; and the managerial breakdowns or skill gaps within individual firms and institutions to which the coordination problems point.

Firms ready to participate in these sorts of collaborative, participatory rule-making processes are what we need in a world where we are pursuing justice by means of democracy.

For several decades now, economic policy makers have focused on jobs from the perspective of what skills firms need to support productivity and how to match workers to skill acquisition and firm need. This is a highly instrumentalizing approach—as if people were but tools to be fitted to the needs of capital. What about the question of whether the jobs on offer fit the needs of the people to be employed? No economy can be healthier than the people who power it. It's time for us to organize our economic policy from the ground up by asking what opportunities can help people live the lives they seek while also contributing to the greater good of a healthy economy—and how can we ensure these opportunities are equitable and inclusive. It's not just that workers should acquire the skills that firms need; it's that firms should offer the job experiences that people need. A good-jobs economy would include tailored supports and strategic investments that broadly spread opportunity to participate in an inclusive, dynamic economy. This includes attention to issues like housing and transportation. Wherever policy makers are focused on "job training" and "skills development," they should shift focus to achieving "opportunity with equity" and ensuring that all residents are connected to the good jobs of today and tomorrow in ways that deliver to workers an experience of opportunity and dignity, not instrumentalization (Allen, Gerard, Cerny, et al. 2021–22). The strategic work necessary to build these good jobs requires multistakeholder collaboration. In other words, an economy based on free labor requires power-sharing liberalism.

A good-jobs strategy focuses on the economy's productive structure, so that the economy itself can deliver the bases of well-being, in the form of a sufficient number of good, purpose-sustaining jobs. The goal is to put behind us approaches to political economy that leave significant portions of the citizenry highly exposed to the cold winds of political fights over redistribution. Let's instead choose a path that integrates all sectors of society into productivity. Importantly, the free-labor principle, when pursued in the US in the nineteenth century, built a strong middle-class economy for white Americans only. In the wake of the end of Reconstruction in 1876, African Americans and other minorities were excluded. And as we have seen, realization of the principle depended on the expropriation of land from Native Americans. These same kinds of exclusion characterized the GI Bill after World War II that helped deliver a good-jobs economy to some in the middle of the twentieth century. Our twenty-first-century approach to the free-labor principle must finally be fully inclusive. Recognizing that, then, we can say that what land was to the nineteenth century, technology is to the twenty-first century: a new frontier, a source of innovation and fresh productive possibilities. In order to achieve the equivalent of allocating homestead plots to entrepreneurial workers ready to build on opportunity, we now have to build collaborative participatory processes, based on public-private partnerships, to generate, in the form of "good jobs," an equivalent to those nineteenth-century plots of land. Democracy-supporting firms are necessary actors in the pursuit of a free-labor economy. And so too is democracy itself. Just as the provision of homesteads in support of an empowering economy was steered in the nineteenth century by democratic processes, so too the achievement of a good-jobs economy will be the result of successful democratic steering of economic policy in the twenty-first. This has to include steering of the technology sector, which has yet to recognize its own responsibilities to inclusivity or to recognize that egalitarian participatory constitutional democracy, as the main vehicle of rights protection, is itself infrastructure for a healthy economy.

The Second Design Principle: Investment in Bridging

The need to be more explicit about inclusion in the project of building an empowering economy brings us to the third design principle. The collaborative, participatory rule-making processes necessary to navigate toward a good-jobs economy require investment in bridging relationships.

Scholars have recognized bridging ties as economically productive. For instance, in the case of Irish dairy farming explored by Rodrik and Sabel (2022), farmers, scientific experts, and government regulators had to be brought into productive synergies with each other, and relationships developed linking public and private sector, market firms and NGOs, for instance universities and think tanks. Bridge-building has been shown to support economic dynamism in the tech sector as well. As AnnaLee Saxenian puts it in *The New Argonauts*, Silicon Valley surpassed the Route 128 technology corridor in Massachusetts, and the entrepreneurial West surpassed the "hierarchy of established East Coast corporations," because they created "an industrial system distinguished by open labor markets, continuous entrepreneurship, and information exchange both within and between firms—all the direct opposite of the modern corporation with its hierarchical control of information, detailed division of labor and internal labor markets, and corporate secrecy and self-sufficiency" (Saxenian 2006, 29). In the Silicon Valley case, the striking detail is that information is exchanged not only within but also between firms. This upended a model of competition that shut down information flow and replaced it with a model of networking and cross-pollination that strengthened a whole ecosystem.

Bridges linking immigrants in the US who then chose to return home also helped power the extension of Silicon Valley's entrepreneurial culture to new hubs of technological growth and development such as Taiwan and Israel. Saxenian tells the story of the repeated creation, in the wake of Silicon Valley's influence, of "cross-regional communities" driven by bridge builders able to bring together technical know-how with cultural competencies across a range of diverse communities— from the US to Taiwan to Israel to India to China. Importantly, the strongest success cases for the mobilization of technology sector dynamism in support of economic development also bridged to the public sector to achieve support for a "well-functioning physical and communications infrastructure" and space for a private sector to "support venture capital funding and provide viable liquidity options." In these success cases, all parties across private-public lines were invested in collaborations and bridge-building relationships, not merely in narrowly defined competitive activities. Often the prime movers of these bridge-building relationships were immigrant professional associations, just the sort of associations we considered in chapter 5. They linked Silicon Valley to new hubs of development in their members' countries of origin.

The bridging model to spur economic dynamism is powerful and can be extended to contexts beyond the technological. For such bridge-building work to generate not only a dynamic but also an inclusive economy within any society, investments in bridge-building as a matter of economic policy should also be directed within regions, not merely between regions. Subpopulations that are currently disconnected from economic participation—whether the urban poor or rural communities—need basic investment in bridging relationships. For entrepreneurs and policy makers to know what assets are available in different communities to drive innovation, dynamism, and good jobs, connection, not competition, may be the answer—not industrial espionage but creative and nontraditional trade associations that incorporate participation by historically marginalized entities and people. For members of marginalized communities to be able to leverage opportunities of which they are aware in their local context, they need "market knowledge and connections as well as technology and skill" (Saxenian 2006, 116). It's not enough just to give workers skills-training opportunities predefined by others. They should be integrated into innovation networks of existing entrepreneurs, investors, managers, and others with domain-specific expertise and offered the opportunity to lead in shaping a development agenda. Public-sector investment in such bridge-building advances an empowering economy.

The Third Design Principle: Democratic Steering

It is time now to turn to the next design principle of an empowering economy: democratic steering. The pursuit of the design principles of free labor, democracy-supporting firms, and a good-jobs economy led to a focus on the domain of production within the economy. While the focus on the relational, rather than the transactional, components of the economy, led us in this direction, Rodrik and Sabel, starting from a different theoretical point, also eloquently articulate the relational stakes of the domain of production:

> In contrast to standard remedies that deal with the pre-production (e.g. schooling) or post-production (e.g. taxation) stages of the economy, our approach directly targets production. The motivation is that private producers, left to their own, do not take the social costs of the scarcity of good jobs into account. In the absence of government action, production is not efficient. An important implication is that the traditional distinction between distribution and production no longer makes sense. Efficient production and distributive inclusion are two sides of the same coin. One cannot achieve one without the other. Questions of production—how goods and services are provided, which types of investments are made, what is the direction of technological change— are placed right at the heart of political economy and justice analysis. (Roderik and Sabel 2022, 88)

The fundamental relational question about how the economy is structured is whether it generates empowering forms of relationality. To provide the material bases of empowerment, an economy must generate good jobs; to pursue this is via participatory processes is also to maximize productive efficiency. We took that idea a step further by proposing investment in bridging as one of the key design principles of an empowering economy. And, importantly, bridging investments must be fully inclusive. The goal with the successful production of good jobs and inclusive bridge-building is to take the economy to its productive limits and thereby deliver the material basis of democratic empowerment. This does not mean that preproduction investment or postproduction redistribution are off the table, only that they are complements to the core goal of fostering empowering relations of production.

To reiterate, successful production of good jobs is a desideratum of democracy specifically. This is because democracies need good jobs to achieve an empowered citizenry. For this reason, it is above all a democracy's representatives who will recognize this goal and who must be charged with pursuing and protecting it. Achieving a good-jobs economy will therefore require steering of the economy by those elected representatives. Only such democratic steering can be expected consistently to deliver good-jobs policy that puts questions of production and relationality front and center in policy-making. An economy steered primarily by firms or by the holders of capital may lose sight of the important foundation of justice in free labor. As a result, the ideal of an empowering economy consists not just of the empowerment of individual residents of the polity, as supported by free labor and democracy-supporting firms, but also of the empowerment of the national legislature, specifically, to steer the national economy.

This is a strong claim. For much of the past few decades, the goal has been to insulate economic policy-making from politics by entrusting it to independent bodies such as the Federal Reserve. The requirement for democratic steering is not that we should abandon such independent bodies but, rather, that the legislature should more actively take responsibility for establishing the objectives of those agencies. When the Federal Reserve was originally chartered in the early twentieth century, it was to be rechartered every twenty years. This has not occurred. Yet policy targets of independent central banks should not be assumed to be permanently stable, and any given set of policy targets involves trade-offs that have political implications (Downey 2021, 2022, forthcoming). Annual legislative review of credit guidance and an every-twenty-year rechartering of the central bank would permit appropriate democratic accountability over the direction of monetary policy, balanced with respect for the role of technocratic expertise in managing monetary policy (Downey 2021, 2022, forthcoming). In recent years it became common to observe that the fundamentals of the economy in the years 2000–2020 suggested that inflation cannot be understood merely as it was in the 1970s. This observation led to an exploration of the idea that central banks should perhaps not have inflation targeting as their primary duty. Central banks took up study of this question, investigating potential alternative areas of work pertaining to the stability of the financial system and climate change. They began exploring individual accounts and digital currencies. And now, of course, robust postpandemic inflation has returned their attention to that original inflation-fighting mission. But while central banks should tee up the analysis, they should not be the ones to make the final call on the trade-offs that face them as they set new directions for their policy work. Elected representatives should have a routinely established opportunity to review and approve the objectives selected by central banks.

Monetary policy—and the trade-offs it establishes between inflation and jobs—is not the only aspect where democratic steering is pertinent. The specific forms of private-public partnership that can accelerate and expand the development of good jobs will be place-specific. Success will require aligning natural and actual polities (as discussed in chapter 3). The work of building and steering these partnerships should therefore proceed by means of devolution to states, cities, and towns.

Democratic steering of the economy should also occur across all three domains of the economy: preproductive and postproductive as well as the productive domain. In no domain should the democratic legislature abdicate to technocrats, even if it should routinely call on their expertise and advice. To propose democratic steering of the economy's productive structure is, as we have seen, to introduce a focus on public-private partnerships for rule-making in support of good jobs. It is to call attention back to the role of fiscal policy in steering a healthy economy, via investments in infrastructure that supports productivity. It is also to foreground the need for democratic steering of antimonopoly and competition policy. Finally, the ideal of an empowering economy ought to include a jobs guarantee, a form of stabilization of the economy in periods of economic contraction that avoids the erosion of skill and capacity, and therefore of empowerment, in the citizenry.

As Rodrik and Sabel point out, current policy regimes have the following problems:

Ex post redistribution through taxes and transfers accepts the productive structure as given, and merely ameliorates the results through handouts. Investments in education, universal basic income (UBI), and social wealth funds seek to enhance the endowments of the workforce, without ensuring productive integration. Broadly speaking the same can be said about the Keynesian approach to job creation, through aggregate demand management. (Rodrik and Sabel 2002, 62)

An empowering economy seeks productive integration, as Rodrik and Sabel put it. The combination of the design principles—for free labor, a good-jobs economy, investments in bridging relationships, and democratic steering—add up to a fundamentally different economic vision than has reigned in the US for the past forty years—to a paradigm change, in effect. We can best see how the different elements of the paradigm change come together by looking closely at how the "empowering economies" framework yields an alternative view about the place of education within economic policy, a critical preproductive investment.

Economy and Education

The question of whether an economy integrates all members and sectors in productivity itself and thereby directly in the gains of productivity is answered by political decisions made by that nation's legislatures. Yet mainstream scholarship in political economy has not focused on restoring political capacity within the citizenry as a method of correcting problematic patterns of production and distribution. Instead, the main line of technocratic attack on inequality has served to erode the foundation for political equality.

In the late 1980s, economists began to notice a dramatic increase in wealth and income inequality, particularly in the United States and Canada. By the early 1990s, economists had identified technological change, which biased available jobs toward highskilled workers, as the primary culprit. From this diagnosis, they then took a short step to an argument that education—specifically, vocational education and education in science, technology, engineering, and math (STEM)—was the remedy. That is the lesson of Claudia Goldin and Larry Katz's important book

The Race between Education and Technology (2008). They argue that the best way of reducing the wage premium on education is to disseminate technological skills as broadly as possible throughout a population; this dissemination of skills would be expected to drive down the wage premium on expertise and compress the income distribution.

Indeed, in the US, starting with the Cold War competition with the Soviet Union, educational policy makers have steered educational institutions toward increasing vocationalism and emphasis on science and technology. The argument from economists that the only way to reverse the dynamics of income inequality is to accelerate the dissemination of technological skills through the population further entrenched this policy direction. It has been widely adopted at the highest levels of government. President Obama, in his 2013 State of the Union address, announced a competition to "redesign America's high schools." Rewards would go, he said, to schools that develop more classes "that focus on science, technology, engineering, and math—the skills today's employers are looking for to fill jobs right now and in the future." And in his 2016 State of the Union address, Obama announced a Computer Science for All initiative that would make students "jobready on day one." A result of this focus, one shared by Obama's predecessors, has been a precipitous decline in the US, over the past twenty years, of time spent in school on social studies, the arts and humanities, and programs like Model United Nations, youth simulation of politics and policy-making (Allen 2016d). In parallel, colleges and universities have seen a precipitous decline of enrollments in these areas, as students flock to the "big four" fields of business, computer science, economics, and medicine.

Piketty, too, has pursued this line of technocratic response to inequality. Leaving aside his global wealth tax, his other proposals for addressing inequality fit squarely within this now conventional frame, focused on the dissemination of technological skills. He writes, "Historical experience suggests that the principal mechanism for convergence [of incomes and wealth] at the international as well as the domestic level is the diffusion of knowledge. In other words, the poor catch up with the rich to the extent that they achieve the same level of technological knowhow, skill, and education" (Piketty 2014). To the degree that Piketty's recommendations turn to educational policy, he focuses on access. When he considers curriculum, he is explicit only about vocational goals. He argues that educational institutions should be made broadly accessible; elite institutions, which serve mainly privileged youth from the highest income brackets, should draw students from other backgrounds; schools should be run efficiently; and states should increase investment in "high-quality professional training."

But there is a flaw in the argument that technology's inexorable forward march, and its creation of inequality, can be remedied only through the dissemination of technological skills and transactional practices of redistribution. As economists Daron Acemoğlu and Jim Robinson argue,

> The quest for general laws of capitalism is misguided because it ignores the key forces shaping how an economy functions: the endogenous evolution of technology and of the institutions and the political equilibrium that influence not only technology but also how markets function and how the gains from various different economic arrangements are distributed. (Acemoğlu and Robinson 2015, 3)

Similarly, as Rodrik (2016) puts it, "Today's world economy is the product of explicit decisions that governments had made in the past.... It was the choice of governments to loosen regulations on finance and aim for full cross-border capital mobility, just as it was a choice to maintain these policies largely intact, despite a massive global financial crisis." Again, these economists are making the point that the economy is embedded in society.

The pursuit of free labor, democracy-supporting firms, a good-jobs economy, and bridging investments constitutes a powerful alternative framework for government decision-making in support of an economy that would be not only productive but also egalitarian. Yet achieving that policy framework depends on advocacy on its behalf by a democratic citizenry. Rather than supporting such advocacy, however, the standard policy response to income inequality—the dissemination of STEM skills—actually erodes political equality. The very modes of education advanced by the technocratic policy fail to prepare people for democratic participation. In the US, at least, attainment in the humanities and social sciences correlates with increased engagement in politics, but attainment in STEM fields correlates with lower political engagement. Data from the Department of Education reveal that, among 2008 college graduates, 92.8 percent of humanities majors have voted at least once since finishing university. Among STEM majors, that number is 83.5 percent. And, within ten years of graduation from university, 44.1 percent of 1993 humanities graduates had written to public officials, compared to 30.1 percent of STEM majors.[8] These are statistically significant differences. These college graduates are generally of similar socioeconomic backgrounds, suggesting that factors other than relative wealth or income must account for the difference in political engagement. The emphasis on STEM appears to leave people underprepared for civic engagement and empowerment. The technocratic policy we have is working against the ends we need.

Of course, the self-selection of students into the humanities and STEM majors may mean that these data reflect only underlying features of the students rather than the effects of teaching they receive. Yet the same pattern appears in a study by political scientist Sunshine Hillygus (2005), which controls for students' preexisting levels of interest in politics. Hillygus also finds that the differences in political engagement among college graduates are mirrored in primary education. High verbal scores on the SAT (an achievement test used for college entrance exams in the US) correlate with increased likelihood of political participation, while high math scores on the SAT correlate with decreased likelihood of participation. Again, since socioeconomic effects on SAT scores move both verbal and math scores in the same direction, this difference between the effects of high verbal and high math scores on the likelihood of participation must be telling us something about the relationship between attainment in specific subject domains and participatory readiness. Moreover, the SAT effect endures even when college-level curricular choices are controlled for.

In a 2006 article, "Why Does Democracy Need Education?," economists Edward L. Glaeser, Giacomo Ponzetto, and Andrei Shleifer argue that education is a causal force behind democracy. Specifically, they point to a causal relationship between education and participation, considering three hypotheses for why the former might be a source of the latter. They consider whether education drives up participation through indoctrination, through the cultivation of skills that facilitate participation (reading and writing and "soft skills" of collaboration and interaction), and through the increased material benefits of participation. (On the last, the idea is that education increases income, and participation correlates to socioeconomic status.) The authors reject the first and third hypotheses in favor of the second. Education, they argue, fosters participation because it prepares people for democratic engagement. Reading, writing, and collaboration are, after all, the basic instruments of political action. In short, Glaeser, Ponzetto, and Shleifer conclude that it is indeed attainment in the verbal domain that correlates with participatory readiness.

To identify a correlation is not, of course, to identify, let alone prove, causation. But those with more sophisticated verbal skills and skills at sociopolitical analysis are clearly more ready to participate in civic life. Another source of motivation may have engaged them in politics, leading them, once engaged, to seek out the verbal and analytical skills needed to thrive as civic participants. Or verbal competence and social analytical skills may make engagement easier in the first place. We don't have a study that considers levels of engagement before and after significant increases in these kinds of competence. Nonetheless, data suggest that the work of the humanities and social sciences on verbal empowerment and social analysis is intrinsically related to the development of participatory readiness.

Of course, science, technology, engineering, math, and medicine have done much to create the contemporary condition in which we find ourselves residents of mass democracies. Thanks to the industrial, aeronautical, biomedical, and digital revolutions, the world's population has grown from one to seven billion in little more than two hundred years, a profound historical transformation. We surely need the STEM fields to navigate this new landscape. But if the STEM fields gave us the mass in "mass democracy," the humanities and social sciences gave us the democracy.

The European and American colonists who designed systems of representative democracy capable of achieving a continental scale—also tragically employing genocidal techniques—were broadly and deeply educated in history, geography, philosophy, literature, and art. This is the sort of education necessary for citizenship. After all, citizens must judge whether their governments are fulfilling the responsibility to secure basic liberties and the conditions in which private and public autonomy can emerge. If a government fails in its core purposes, citizens have the job of figuring this out and deciding how to change direction. When those early founders failed at inclusion, it was figures steeped in the humanities and social sciences who pointed this out—from Abigail Adams to Frederick Douglass to Ida B. Wells to Martin Luther King Jr. Changing direction requires diagnosing social circumstances and making judgments about grounding principles for the political order and about possible alternatives to the formal organization of state power. Properly conducted, the citizen's intellectual labor should result in a probabilistic judgment answering this critical question: what combination of principles and organizational form is most likely to secure collective freedom, safety, and happiness? Such labor is best supported not by the STEM components of an education but by the humanistic, social scientific, and critical components (Saxenian 2006, 86–87). Rather than blindly "following the science" in political decision-making, we need to cultivate capacities for judgments based on actionable intelligence. Such equality as the world has managed to achieve—whether political or economic—can often be traced to the operations of these latter human capacities. This is not an argument that we should have education in the humanities and social sciences *instead of* STEM education but, rather, an argument that *we need both.*

Democracies cannot afford to dispense with those kinds of education that nourish the capacities needed in a democracy. And to the degree that science education as currently practiced undermines democracy, we ought to revisit our STEM instructional strategies.

In contrast to the technocratic, transactional approach to the role of education in combating income and wealth inequality, this line of argument, which returns to the relational, introduces significantly different needs for an educational system. If political choices determine the rules that shape productive and distributive patterns, it makes sense to focus on ensuring the emergence of political equality and forms of democratic empowerment in which citizens are equipped to secure modes of economic arrangement that in turn reinforce their freedom. If we choose political equality as our orienting ideal—empowering all to participate capably in the life of a polity—a different view of education's purpose, content, and consequence comes into view. We clearly need not only technology-oriented but also civic education. This means investment in all those liberal arts subjects described above. But not only that; at this point, digital literacies, not merely STEM knowledge, are a form of linguistic competence that itself can work powerfully in support of democracy. Education in the technological infrastructure of democracy needs to be incorporated into the other core building blocks of civic education. STEM education itself can be reconfigured in support of empowering, rather than neoliberal, economies.

Implicit in my argument thus far is that a civic education will not only support political equality but also lead to increased economic fairness—by lodging decisions about the steering of the economy with a broadly engaged public of ordinary citizens. As Acemoğlu and Robinson argue, the expansion of political participation drove egalitarian economic reforms in Britain in the nineteenth century and in the United States in the early twentieth. We are currently seeing a resurgence of participation on both the right and left. These movements, dubbed populist by many commentators, are putting issues of distributive justice on the agenda once again. Their populist dangers flow from their direct connection with charismatic party leaders, aspirations to unchecked majoritarianism, and alienation from respect for legisla-tures, processes of representation, full inclusion, minority-protecting mechanisms, and synthesis and compromise. In other words, populists reject egalitarian participatory constitutional democracy, as described in chapter 3.

Nonetheless, in the cases of the US, the UK, and France, the pop-ulists have restored valid questions, marginalized for too long, to the agenda of political economy. They have raised questions about the structure of the labor market and its relation to migration. They have raised questions about the fairness of the distribution of the gains from productivity. The question is whether populism can evolve from the expectation that a charismatic leader will change things by executive fiat into an embrace of egalitarian participatory constitutional democracy, where representatives seek compromises that permit them to steer the economy in ways that rest on the perspectives of the polity's diverse stakeholders. This resurgence of populism increases the stakes of edu-cating people for civic participation. While the technological view of the link between education and equality reinforces a vocational approach to curriculum and pedagogy, a civic view demands a renewed focus on the humanities and social sciences and a civics-oriented approach to technology. Justice by means of democracy will depend on investments in public goods, among them education, and, even more specifically, civic education.

Conclusion

In order to develop a political economy for "empowering economies," I have turned away from the transactional and toward the relational, asking how the overarching principle of difference without domination might be extended to the economic realm. Following Rodrik and Sabel, I identified the productive sector of the economy—the job-creating sector—as that portion of the economy that can generate both pro-ductivity and reasonably egalitarian distribution of its fruits. I used the principles of free labor, democracy-supporting firms, and good jobs;

of investment in bridge-building; and of democratic steering of the economy as guides to the specific policies we might pursue. Throughout I have assumed as a basic requirement of any policy that it must be structured to protect the positive and negative basic liberties both directly and indirectly.

A focus on achieving difference without domination in the economic realm widens the lens beyond Rawls's redistributive questions and, as in the social realm, requires recognizing a broader swath of the policy landscape than we typically acknowledge as relevant to the question of how to protect equal basic liberties. In this sense, the principle of difference without domination is more strenuously egalitarian than the difference principle. It establishes a higher standard for our decisions about how we protect our equal basic liberties and pulls a larger swath of the policy landscape under the umbrella of that to which the equal basic liberties pertain.

This approach to political economy protects freedom of contract and property but seeks to ensure that the relational environment in which contracts are developed supports stakeholder, not shareholder, capitalism. This requires egalitarian political empowerment, social connectedness, and a standard of disconnecting difference and hierarchy from domination in all contexts—public and private. This political economy also identifies the policies that organize land, labor, and capital as elements of the structure necessary to secure the basic liberties, positive and negative, and therefore to secure private and public autonomy. The combination of egalitarian political empowerment, social connectedness, and a relationally oriented political economy should result in a productive structure that secures more egalitarian distributive outcomes than our current productive structure.

But even under this egalitarian political economy, the patterns of distribution that flow from underlying arrangements of production will not escape the problem of those who would fall outside the structure of employment and, therefore, absent a foundation for flourishing, would fall below the threshold of material security necessary for political empowerment. This political economy, too, will need to secure a transactional welfare state, but the design of services should be understood conceptually as a second step after the design of the relational infrastructure. Moreover, the design should focus on providing a foundation for participation in economy and society—not a safety net in which to become entangled but a stable floor, anchored by housing security, on which to stand and thrive. The goal is an economy organized such that the least well-off still have access to egalitarian political empowerment, and this means a foundation for flourishing through access to housing, transportation, education, and health. But it also means a system of employment and a market economy compatible with political agency and democratic social connectedness. Thus conceived, we might develop a political economy aimed at securing freedom in its fullest sense—including not only private but also public autonomy, with both strands aligned with freedom from domination. This is a political economy for power-sharing liberalism.

Finally, there is the question of how a vicious cycle of income and wealth inequality and political domination of democratic institutions by wealthy elites can be converted into the virtuous circle of egalitarian empowerment, social connectedness, relational economies, and stakeholder capitalism that I have sought to describe here. The answer is through the democratic exercise of power in political institutions. We need to pursue justice by means of democracy. For this, we need to focus on the practice of democratic citizenship. This is the subject of the final chapter.

PART III

From Ideal to Design Principles to Practice

7

A New Model for the Practice
of Democratic Citizenship

Introduction

Justice, I have argued, begins from securing basic liberties—positive as well as negative. Fully inclusive egalitarian participatory constitutional democracies are the only governance structure that can achieve this. Justice therefore requires egalitarian participatory constitutional democracy. Sustaining protections for positive and negative basic liberties requires protecting them not only directly—through political institutions—but also indirectly. The guiding design principle of difference without domination provides this indirect protection of basic liberties. Its application is not only to the realm of political institutions but also to civil society—both the social realm and the economy. A polypolitan conception of political membership supports extension of this view of justice to the broadest possible range of participants. A polypolitan approach opens up the possibility that any given democratic nation-state can pursue justice within its borders without relying on injustice beyond its borders to achieve its domestic goals. An economy empowering for all will deliver a foundation for participation for all, both in an inclusive, dynamic economy and in the democratic steering of that economy. That democratic steering toward a healthy economy requires support through investment in civic education. But how exactly should we characterize the practice of democratic citizenship for which people should be educated?

We need a model for a citizenship practice that will help realize the overarching design principles of securing basic liberties and difference without domination, as well as the specific design principles for each domain (politics, society, economy). In the domain of political institutions, the design principles I have set out are accountability, checking-and-balancing power, inclusion, and achieving a balance between energy and republican safety. In the social domain, they are the bridging principle and a "polypolitan" bonding principle. In the domain of membership, the core design principles are support for the maximal possible free movement of labor, policies of integration in receiving societies, and support for noncitizen voice. Finally, in the economic domain, the design principles are support for free labor, democracy-supporting firms, good jobs, bridging investments, and democratic steering. A model for the practice of democratic citizenship that internalizes an orientation to all the overarching and domain-specific design principles is a tall order, but achievable.

In sketching a picture of the practice of democratic citizenship for this conception of justice, I focus on the US case. My hope, though, is that the example might spark creative application in other contexts as well. This theory of justice by means of democracy has reoriented political economy toward alignment with power-sharing liberalism. Place-specific approaches to economic policy, rather than boilerplate universalizations, were central. The same is true for the practice of democratic citizenship. I will offer a place-specific answer, but by drawing out design principles that might also be adapted with integrity and place specificity elsewhere.

Reckoning with the demands of the practice of democratic citizenship requires facing three challenges: an existential challenge for democratic citizens about their role and function, an epistemic or intellectual challenge, and a relational challenge. I will outline each challenge. Then I will explore preexisting historical and theoretical models for the practice of democratic citizenship, with a view to drawing from but also revising them into a new model. The good citizen isn't first and foremost informed or engaged but authentic and equitable. The authentic, equitable citizens forges a civic identity that starts from a clear sense of personal purpose and integrates into that understanding a recognition that the good of the community is also to their own benefit. Herein lies their equitability. The authentic, equitable citizen then makes a personal choice of which among many available civic roles to adopt. That authentic, equitable citizen also needs to become reasonably informed in the subject areas in which they choose to engage. In addition, in adversarial contexts, the good citizen understands what it means to fight fair. Good citizens are able to be both effective and self-protective because their civic action is anchored in authenticity and equitability.

Challenge 1: Multitasking

We can quickly identify the first core challenge of the practice of democratic citizenship by beginning with two thinkers—Plato and Benjamin Constant—who dismissed the value of political equality, and by homing in on the challenge they saw with embracing positive liberties. A commitment to political equality requires supporting citizens in developing a multitasking lifestyle. This is democracy's existential challenge. Can we all, or at least enough of us to keep democracy alive, embrace a multitasking lifestyle?

Plato was the first theorist to take on the question of how the daily activities of ordinary citizens relate to the health of a society. His example remains instructive. For Plato, civic life was at its base hierarchical—a select few were cut out for leadership, a small elite cohort for the work of maintaining geopolitical security, and the rest were left as mere producers. Those who possessed the requisite talent and virtue for leadership needed to be taught to make use of their gifts and to develop a sense of civic agency fully. Underlying this was Plato's conviction that solutions to political problems required aligning practical realities with abstract permanent truths and that these were accessible only to true philosophers. Philosopher-kings and queens (and Plato, unusually for his time, did include women in his conceptualization of those elite leaders) would have the job of achieving this alignment. Because the goal was to understand a fixed and a priori external truth, politics would have little need for perspectives beyond those brought to bear by the philosopher-rulers. Other people should be educated to make the best use of their own skills for some circumscribed social role like craftsmanship, agriculture, or the military. Their civic education would consist of inculcation in the laws and moral norms laid down by the philosopher-rulers. Because their civic agency was limited to obedience to the law, those citizens had no need for an empowerment model of civic practice. A stratified education system for a stratified society would maximize happiness and virtue. Most importantly, Plato believed the society would optimize its flourishing if each member in it focused on maximizing excellence in the single role for which each was best suited.

Plato was arguing against an alternative perspective cultivated by the Athenians, citizens of the world's first institutionalized democracy: that democratic citizens can do many things well simultaneously. This alternative perspective was best articulated by one of Athens's leading political figures, the general Pericles. He led the city through a period of great growth in power, effectiveness, and wealth. In a funeral oration given to commemorate soldiers who had given their lives in the Peloponnesian War against Sparta, Pericles celebrated the Athenians for their ability to bring excellence to private and public affairs simultaneously. According to the historian Thucydides, he praised his people for their multitasking:

> Our public men have, besides politics, their private affairs to attend to, and our ordinary citizens, though occupied with the pursuits of industry, are still fair judges of public matters . . . I doubt if the world can produce a man, who where he has only himself to depend upon, is equal to so many emergencies, and graced by so happy a versatility as the Athenian. (Thucydides, *History of the Peloponnesian War*, 2.34–46).

Plato's political project was to dispense with this multitasking citizen. In fact, one of his core objections to democracy was that it produced a society "embroidered like a multicolored coat," a society of citizens who didn't just settle on a single activity and single excellence (Plato, *Republic*, 557c–d).

Like Plato, Benjamin Constant also rejected belief in the value to human beings of multitasking—of pursuing those interests protected by negative liberties simultaneously to availing themselves of the empowerment secured via the positive liberties. Constant's rejection of the political liberties of the ancients in favor of the commercial liberties of the modern arose from the view that the access to wealth available through commercial enterprise would require single-minded focus. Politics would just distract from and diminish the benefit to be had from that pursuit.

Standing against these views is W. E. B. Du Bois's point about the necessity of the ballot. Du Bois's articulation, as we have seen, rests on the recognition that protecting the space to pursue private interests— whether those interests are commercial or take some other form— requires active public engagement. You don't get the negative liberties, in other words, without positive liberties. Consequently, the full pursuit of sustainable forms of justice does not simply suggest but in fact requires a form of multitasking. This multitasking is at the heart of the practice of democratic citizenship.[1] At its core, this existential challenge of democratic multitasking is fundamentally about how we connect our private and public personal interests. Whatever habits, interests, practices, and values members of a democracy may adopt to give shape to pursuit of their private purposes protected by the negative liberties, they will also need some bare minimum set of practices that make real their public autonomy. We will characterize the necessary practices when I lay out a new model for civic practice below, but first we must sketch the epistemic and relational challenges.

Challenge 2: Democracy and the Life of the Mind

The next challenge for the practice of democratic citizenship in an egalitarian, participatory constitutional democracy is epistemic or intellectual. Among regime types, democracies and republics stand out as placing exceptional intellectual burdens on the citizenry. The names themselves signal this. Both words—"democracy" and "republic"— require engagement with the abstract. Democracy, of course, in its original Greek etymology, refers to the power of the "people." But where precisely is this people, or who is this people? One can't point to a person or a concrete object in the world to make sense of this idea. Contrast this to "kingship," "monarchy," "aristocracy," or even "oligarchy." If you need to explain kingship to a young person, you point to a picture of a king and say, "This person makes the rules and has an army to enforce them." The same can be done with an aristocracy or an oligarchy. You can point to a list of identifiable individuals and say, "These people are in charge." A democracy, instead, requires somehow conjuring up an imagined community, to use the term that Benedict Anderson applied to nations. Whether the people is the citizenry of a city-state or a nation, some abstract intellectual work has to go into explaining how they can come to be thought of as a single, coordinating agent rather than as a multiplicity of diversely willing souls.[2] In chapter 3 I discussed the depersonalization of power as an important feature of any democracy. The point I make here is that this depersonalization of power requires democratic citizens to engage in abstract thinking. The same is true of the idea of a republic. Here the etymology is perhaps even more directly abstract; the word "republic" means "the public thing." What on earth such a phrase might refer to—again, when there is no concrete referent in the world that it picks out—is a quite perplexing question.

The various answers to the questions of what a democracy or a republic is have similar shapes. Such words pick out a group of people who reside in some territory with identifiable boundaries and develop processes of coordination toward shared decision-making that receive acceptance from the population as a whole as legitimate.[3] Those processes of coordination combine what has been called "will formation" with delegated action—that is, decision-making and action on the part of those public servants to whom business of the community has been delegated.[4] By "will formation" I mean the work of consolidating a majority or supermajority opinion of some kind—to establish the directionality and constraining parameters for decisions and actions by those public servants acting in the name of the people (Downey, forthcoming).

As a reminder, the basic elements of political decision-making are as follows: (1) discovery or diagnosis of social circumstances that require correction or improvement via collective action; (2) decision about which principles should guide collective decisions and which modes of organizing the powers of government (policies and laws) should be employed; (3) development of specific prescriptions or proposed courses of action; (4) deliberation and decision on those possible pathways; (5) dissemination of decisions made with regard to both framing principles and recommendations for how to organize the powers of government; (6) implementation of those decisions; and (7) review of the effects of that implementation, and a return again to the beginning of the cycle, with the work of diagnosis and discovery. These steps might also be thought of as the different phases of will formation.

These processes of will formation and decision-making are what convert a democracy or republic from an abstract idea into an operable political regime. They place intellectual burdens on the citizenry. People are asked to participate by convening in assemblies, periodically picking representatives, voting on substantive ballot measures, serving on juries, joining protests, running for office, chairing public committees, and serving on commissions, among other activities. To do any of these things, people have to have some sort of view of the direction in which they'd like to see their society move. That view may be as simple as the hope that the society moves in a direction that advances their own immediate interests, or that it rectify some immediately felt unfairness or injustice. Or it may be a more complex view about what constitutes some sort of common good or desirable shared fate. Either way, citizens have to come to a judgment. The intellectual burdens placed on citizens by democracy or republic are, then, of two kinds: (1) an initial need to process abstract conceptualizations of power and agency to a degree that can sustain seeing the decisions of public bodies as belonging to the society as a whole; and (2) an ability to make judgments about collective social directions.

Figures from Pericles to John Stuart Mill and John Dewey have recognized the intellectual labor involved in participating in a democracy and have therefore considered one of the great values of these regimes to be their necessary support for the development of human mental faculties. Athens was, Pericles argued, the school for all Greece. Even more important, its political life schooled its own citizens. Mill and Dewey saw the intellectual requirements of democracies as valuably inspiring experiments in living that could generate human progress over time. Their points were not merely that democracies need the support of strong educational systems so that citizens can do their jobs; they also emphasized that the very opportunity to participate in democracy is itself a necessarily educative and developmental experience. Democracies need schools, but democracies also school.

What can justify placing this intellectual burden on people? Not everyone has believed that it was right or wise to do so; or, from the citizen's point of view, not all citizens feel that it would be prudent or even desirable to assume that burden. Plato, of course, argued against it, taking the position that most people should be relieved of the intellectual burden of conceiving of the social whole and making political judgments. For his part, Benjamin Constant thought this burden undermined the opportunity to pursue wealth.

To ask about the justification for burdening people with democracy's intellectual work is to ask once again what justifies the selection of a democracy as a regime type in the first place. The answer still lies in fundamentals of human experience—in particular, the fact that human beings are purposive. Human beings seek to make choices to do this or that, to guide their lives in this or that direction. In the language of the Declaration of Independence, we all "pursue happiness." Importantly, we typically make our judgments about what to do in contexts where life within a community helps shape the parameters of what we consider choice-worthy. Our purposiveness is shaped not so much by an architecture of rational choice as by what the philosopher Amartya Sen has called "justified choice." We choose what we consider justifiable; the concept of justifiability, however, is far wider than the technical definition of rationality that we owe to economists and their fellow travelers. As, day by day, we choose actions that we think we can justify to ourselves and to the community or intersecting communities to which we understand ourselves to belong, we forge our idiosyncratic courses through life. To attribute this general purposiveness to human beings is to give content to the desire for freedom that we comfortably attribute to ourselves. To assign that general purposiveness to all human beings is also to identify the core content of our human equality. The purposiveness of human beings explains both the desire for freedom and the sense in which we are equal to each other. Each and all of us hope to achieve the realization of our purposes. To focus on human purposiveness as a basic feature of human experience is not, however, to say anything about what human purposes are or should be, only that our paths through our worlds are shaped by our purposiveness—to the degree, that is, that freedom from domination makes it possible for us to pursue our purposes. The political forms that best provide freedom from domination and equal liberty best support human flourishing. Insofar as the goal in protecting positive liberties and political equality is to secure the opportunity for that realization of purpose, the necessary intellectual burden placed on human beings by life in a democracy is best understood as no less but also no more than a necessary extension of the intellectual work inherent in human purposiveness. Democracy places no burden on us beyond that which we already bear simply by being creatures with purposes.

In requiring collective will formation—and therefore processes of conversation, deliberation, debate, and contestation—democracy shapes and reshapes the preferences of its community members. This is democracy's constructive work (Sen 1999b; Woodly 2015). Citizens change the terms and conditions of justified choice by participating in democracy, and in this regard they constantly re-engage in defining the terms of their own approach to purposiveness. The processes of will formation serve a direction-setting purpose that sets the terms for collective actions in the name of the people and also continuously reshapes the choice context for members of the community. Democracy schools us not only in collective action and our policy options but also in our fundamental values and how those intersect with the values we develop from participation in other shared communities of meaning, whether those are regional, ethnic, religious, professional, cultural, or of some other kind.

All citizens must be thinkers. Inevitably to participate in democracy is to participate in collective epistemic processes. Doing so is an extension of the purposiveness enacted in one's private sphere. The minimal set of practices that democratic citizens will need in order to contribute to the pursuit of justice by means of democracy therefore must include epistemic practices that make the extension of purposiveness into the public realm possible. Again, we will characterize this minimal set when I sketch my new model for civic practice, but before we do that, we must sketch democracy's core relational challenge. Although power is depersonalized and citizens must engage in some sort of abstract conceptualization of "the people" that holds power in a democracy, they must also claim a part in it for themselves; they need a feeling of belonging. The abstract needs to be squared with the immediate and connected. To characterize the relational challenge, we will lean on the philosophical work of Martin Luther King Jr.

Challenge 3: Democracy's Relational Challenge

In the wake of long legacies of enslavement, Jim Crow, and discrimination in the US, the hardest of the challenges to democracy in this country is the relational challenge. This is the challenge of ensuring that all people have an experience of ownership, belonging, and equal footing in relation to our political institutions. To give detail to this challenge, I will draw on King's characterization of the challenge of integration.

Of course, it is not merely histories of racial domination that shape the relational challenge defining twenty-first-century democracy. As we discussed in chapter 3, liberal democracy was originally conceived in a fashion that limited rights of participation to a subset of the population: typically, white property-holding men. The limitation of political power in this way both stemmed from and, to a meaningful degree, extended long-standing forms of social hierarchies—not only of race but also of class, gender, sexual identity, and religion. That the Constitutional period not only built on preexisting patterns of domination but in some places even extended them can be seen from the fact that in the years between the American Revolution and the writing of the US Constitution, women had the right to vote in several states, but by 1807 they had *lost* that right everywhere via decisions at the level of state law (Museum of the American Revolution 2020). The written Constitution was never the whole of what gave US society its order. Social hierarchies served as the informal constitution for the country. They determined who could wield power through political institutions and underpinned the legal Constitution, often manifesting their reach in the form of state law.

Even outside the US, more broadly, the wielders of power in liberal democracy had primarily been men until the middle of the twentieth century. Women in Switzerland finally gained the right to vote in federal elections in 1971. Revision of the concept of constitutional democracy in the direction of full inclusion and therefore in the direction of egalitarian participatory constitutional democracy is as recent as this—scarcely fifty years old in the Swiss case. And in the US, only in the final decades of the twentieth century did large parts of the population (though not all) embrace the project of replacing the old informal constitution with a new, egalitarian one (Allen 2004, chaps. 1–4). As we saw in chapter 4 in discussing the ideal of a connected society, the challenge of this transformation comes at the level of social practices: Can we build the habits of bonding and bridging that can support for all an experience of belonging and membership in an all-inclusive egalitarian participatory constitutional democracy? What would it take to build the habit that elsewhere I have called "political friendship"?

Integration is a word that has fallen out of favor, largely because of its long-standing connection to a concept of assimilation. But King's theory of integration is far richer, and it's worth borrowing his word and term for that reason. In an important essay, "The Ethical Demands of Integration," he articulates the relational challenges of democratic citizenship in conditions of full inclusion, defining integration as the "welcomed participation of Negroes," or out-groups generally, "in the total range of human activities" (King 1986a, 118). This is also like Rodrik and Sabel's concept of the need for integration of all in production. As a part of his argument, King makes a sharp distinction between desegregation and integration. Although both concepts respond to segregation, they are different modes of response. Desegregation entails the end of "prohibitive systems" that deny "equal access to schools, parks, restaurants, libraries, and the like." Here King implicitly invokes Berlin's distinction between negative and positive liberties. He identifies desegregation as "eliminative and negative, because it simply removes these legal and social prohibitions." Integration, in contrast, is positive, and also, in King's vocabulary, "creative." It is the "positive acceptance of desegregation and welcomed participation of Negroes into the total range of human activities. Integration is genuine intergroup, interpersonal doing." Desegregation provides freedom from prohibition and interference. Integration, in contrast, provides the freedom to "do." Only integration, King writes, "unchains the spirit and the mind and provides for the highest degree of life-quality freedom" (1986a, 121).

Like Du Bois, King places significant emphasis on positive liberty and is not satisfied simply with negative liberty. He writes: "I cannot be free until I have had the opportunity to fulfill my total capacity untrammeled by any artificial hindrance or barrier" (1986a, 121). Whereas liberals from Kant, Constant, and Berlin onward through Rawls focused on securing the negative liberties as a route to securing autonomy, their most prized form of human development, King seeks instead "the fulfillment of total capacity" (121), the chance to achieve one's purposes, a chance that requires fulfillment in and through participation in human community (Allen 2018). This is not a project of assimilation but a project in which all participants can occupy the position of creators—cultural, political, and economic. Think again of the need for productive integration. King picks up Du Bois's argument that the final phase in the achievement of freedom would be the inclusion of all as cocreators in the kingdom of culture. Human beings don't set laws individually for themselves, as isolates. They are social creatures who, together, weave the fabric of human culture that establishes the horizons of possibility for any given generation and community. Full freedom, the fulfillment of total capacity, entails the absence of artificial hindrances or barriers to participation in that process. This is the job not of desegregation but of integration. This union of negative and positive liberties into a foundation for personal completion is what King means by the phrase "life-quality" freedom.

The relational challenge, then, is how civic participants in a pluralist democracy can come to empower each other as cocreators. King breaks the challenge down into three parts: First, to create a relational standard that supports cocreation, in our hearts we have to grant "thouness" to other human beings. This is King's vocabulary for the view that justice requires that we treat our fellow human beings as ends, not means. Second, the challenge requires that we recognize and enable the equal capacities of all to deliberate, decide, and take responsibility. Third, we must contest the failure of others to fulfill those first two duties through the techniques and discipline of nonviolence. The techniques of nonviolence constitute a mode of fighting that fully embodies the principles being fought for—an attribution of "thouness" to all and an acknowledgment of the capacity of all to deliberate, decide, and take responsibility.[5] Adopting those techniques is the hardest part of the relational challenge, but I will spell out all three elements of the challenge in turn.

The key feature of the challenge to recognize the "thouness" of other people is that we not treat them as means, or as "things." We convey that we treat others as "things" when we concern ourselves not with their well-being but only with how well they perform some function of instrumental value to us. Consider again the talk of "skilling" workers. This instrumentalizes. Take, as another example, criminal justice policy. When we focus on prisoner re-entry by seeking above all to reduce recidivism, in order to minimize the damage of criminal offense to a broad community, we fail to consider the question from the point view of the well-being of the former inmate. We might instead focus on the conditions of success for re-entry as a way to measure how well we are supporting and achieving the well-being of former prisoners. To live up to a standard of non-domination, any given policy question would need to be addressed to considerations of the well-being of all those affected by it. Here is another way of putting the first relational challenge: it's about you, not me.

The second feature of this challenge lies in the need to recognize and enable the capacities of all to deliberate, choose, and take responsibility. Segregation blocks these capacities by imposing "restraint on my deliberation as to what I shall do, where I shall live, how much I shall earn, the kind of tasks I shall pursue" (King 1986a, 120). It has the consequence of forcing people to live in "some system that has largely made these a priori decisions for me." The result is that "I am reduced to an animal." Importantly, desegregation without integration only partially removes this element of domination. Unless members of out-groups are positively welcomed into all decision-making contexts with social significance, they are continually required to live in that "system [that] has already made [those] a priori decisions." Without positive liberties, and active participation in cultural and political creation, "I have been made a party to a decision in which I played no part in making." When this occurs, "the very nature of [a person's] life is altered and his being cannot make the full circle of personhood because that which is basic to the character of life itself has been diminished" (King 1986a, 121). Alongside the "well-being" requirement, then, King here poses the challenge that inclusion cannot be merely formal. If the social practices that structure decision-making ensure that for some participants the results are always like decisions made for them a priori by others, then non-domination has not been achieved.[6] A way of putting the second relational challenge is this: nothing about us without us.

This brings us to the third feature, the need to use practices of nonviolence when people fail to meet the "well-being" and "inclusion" challenges. Here King builds on the Gandhian concept of "noninjury" to build a theory of action that rests on recognition of the sacredness, the "thouness" and need for freedom, of every human being. The discipline of nonviolence provides a mode of contesting oppression and domination without turning the oppressor into a "thing." Indeed, the commitment to nonviolence demands that the practitioner "respect the personhood of [the] opponent." Thus, King writes, "nonviolence exalts the personality of the *segregator* as well as the *segregated*" (1986a, 125). This principle might help us clarify contemporary debates about microaggressions and how to counter them. Microaggressions—subtle, even unintended insults that put down members of marginalized groups on account of their group membership—are part of the fabric of social practices of domination. They represent failures to recognize the "thouness" of others and a related failure to frame interactions with others through an orientation toward their well-being. They also can often serve to degrade the opportunities of members of marginalized groups to participate effectively in joint decision-making. In other words, microaggressions can, and often do, work against full participation. Regardless of whether a given microaggression is, in its essence, a failure to recognize the "thouness" of others or a blockage to full participation by members of marginalized groups, the microaggressor can become the target of nonviolent resistance. But what does this mean? Not, in fact, that one must stage a protest or occupy a building in response to a particular microaggression, but only that one must ensure that whatever response one pursues accords with exalting the personality of the person who has inflicted the insult. Under King's principles for an ethics of non-domination, one would respond to a microaggressor not by seeking to insult or humiliate or shame in turn but in some other way—for instance, in the mode of a teacher, a figure who corrects or improves someone for the good of the person so educated, as well as for the teacher's own good. We might also call this "no-blame problem-solving."[7]

King acknowledges that this particular burden falls heavier on those "who have been on the oppressed end of the old order." He writes: "I cannot conclude without saying that integration places certain ethical demands upon those who have been on the oppressed end of the old order" (1986a, 124). This is precisely where King's trio of challenges helps bring to the surface the multiple ways democratic citizens ask things of each other and demand sacrifices. It pinpoints how even differentiated burdens can be rendered compatible with an egalitarian political project. If the third challenge falls harder on those who have been "on the oppressed end" historically, then the second challenge, to transition to fully inclusive decision-making, falls harder on those who would have had the upper hand under maintenance of a status quo order. Yes, as King says, transitioning to modes of decision-making in which all participate is the right the thing to do, but this does not make it costless. To adjust King's words, we might say that we "cannot conclude without saying that integration places certain ethical demands upon those who have been on the privileged end of the old order."

As members of each group seek to shoulder their integration burdens—for the privileged, of transitioning to fully inclusive decision-making; for the formerly oppressed, of responding with noninjurious pedagogy to witting and unwitting efforts to continue practices of domination—each in fact also responds to the first challenge of considering their fellow citizens, including those from whom they have historically been divided, as ends in themselves, not means; they address one another with reference to their well-being, not the question of how others can be made to do for me.[8] And, to put the general idea simply, the work is to call in, not call out.[9]

The practice of democratic citizenship, then, in the egalitarian participatory constitutional democracy that we should seek to build in the twenty-first century, must provide civic participants with the resources for meeting the existential challenge of multitasking, the epistemic challenges of democratic reasoning and judgment processes, and the relational challenges of making it about others and not just ourselves; of making sure that all those who are affected by a decision are included in its creation; and of calling in, not out, those who get these practices wrong. What model of democratic citizenship can deliver this? This model needs to be minimalist, in order to make the necessary multitasking viable. It also needs to foreground the epistemic and social roles and responsibilities of democratic citizens, as described above. In order to sketch a picture of the democratic practices we need, I will first explore preexisting models for the practice of democratic citizenship, both historical and theoretical. Then I will draw on these preexisting models but also reassemble and revise them to offer a new model for the practice of democratic citizenship.

Earlier Models of the Good Citizen

Models of democratic citizenship are often captured in pithy phrases, for instance, when people say that it's important for us to be "informed voters." To ask what model of democratic citizenship can help us cultivate the practices we need now when we seek justice by means of democracy is an opportunity to hold up for examination a set of models that have existed historically and to consider what will work for us now, and what we want to modify.

Sociologist Michael Schudson, in his book *The Good Citizen* (1998), argues that over the course of US history models of good citizenship have evolved concomitantly with predominant political ideologies and the changing incentives of political elites and mass movements. Schudson points to four models that have arisen since the nation's founding, each of which emphasizes different skills, duties, and values. Notably, an artificial juxtaposition between "the civic" and "the political" emerges in part from these competing conceptions of citizenship, as periods of contentious politics produce views of citizenship at odds with those favored during periods of dampened political conflict and greater public consensus.

In the fledgling years of the American republic, the view predominated that politics ought to be the purview of exceptional, virtuous (white, property-owning) men, in Plato's mold. As Publius articulated in the *Federalist Papers*, the goal was to design a republican system that tempered the potential for faction and mobocratic excess by encouraging the election of the "most diffusive and established characters."[10] The ideal citizen-leader, drawn from the "learned professions," would possess the "wisdom to discern" the interdependence of local communities and the "virtue to pursue, the common good of the society" (*Federalist* 35, 57). Civic education would cultivate the civic and epistemic virtues of this exceptional few. The rest merely needed to be educated to make wise selections of those leaders, and hold them accountable in periodic elections.

The arrival of Andrew Jackson, organized parties, and the increasing enfranchisement of unpropertied white men starting in the late 1820s shifted this paradigm. Mass parties demanded newly enfranchised voters' solidarity and strong bonds of party loyalty, often independent of the parties' actual platforms or their members' conduct in office. Like the "virtuous few" model of the early founding, the "party solidarity" model made minimal cognitive demands on most citizens but greatly strengthened the idea of a civic duty to participate. You did not need to read, but you did need a party affiliation, and you did need to show up to the ballot box.

Party realignment after the 1890s and the surging reformist spirit of the Progressive Era led to overlapping interest in constructive reform among Democrats and Republicans. The piecemeal enfranchisement of women, culminating in the Nineteenth Amendment in 1918, produced a massive, diverse new voter bloc that split between the two parties. Women's groups like the League of Women Voters prioritized the national struggle for suffrage over party politics and remained nonpartisan once suffrage was won, adopting an emphasis on "informed" voting. In their estimation, the good citizen made good vote choices based on knowledge of party platforms and rational weighing of high-quality information from a newly professionalized news media. The unthinking party loyalist was replaced with a citizen with a duty to research and reflect before making political decisions. The development of this paradigm was paralleled by changes in journalism and the development of a code of professional ethics aimed at replacing so-called yellow journalism with objective, fact-based reporting. Such forms of media had the job of providing the resources "informed citizens" would need.

The model for the good citizen shifted again during the civil rights movement, when African Americans mobilized outside electoral politics to shatter a bipartisan consensus that protected oppressive Jim Crow laws in the South. The social movements that began in the 1950s required another iteration of the cognitively engaged citizen. Such citizens would be self-aware about the rights they possessed and how they were being violated, and they would make demands on how the violations could be fixed. Their motivations would rest on authentic understanding of their own values and commitments and a willingness to speak up in public space for their intentionally and independently developed commitments. The new "rights-conscious" citizen was less focused on informed choices between existing options than on challenging and changing those options by mobilizing public opinion. This was made possible by a new set of tools: public litigation, public acts of civil disobedience, mass media coverage, and consciousness raising. Put most broadly, citizens acquired the tool of voice that now lives alongside the tool of voting, as another instrument of influence.

The models of the virtuous few and the "informed" voter reflect an ideal of reasoned deliberation toward a common good acceptable to all. The models of the loyal partisan and the authentically motivated rights advocate put conflicts over interests and goals at the center of the model and start from acknowledging the necessity of winners and losers in politics. The first two models are typically seen as examples of "civic engagement," the latter two as examples of "political engagement." Yet it would be wrong to suggest that the four historical models represent truly discrete moments in American history, oscillating between conciliation and conflict. Rather, they represent the multivalent character of political participation, where civic agents are faced with the overarching task of modulating and switching between demands for consensus and conflict, where civic participants are always both "civic" and "political."

In addition to these four historical models, in the past two decades political philosophy has also offered a fifth model for the practice of democratic citizenship, namely, the model of deliberative democracy and the deliberative citizen. The two leading advocates have been the

German philosopher Jürgen Habermas and, once again, John Rawls. While there are important differences between their views, they are ultimately close enough that we may capture them both in a capsule summary: Deliberation involves coming to decisions as a group through means that focus on reaching, or using methods in concordance with, consensus among all members. From the individual perspective, deliberation involves a mode of communication that is abstracted from individual interests and is focused on justifying certain policies or alternatives on grounds that are equally accessible for all persons. The standards of public reason and disinterestedness make deliberation more demanding than regular conversation. They require civic actors to leave their personal identities at the door when engaging in deliberation. Civic actors are expected to take up the standpoint of an identity-neutral group member or that of the group as a whole when endorsing or criticizing potential decisions.

These five models of citizenship provide different answers to the question of how to meet the challenges of democracy. That is, they offer different pictures of what the basic activities of citizens are, what their epistemic roles are, and what their ethical orientations toward their own self-interest and the broader society should be. In some of the models, the citizen's primary activity is simply to vote for representatives. Other models involve more participatory elements, like displays of party solidarity, litigation, protest, running for office, and participation in deliberative citizen assemblies. With regard to citizens' epistemic roles, some of the models articulate the expectation for a division of labor, for instance, between elite, "learned" leaders and citizens who simply need to know how to identify the elites who will best represent them; or between citizens who seek to be "informed" and the journalists who "inform" them. Other models focus on what all citizens can do epistemically: for instance, understand their rights and their own commitments and values and, on the basis of authentic purposes, advocate in good faith for change in the political universe; or, as another example, engage in deliberative discourse with others. Finally, across the range of models we see very different conceptualizations of where self-interest should fit in. In the model of the solidaristic party partisan and the authentic activist, citizens are understood to be pursuing their own interests passionately. In the models of deference to statesmanlike leaders, of the informed citizen, and of the deliberative citizen, there is an expectation that citizens will put aside their own interests in the pursuit of a common good.

But what model do we need now for our own times? And how can these historical models inform our development of our own model?

A New Model for the Practice of Democratic Citizenship

Justice by means of democracy ultimately comes down to what citizens *do*. The practice of citizenship requires meeting three fundamental challenges: the multitasking, intellectual, and relational challenges of democratic citizenship. None of the older models for the good citizen gets us quite to where we need to be to understand the practice of citizenship within this new framework for understanding justice. Although each of the models reviewed above individually falls short, collectively they point us in the right direction. Rather than expecting any one model to be fit for purpose, we need to look across the models, elicit commonalities, and build a new model from there, adopting insights where feasible, and correcting where necessary.

Let's start with the multitasking that's required to engage in democratic citizenship. Three core activities underlie the several prior conceptions of the practice of democratic citizenship: (1) deliberation, or consensus-oriented group decision-making; (2) fair fighting, or adversarial advocacy for goals within a framework of tolerance, mutual forbearance, and respect for one's rivals; and (3) prophecy, or frame and value shifting. In reality, these are not three separable activities but can exist together in a variety of different configurations and are often allocated to different persons or roles (voters, politicians, activists). A complete model for the practice of democratic citizenship will include all these activities, while recognizing that not all citizens will undertake all of them. Instead, as each citizen develops a multitasking role, civic participants ideally cultivate the capacity for all three of these tasks, understand which tasks are best suited for each context, and decide for which they themselves are best suited. What matters is that citizens have the chance to develop their own multitasking personas, their own civic identity, as best suits and empowers them (Allen and Kidd 2023). There may be a division of labor, but its shape should emerge from the autonomous choices of the citizenry, in contexts of full opportunity.

How do we support development of this multitasking capacity? Civic education needs to make these different activities visible for learners so that they can find their way to the specific practices that are the right fit for them. Beyond this developmental question, the chance to engage in these activities also requires time. That means that an empowering economy will be one that secures people free time away from work to participate in their necessary civic multitasking. Just as businesses currently support employees' participation in charitable endeavors, they ought to find ways, too, to support their participation in civic endeavors. Housing policy is important here too. Those who are rent-burdened often don't expect to stay in their community for long, and therefore choose not to engage. Stable, sustainable housing situations are also necessary to support the multitasking needed for democracy. Ultimately, we need a virtuous cycle linking what happens in economic and social domains to support for citizens' multitasking in the political domain.

But what about the intellectual and relational challenges of the practice of democratic citizenship? The key intellectual challenges were (1) how individuals understand themselves to be connected to a whole and (2) how judgments about collective direction are made. The relational challenge was whether rich integration can be achieved. Here the historical models bring something interesting to the fore. The epistemic and ethical-relational challenges are actually closely linked. They are linked via the question of how self-interest should factor into the practice of democratic citizenship.

The partisan and activist models provide an answer to the first epistemic problem. They explain how each of us is connected to the outcomes of our democratic machinery. The answer is that we are connected when we forge strong bonds of associational alliance that mediate the relationship between a civic participant and their own perspective and the decisions that emerge from the political process, driven by parties or movements. A civic participant's self-interest takes them into a set of associations, and then these associations help shape the outcomes, thereby ensuring that the participant's interests inform the final results. The abstract effort to understand a relationship between part and whole is turned into a concrete relational experience of associational life.

In contrast, the models that focus on the virtuous leader, informed voter, and deliberative democrat answer the second epistemic question: how citizens can make judgments about collective direction. These models advocate for citizens to shape their judgment by inculcating habits of somehow putting interest aside and hooking up their judgment to elite wisdom, or "the facts," or "what science says," or an abstract "common good." The epistemic conundrum is again solved via a relational commitment. I put aside my own interest and bring an orientation of altruism to the work.

But as we look at how different sets of these models answer one or the other of the epistemic challenges, they almost offer the impression that we have to make a hard choice about whether self-interest is or isn't at the basis of the practice of democratic citizenship. One set of models says we need it in, to address the first epistemic challenge. The other set of models says we need it out, to address the second.

The mistake here is to understand the practice of democratic citizenship as originating in self-interest. Instead, as I have been suggesting throughout, the relevant phenomenon that drives citizenly engagement is not interest but purpose. The goal should not be to pretend that people do not have interests or that they can shed them when they enter the deliberative assembly, as is suggested by the fifth theoretical model. Instead, we should start from the recognition that the point of civic and political engagement simply *is* the pursuit of one's purposes. In distinguishing between interest and purpose, we open up space for reconsidering accounts of how people ought to engage with their own commitments in public spaces. The goal should be not to elide one's purposes or hide them from view but to build forms of civic practice around equitable engagement with those purposes, a case I have made in *Talking to Strangers*. The question is how to connect our purposes with those of others. This is the creative work with others that lies at the heart of meeting the relational challenge of rich integration. We connect our purposes to others by holding their "thouness" in our hearts, by including all affected in the processes of decision-making, and by using principles of nonviolence to respond to injury. By coming to see how our purposes get linked with those of others, and by thinking about how we make judgments about our purposes and connect them to broader efforts, we address both intellectual challenges simultaneously. We learn how we are connected to others; we find in those connections an orientation for making judgments about social direction. Getting our purposes right is about hooking them up to those of others; this necessarily requires relational work. Purpose helps us see how the pieces fit together.

Indeed, the three tasks of democratic citizenship—deliberation, fair fighting, and prophecy—all require the same ethical practice: regulating and transforming self-interest in the direction of purposiveness. Yes, deliberation involves coming to decisions as a group through means that focus on reaching, or using methods in concordance with, consensus among all members. But contrary to the view in the deliberative democracy literature that deliberation involves a mode of communication abstracted from individual interests, deliberation should instead involve communication that focuses on acknowledging but seeking to counteract self-interest, and to convert rivalrous into equitable self-interest. Equitable self-interest is where a sense of one's own good is hooked up to a concern for the ongoing health of the community of which one is a part. When this concern is operable, then one can work with others to find a shared or common purpose (Finnemore and Jurkovich 2020; Allen 2021). To do this, those participating in deliberation make a routine practice of testing their view for "universality," for its broad value to the community as a whole. This differs from the idea that the grounds of arguments made in the deliberative context should be equally accessible to all. While those who participate in deliberation will draw on the different intellectual and moral resources to shape and communicate their commitments, they will actively test the value of what they propose from the perspective of others, entering into the intellectual and moral frames of others as well as of themselves (Stout 2003). In support of this work of testing their propositions, they will focus on equipping themselves with high-quality information on a wide array of issues, as well as with knowledge about how the world looks from different perspectives. The work of deliberation requires broad understanding of pertinent civic issues and perspective-taking, not shedding one's own purposes, or abandoning the cultural resources through which one has come to understand them. And the process of deliberation should, as Amartya Sen (1999b) proposes, lead to the evolution of participants' purposes.

Fair fighting also begins from an acknowledgment of one's own purposes, as the partisan and activist models come closer to conveying. Through these roles and through the activity of fair fighting, civic participants take up causes they care passionately about and pursue them as advocates. They must have clarity about their goals. Rather than seeking to ascertain how best to integrate their proposals with the perspectives and proposals of others, they seek to make the best case for their own point of view and to advance the influence of their case throughout the structures of political decision-making. This inevitably requires research and information acquisition, but it is driven by personal salience. Citizens don't seek to become broadly informed but to become informed as specialists about their domain of purpose— maybe climate, maybe gun rights, maybe justice reform. They choose their own specialty and leave other specializations to others. And, of course, passionate advocates seek efficacy in relation to those goals. This drives a second kind of information acquisition. Advocates need tactical understanding. They must understand how different decision points within the structure of political institutions can be used to drive change, and must be good at pulling these "levers of change." But the knowledge they need is not merely informational. It is also ethical. Since they are pursuing specific ends, motivated by their own purposes, they will also need ethical parameters that help them reason about how to link means to ends. Under a "fair fighting" paradigm, both their ends and their means will be shaped by a commitment to the ongoing existence of the community and shared political institutions through which they act (Mantena 2012, 2018). Fair fighters seek to best their opponents within the scope of agreed-upon rules by mobilizing noncommitted groups to their side. They do not seek to obliterate their adversaries, nor to alter those rules to prevent subsequent competition (see Levitsky and Ziblatt 2019). "Fair fighting" is characterized by recognition of the dignity and rights of ones' rivals (King's "thouness") and by norms of forbearance and tolerance (King's commitment to nonviolence). But as King and Gandhi have shown, there is remarkably efficacious and transformative power to be had from adhering to those limits (Mantena 2012, 2018; see also Ricks 2022). By recognizing that one's purposes have to be shaped by the requirements of fair fighting, one has a context for making judgments about purpose that also connect one's purposes to those of others.

Finally, prophecy, the third activity of civic agency, mediates between the two poles of deliberation and advocacy and directly takes up the question of what our purposes should be. Prophetic work is intended to shift a society's values; in the public opinion and communications literature, this is now called "frame shifting." Think of the rhetorical power of nineteenthcentury abolitionist Harriet Beecher Stowe; of Martin Luther King Jr.; of Occupy Wall Street activists, with their rallying cry of "We are the 99 percent!"; of the Movement for Black Lives and the hashtag #BlackLivesMatter; of artist and community developer Theaster Gates, who with art re-sacralized an abandoned neighborhood on Chicago's South Side; or of Bryan Stevenson's work to build the Memorial to Peace and Justice in Montgomery, Alabama. In all these cases, civic actors reshaped the terms by which individuals interpret their social conditions and articulate their values. Prophecy is public speech and action (broadly conceived) that looks to replace reigning values, interpretive systems, or public narratives. It changes the contexts of deliberation and is an important resource for advocates, but it may also be used by civic actors who pursue changes in cultural understandings, disconnected from any particular policy proposal (Stevenson and Lewis 2018). Prophecy undertakes to reshape the purposes that people bring with them into the political arena in the first place. Efficacy here derives from changing the game being played.

If purpose is at the base of civic participation in the democracy we need in the twenty-first century, then the ideal citizen is first and foremost authentic—clear about what matters to them and why. This citizen will forge a civic identity in which they choose the right multitasking package of roles for themselves—given their personal inclinations and habits, life circumstances, and background identities and affiliations. And given their purposes. Some may choose several civic roles; others only one; some no role at all—a choice to abstain. In making the right choice for themselves, they will be exercising a form of self-protection—working to achieve alignment between the purposes that shape their private lives and those that motivate their public participation. This is just the spirit of self-protection expressed by W. E. B. Du Bois when he laid claim to the ballot. The informational needs of these authentic citizens will vary depending on the civic roles they have selected and civic identity they have forged. We will need partners and collaborators to practice democracy because no one can be fully informed about everything. In other words, we will extend our intellectual capacity through our relational work with others. Good citizens will be well informed *because* they put relationships with diverse others at the center of their civic practice. Good citizenship, then—truly well-informed, well-directed, and effective citizenship—will be not only purposive but equitable—the mode of purposiveness that emerges when we hold the "thouness" of others in our hearts and fold the ongoing health of our community into our understanding of our purpose. We are able to fold a concern for the ongoing health of our community, and understanding of how to pursue it, into our sense of purpose only if we have *asked* others what they think and actually listened. In short, the intellectual and relational work of civic participation in egalitarian participatory democracy starts from listening to strangers.

"Choose unity," I said above. Why? Insofar as democracy is the vehicle for empowerment and public autonomy, and these are necessary for human flourishing, preserving the vehicle of our flourishing—the durable and sustainable union of a set of fully inclusive democratic political institutions—should be a nonnegotiable commitment for the ideal democratic citizen. But unity is a word we cannot use honestly unless we are putting in the work to develop the intellectual and relational capacities needed for the social wholeness of a connected society, for egalitarian participatory constitutional democracy, and for the inclusive dynamism of an empowering economy.

How do we do that? Civic education needs to help learners deepen their understanding of their own purposes and the sources of those purposes, how they intersect with the purposes of others, how to become well informed in relation to their purposes, and how to learn from and about the purposes of others. To support the last element, civic education needs to foster development of skill at civil disagreement, perspective-taking, and bridging relationships. And civic education needs to help learners understand the ethics of the practice of democratic citizenship—norms of fair fighting and nonviolence (Educating for American Democracy 2021). In addition, we need to reform policy-making and electoral politics to deliver access and voice to those who have historically been put-upon or done-to—and left uninvited from full integration into the shaping of our shared purposes in the first place. The democratization of policy-making through participatory processes will itself drive the education we need. As we participate in these processes, civic participants will get things wrong. They will insult and offend one another. They will dominate each other. To address this, we need to call each other in, not out. We need to call each other in to the project of holding "thouness" toward others in our hearts. We need to strengthen the ethic of nonviolence and put it at the center of our politics. We need a culture not of blame and shame but of acknowledging fallibility and of calling one another in for course correction. That calling in is an act of invitation to a full sharing of power and responsibility.

Conclusion

How does the model of the authentic citizen—of the equitable, effective, and self-protective civic participant—sketched above support justice by means of democracy? This is to ask how the model supports all the principles with which I concretized the project of justice in each of the three core domains of politics, society, and the economy. All of the principles work toward establishing the conditions and practices of shared power. Consequently, the answer is a simple one. The practice of democratic citizenship thus conceived equips people to share power and responsibility. Justice by means of democracy will exist when all people, regardless of background, fully share power and responsibility.

The test of whether these ideas have any merit will be in the trying—if in pursuit of them we find that more space has been made for human purpose, if we find that we feel the sweet balm of justice more frequently, then we will know our striving pulls in the right direction.

Epilogue

The focus offered here on political equality, justice by means of democracy, and a political economy and civic practice built on such commitments should help us avoid being surprised by a Brexit or the election of a Trump and help us prepare to govern through a crisis. Such a focus should even help our polities track a steady course in pursuing general welfare while avoiding radical upheavals or existential challenges to democracy itself. In the first place, a political economy built around the need to secure political equality requires deeper contextual knowledge of the political situation of any given place. One can't think well about policy on this model without thinking about the distribution of power and about how arrangements of land, labor, and capital contribute to power's structural allocation. In the framework I offer, economic policy questions will necessarily require social contextualization, and that effort will increase the amount of knowledge our technocratic professionals have about the societies for which they are designing policies. A civic practice of bridge-building and listening would similarly deepen the knowledge base in use for policy-making and problem-solving.

An approach to political economy grounded in the nonsacrificeability of political equality also foregrounds human dignity, people's desire to be cocreators of collective life. The approach asks us to consider the impacts of policy on that aspect of human experience.

A political economy that takes sociopolitical context and human dignity seriously would help avoid future failures on the part of our policy makers to understand our political circumstances. Democracy is one of the most powerful tools of understanding and social discovery ever invented by humanity. While the importance of prices (and therefore market mechanisms) to the distribution and productive use of knowledge has been long heralded, the value of democratic governance processes has not as commonly been identified as an equally important human invention in support of human flourishing. Yet its power is at least as, if not more, significant.

Justice by means of democracy requires securing both the negative and the positive liberties. In securing both sets of liberties, the pursuit of justice so defined equips humanity with the most powerful tools it has yet created for securing safety and happiness—not only markets but also democracy. Markets come in many variants; we should choose only those forms—and undergirding rules—that best work in support of democracy. This is the pathway to a new political economy, a power-sharing liberalism, and a society where communities can prosper and beautiful differences can flourish without being devoured by the parasite of domination.

We choose our political economy not as an end in itself but to secure the foundation on which human beings can live their best lives. The flourishing that comes from human empowerment—from self-government in our private lives and shared self-governance in our public lives—is the goal. The economy is only a tool. As for the flourishing that comes from fulsome opportunity to discover and pursue, in concert with others, our chosen purposes, this is the fruit of justice pursued by means of democracy.

Acknowledgments

I grew up in an opinionated, fractious, loving family. In the 1970s we were a big network of aunts, uncles, and cousins in Southern California. My dad had grown up in a big family of twelve siblings in Northern Florida. My grandfather had helped found one of the first NAACP chapters in that part of the state—a pretty dangerous undertaking. The lynching of Emmett Till changed everything, my father told me. Half of the siblings fled the Jim Crow South for LA, seeking freedom and opportunity. They were politically engaged. My father sported a beret. And their engagement spanned the political spectrum. In one year, in the early '90s, my aunt Roslyn was on the ballot for Congress in the Bay Area for the Peace and Freedom Party while my dad, William, was running for Senate from Southern California as a Reagan Republican.

Throughout those decades, our holiday dinner-table conversations were something to behold. Knock-down, drag-out political debates between my dad and Aunt Roslyn: he, lean and bald, with a wreath of pipe smoke curling around his head; she, also with a receding hairline, lesbian and built like a Mack truck, with a huge belly laugh. They agreed on *what* they were pursuing. They were both trying to find a path to empowerment for themselves, for the people they loved, and for every community. They wanted the empowerment of self-government and a foundation on which they and those around them could stand upright and flourish. But, boy, did they disagree on *how* to get there. He made the case for market freedoms, libertarian choice rights, and personal virtue. She argued for public-sector investment across all segments of society and experiments in living. Neither of them chose the Democratic Party—after all, back then, it ruled the South they'd fled. And one other thing stood out. Never, as they argued, did they break the bonds of love. They never attacked each other personally. They were never anything but loving to the other human in front of them. Nor was there ever any question that each would be there for the other in a time of need, as they were.

I was caught between them, quiet, taking it all in, just trying to keep up. Eyes darting back and forth, like watching a ping-pong match, trying to figure out *the answer*. In my childhood, I couldn't. But I knew my dad and aunt were my models for the civic and political life I wanted. Like them, I have tried always to engage in all political debates with a loving spirit, even with strangers, even with those who seek to wound. This has been a reliable and calming anchor for me. Now, after many years of labor, I can enter into their substantive debate with my own considered contribution.

Yes, Dad. Yes, Aunt Roslyn, I agree with you both on the *what*. We flourish when we govern ourselves in our private lives and through shared self-governance in public institutions. And as to the *how*, I offer you a blend of the two of you—a bit of market, a bit of public sector, civic virtue, and room for experimentalism. Justice by means of democracy. Call it a productive integration.

I owe uncountable debts of original thanks, not only to my dad and my aunt, my mom, my brother, my stepmom, my first husband, my stepsons, and the rest of my family, but also to all those who have traveled with me over my academic career. All of my earlier efforts show up in this book. There are too many generous souls to recount by name. But I want to give special thanks to the wonderful teams of scholars I've had the chance to work with on a set of edited volumes published by the University of Chicago Press (*Education, Justice, and Democracy; Education and Equality; From Voice to Influence; Difference without Domination;*

and *The Political Economy of Justice*). I also want to thank my colleagues at the Edmond and Lily Safra Center for Ethics who have read too many versions of these essays. I am especially grateful to Tim Scanlon, Dennis Thompson, Jenny Mansbridge, Michèle Lamont, Eric Beerbohm, Arthur Applbaum, Deb Chasman, Tommie Shelby, Brandon Terry, and Mathias Risse for exceptionally detailed comments on earlier versions of this book. I also owe a special debt to Glen Weyl, Dani Rodrik, and Mal Salter for many conversations about political economy. Students, too, have made invaluable contributions, most recently Leah Downey, Josh Simons, and Justin Pottle. And colleagues at the Democratic Knowledge Project—David Kidd, Chaebong Nam, Katie Giles, Adrianne Bock, Tina Blythe, Carrie James, Adrienne Stang, and Jenny Chung—have been indispensable for thinking about civic education. Fellow commissioners and team members on the American Academy of Arts and Sciences Commission on reinventing American democracy for the twenty-first century have also been superb thinking companions. Chuck Myers, Tamara Ghattas, and Nick Lilly have made the editorial process a breeze. The two anonymous reviewers for the press challenged me in all the right ways. They were master teachers. I am profoundly thankful for the smart, caring team at the Safra Center and Erica Lutcher in our home, who have kept everything on track.

But the greatest thanks are reserved for last: to Jimmy, Nora, and William, for everything, always.

Cambridge, MA
July 4, 2022

*   *   *

Earlier versions of sections or chapters in this book have appeared in Earl Lewis and Nancy Kantor, eds., *Our Compelling Interests: The Value of Diversity for Democracy and a Prosperous Society* (Princeton University Press, 2016); *Boston Review* (Allen 2016d); *Politische Gleichheit* (Suhrkamp 2017); the *Atlantic* (Allen 2019); Tommie Shelby and

Brandon Terry, eds., *To Shape a World: Essays on the Political Philosophy of Martin Luther King, Jr.* (Harvard University Press, 2018); Danielle Allen and Rohini Somanathan, eds., *Difference without Domination: Pursuing Justice in Diverse Democracies* (University of Chicago Press, 2020); and Danielle Allen, Yochai Benkler, Leah Downey, Rebecca Henderson, and Josh Simons, eds., *A Political Economy of Justice* (University of Chicago Press, 2022).

Notes

Prologue

1. This book proposes new questions for economists, and economist Glen Weyl is answering the call (see Weyl 2022a, 2022b). Other work by economists is also developing in this spirit, including Bowles and Carlin (2021) and Rodrik and Sabel (2022); see also Allen et al. (2022). My hope is that the combination of the work in this book and the work of Weyl, Bowles and Carlin, Rodrik and Sabel, and others might provide the foundation for a reorientation of political economy.
2. See my book *Cuz* (Allen 2017) on the US war on drugs for an example of a negative equilibrium that depends on the interaction between structures of governance and the emergence of self-organizing systems.
3. In this regard, a theory of justice contrasts with sociobiology's arguments about justice that claim to describe morality as it has evolved, as a matter of evolutionary biology and the evolution of the human brain.
4. For Rawls, a theory of justice has the job of articulating the right, not the good. Yet here, too, the argument is about an overall picture of human well-being, namely, that it is by agreeing to focus for our collective decisions only on the "right," and not on the "good," that we make it possible for people to pursue and experience the good as they define it. Rawls, too, has at least implicitly a broad conception of what is good for human beings as the final object of his analysis.
5. Mill (1859) 2006, 15–16: "The principle requires liberty of tastes and pursuits; of framing the plan of life to suit our own character; of doing as we like, subject to such consequences as may follow. . . . Each is the proper guardian of his own health, whether bodily, or mental and spiritual."
6. Mill (1859) 2006, 76: "With respect to his own feelings and circumstances, the most ordinary man or woman has means of knowledge immeasurably surpassing those that can be possessed by any one else."

Chapter One

1. Of course, the subfield of behavioral economics—in which every self-respecting econ department must today have at least one practitioner—addresses exactly these questions. The field has not, though, yet displaced the common habits of thought that have migrated from utilitarian theory to common parlance.

2. This is a critique most forcefully articulated by Anderson (1999) and Forst (2011, 2014); and by Honneth (2014). Cf. Risse (2020), part II.

3. That Rawls's arguments work this way in practical contexts is something of an irony. One of his most fundamental points is the lexical priority of the rights. Moreover, fair equal opportunity is prior to the difference principle. There are, in other words, two steps of lexical priority before you get to the difference principle. Yet the difference principle, and a welfarism based on it, has come to define Rawls's influence on public policy.

4. But see Scanlon (2018) for a counterpoint to the dominant tendency. He focuses on the relational foundations of justice as the basis for his several complementary critiques of inequality.

5. Tessema (2020), in a fine study of the historical lineage of concepts of "equity," traced the connection of the term to "social justice" and of both terms to historically developed problems of material distribution that also align with other axes of disempowerment, such as race. It is also important to say something about the meaning of "critical race theory," given current political controversies. Charles Mills (2009, 270–71) offers a particularly helpful review of the concept: "For me, the best way to think of CRT is as analogous to feminism: a broad political and theoretical movement within which there are multiple approaches. In other words, there is a minimal commitment to recognizing the centrality of race to the making of the modern world (equivalent to the commitment to recognizing gender subordination), but after that there will be considerable variation in the causal diagnoses made and the political prescriptions offered." As Mills points out, those prescriptions range from the classical liberal to the Marxist. There is no necessary connection to either approach to political economy.

6. The relevant degree of comfort with discussion of different categories of inequality is probably shifting in the contemporary moment thanks to social movements for racial and gender justice, but the important point is that political inequality as a stand-alone concept typically does not make it onto the list of concerns around inequality.

7. There are exceptions to the tendency of much recent liberal egalitarian political philosophy to tilt toward abstraction—for instance, Tommie Shelby's *Dark Ghettoes* (2016). Shelby's unusual decision to integrate social science research within a Rawlsian philosophical argument is an exception that proves the rule.

8. Ravallion (2016), 87: "The Washington Consensus was too formulaic to be credible as a policy prescription. It listed a single set of policies, but governments of developing countries could see for themselves that there were multiple paths to development success."

9. Mill does not use the term "autonomy," but scholars of his work commonly understand his theory of liberty to be a theory of autonomy.

10. Berlin also extended the meaning of "positive" to include much more than republican liberty, in some instances arguing that positive freedom could exist only in the form of the collective or social whole. He then attacked those extensions, which would obliterate individual freedoms, without distinguishing between them and republican liberty.

11. The revival of republican liberty began with J. A. Pocock in 1975. On the other hand, the whole participatory democracy movement, starting in 1962, very much stressed self-ownership of the law, and one of the earliest and most extensive discussions of "participatory politics" is found in Robert J. Pranger's *The Eclipse of Citizenship* from 1968 (Kang 2012).

12. What are rights? Very generally, they are boundaries in our treatment of each other, secured by incentive structures that both enforce those boundaries and inculcate habits of respecting those boundaries in our treatment of each other.

13. He adds, "These liberties are all required to be equal by the first principle, since citizens of a just society are to have the same basic rights" (Rawls 1971, 61).

14. Rawls (1971), 7: "By major institutions I understand the political constitution and the principal economic and social arrangements. Thus the legal protection of freedom of thought and liberty of conscience, competitive markets, private property in the means of production, and the monogamous family are examples of major social institutions. Taken together as one scheme, the major institutions define men's rights and duties and influence their life-prospects, what they can expect to be and how well they can hope to do. The basic structure is the primary subject of justice because its effects are so profound and present from the start."

15. Rawls (1971), 195: "After this, three problems of equal liberty are discussed: equal liberty of conscience, political justice and equal political rights, and equal liberty of the person and its relation to the rule of law"; 197–98: "In pursuit of this ideal of perfect procedural justice (sec. 14), the first problem is to design a just procedure. To do this the liberties of equal citizenship must be incorporated into and protected by the constitution. These liberties include those of liberty of conscience and freedom of thought, liberty of the person, and equal political rights. The political system, which I assume to be some form of constitutional democracy, would not be a just procedure if it did not embody these liberties"; 199: "The first principle of equal liberty is the primary standard for the constitutional convention. Its main requirements are that the fundamental liberties of the person and liberty of conscience and freedom of thought be protected and that the political process as a whole be a just procedure. Thus the constitution establishes a secure common status of equal citizenship and realizes political justice."

16. Although scholars have not noticed this feature of Rawls's thought, it does in fact structure the book as a whole, as I detail in the chapter, and should be taken seriously.

17. Rawls (1971), 201–2: "Thus one might want to maintain, as Constant did, that the so-called liberty of the moderns is of greater value than the liberty of the ancients. While both sorts of freedom are deeply rooted in human aspirations, freedom of thought and liberty of conscience, freedom of the person and the civil liberties, ought not to be sacrificed to political liberty, to the freedom to participate equally in political affairs. This question is clearly one of substantive political philosophy, and a theory of right and justice is required to answer it. Questions of definition can have at best but an ancillary role"; 230: "One of the tenets of classical liberalism is that the political liberties are of less intrinsic importance than liberty of conscience and freedom of the person. Should one be forced to choose between the political liberties and all the others, the governance of a good sovereign who recognized the latter and who upheld the rule of law would be far preferable. On this view, the chief merit of the principle of participation is to insure that the government respects the rights and welfare of the governed. Fortunately however, we do not often have to assess the relative total importance of the different liberties. Usually the way to proceed is to apply the principle of equal advantage in adjusting the complete system of freedom. We are not called upon either to abandon the principle of participation entirely or to allow it unlimited sway. Instead, we should narrow or widen its extent up to the point where the danger to liberty from the marginal loss in control over those holding political power just balances the security of liberty gained by the greater use of constitutional devices. The decision is not an all or nothing affair. It is a question of weighing against one another small variations in the extent and definition of the different liberties. The priority of liberty does not exclude marginal exchanges within the

system of freedom. Moreover, it allows although it does not require that some liberties, say those covered by the principle of participation, are less essential in that their main role is to protect the remaining freedoms. Different opinions about the value of the liberties will, of course, affect how different persons think the full scheme of freedom should be arranged"; 230: "Moreover, it allows although it does not require that some liberties, say those covered by the principle of participation, are less essential in that their main role is to protect the remaining freedoms. . . . . It is only when social conditions do not allow the effective establishment of these rights that one can acknowledge their restriction. The denial of equal liberty can be accepted only if it is necessary to enhance the quality of civilization so that in due course the equal freedoms can be enjoyed by all"; 233: "I do not wish to criticize Mill's proposal. My account of it is solely for purposes of illustration. His view enables one to see why political equality is sometimes regarded as less essential than equal liberty of conscience or liberty of the person. Government is assumed to aim at the common good, that is, at maintaining conditions and achieving objectives that are similarly to everyone's advantage. To the extent that this presumption holds, and some men can be identified as having superior wisdom and judgment, others are willing to trust them and to concede to their opinion a greater weight. The passengers of a ship are willing to let the captain steer the course, since they believe that he is more knowledge-able and wishes to arrive safely as much as they do. There is both an identity of interests and a noticeably greater skill and judgment in realizing it. Now the ship of state is in some ways analogous to a ship at sea; and to the extent that this is so, the political liberties are indeed subordinate to the other freedoms that, so to say, define the intrinsic good of the passengers. Admitting these assumptions, plural voting may be perfectly just. Of course, the grounds for self-government are not solely instrumental. Equal political liberty when assured its fair value is bound to have a profound effect on the moral quality of civic life."

18. Cf. the argument of the original edition. Rawls (1971, 542–43) continues : "As the condi-tions of civilization improve, the marginal significance for our good of further economic and social advantages diminishes relative to the interests of liberty, which become stronger as the conditions for the exercise of the equal freedoms are more fully realized. Beyond some point it becomes and then remains irrational from the standpoint of the original position to acknowledge a lesser liberty for the sake of greater material means and amenities of office. . . . Increasingly it becomes more important to secure the free internal life of the various communities of interests in which persons and groups seek to achieve, in modes of social union consistent with equal liberty, the ends and excellences to which they are drawn. In addition men come to aspire to some control over the laws and rules that regulate their association, either by directly taking part themselves in its affairs or indirectly through representatives with whom they are affiliated by ties of culture and social situation."

19. Earlier in section 32 he has rightly explicated, with reference to Constant, how the long-running arguments over how to define the liberties of the ancients and of the moderns are really arguments about the relative value of the different basic liberties. Formally, he puts the question of relative value to the side, but he nonetheless seems to suggest that he would come down with Constant for the view that freedom of thought and conscience ought not, he argues, to be "sacrificed" to political liberty.

20. In section 82, Rawls does discuss the emergence of a principle of the inviolability of political liberties in the well-ordered society. In this and the preceding paragraphs, however, I am suggesting that he has misunderstood the role of principles of inviolabil-ity; they should help us achieve a well-ordered society while we are under nonideal conditions, they should not be that which we secure with and only with the well-ordered society. Rawls's prioritizations among the basic liberties, and his differential application

of a principle of inviolability to the negative and the positive liberties, established a framework for political judgment, which is in itself an ideal framework even if deployed in nonideal circumstances. I am criticizing that framework for political judgment.

21. Kamm (1993) discusses the case-based method for moral reasoning in groundbreaking ways.

22. For a good account of co-originality, see Frank (2005).

23. Rawls objected to views that made more extensive claims about the inherent good of democratic equality, for instance, Habermas's argument that democracy is valuable in itself because political participation is necessary to full human flourishing and not merely to self-respect. Rawls rejected the idea that "civic humanism is true: that is, the activity in which human beings achieve their fullest realization, their greatest good, is in the activities of political life" ([1993] 2011, 5–6, 420). Some people, he argued—for instance, a George Washington or an Abraham Lincoln—may develop such a conception of the good for themselves. They may need the activities of a political life to achieve their full flourishing. But we ought not to impose that conception of the good on everyone else.

24. Susan Okin (1991) makes a parallel point concerning Rawls's nonattention to the impact of family structure on justice in *Justice, Gender, and the Family*.

25. I am using a conception of autonomy that extends to embodied autonomy, not simply the giving of moral laws to oneself, as in a strict Kantian sense. Instead, I am using autonomy as an antonym to domination.

26. This is not a new path, not in fact an abandonment of classical liberalism, as Rawls suggests, but a return to a moment before liberalism, via Constant, divided the two sets of rights from each another and prioritized negative liberties. Prior to that point, eighteenth-century traditions of liberalism—rights-based political theories—were commonly republican, emphasizing the importance of positive liberties and participation. As Melvin Rogers has shown (2020, forthcoming), republicanism did not die off when liberalism began to focus on negative liberties with Constant as well as with John Stuart Mill. It lived continuously in the tradition of African American political philosophy. The argument that I make throughout this book draws on the durable commitment of those who have experienced political marginalization to affirming the intrinsic value of positive liberties.

Chapter Two

1. For an excellent exposition of the core elements of an ideal of democracy, see Ober (2017).

2. Why start an argument about the meaning of justice by asserting that justice must include political equality or democracy? There are two possible answers. Either one thinks that participating in democracy is in itself good for human beings or else one thinks that only by participating in a democracy can human beings secure the elements of justice. The value of democracy may, in other words, be either intrinsic, deriving from what it itself is, or instrumental, deriving from the outcomes that it secures. For the past two centuries, political philosophers in the West (in contrast, for instance, to scholars working on Chinese traditions of meritocracy) have argued that democracy has an undeniable instrumental value—in securing conditions for the exercise of personal autonomy, and possibly in securing various aspects of material well-being. They have also argued that it *may* have intrinsic value. It *may* be the activity in which full human flourishing is manifest. See Jill Frank (2005) for a fine analysis of the difference between intrinsic goods, which inhere in an activity itself, and instrumental goods, which are often the deliverables or outcomes of an activity.

Amartya Sen explores both the instrumental and the intrinsic justifications for democracy and a third "constructive" justification in "Democracy as a Universal Value" (1999b). As an example of the instrumental value, Sen famously argues that the adoption of democratic political institutions ensures that a society will not suffer famines (1999a, chaps. 6 and 7). By a constructive justification, he has in mind the work that democracies do to generate our preferences and senses of value and direction; democratic decision-making mechanisms drive social processes that help populations define goals and values in the first place, thereby shaping personal and collective preferences. I agree that democracy can also be justified on this constructivist basis, but I put that plank of justification aside for the time being.

3. This argument that rights of participation protect rights of private autonomy runs parallel to Sen's argument in *Development as Freedom* (1999a) that political rights protect economic rights.

4. This species property argument has predecessors in Aristotle (see Williams 2009; Sen 1999b) and the Declaration of Independence (see Allen 2014b).

5. Rights were originally conceived of as equal among the rights bearers, and once rights were extended to all human beings, the very nature of what we mean by rights means that those who have those rights have them equally.

6. Why these five facets and not others? My answer is that of a philosophical pragmatist: These are the facets of the concept of political equality that anchor understanding of that ideal within the context of US democracy. They are the five facets limned in the Declaration of Independence, a text that has shaped the normative horizons of this culture for two and a half centuries, whether its arguments have been affirmed or repudiated and whether the text has been intentionally acknowledged (as by Abraham Lincoln, Martin Luther King Jr., the Black Panthers, and the Tea Party) or left unacknowledged. The Declaration in fact made a positive contribution to political philosophy by tethering eudaimonism to pragmatism. Its approach to political equality supports that tethering, and I build on its five facets for political equality for that reason. Cf. Allen (2014b).

7. I've argued for them at greater length in my book *Our Declaration: A Reading of the Declaration of Independence in Defense of Equality* (2014b). Here, for summary purposes, I will simply name the five facets.

8. What follows is a broad-brush paraphrase of my argument in *Our Declaration*. I should note that in the context of this chapter I start from the Declaration of Independence not merely because it is an anchor for the US political tradition but also because I take it to have made an innovative contribution to political philosophy, and particularly to the philosophy of egalitarianism. Its innovation has been less recognized and less followed up on in the philosophical literature than it should be. In particular, I take the Declaration to articulate a liberal-pragmatist theory of democracy grounded in a conception of human flourishing ("the pursuit of happiness") that leaves the people themselves to define and judge experimentally and experientially over time, while hedging their experiment with, the concept of "rights." This hedge is what makes the view liberal; the experimentalism is what makes it pragmatism. Moreover, this pragmatism does posit a final good ("happiness"), but it does not give that final good a metaphysical ground. Instead, the document leaves judgments about happiness to individual people and the people as a whole to be made over time. In this regard, the view articulated in the Declaration rests on commitments both to fallibilism and corrigibilism. Finally, it articulates a constructive justification for democracy insofar as it identified democratic citizenly debate (about principle and about how to organize the powers of government to deliver on those principles) as the only means for developing a view about the content of "happiness." The political philosopher who comes closest, I think, to articulating a philosophical view in line with that laid out in the Declaration of Independence is Amartya Sen. John Stuart Mill in *On Liberty* picked up key aspects of the

argument about happiness and independent human judgment set out in the Declaration of Independence, but the ultimate reduction of the "happiness" concept to "utility" by the utilitarian tradition reduced the power of the original idea and obscured the original constructivist view about the ongoing creation of definitions of personal and public happiness over time by a deliberating and contestatory democratic people. With this mistake, utilitarianism, and other public philosophies that have flowed from it, fundamentally lost sight of politics, reducing decision-making to the work of aggregating given and static preferences.

9. Protection from domination includes protection that comes in a positive form—via instances where law is required to solve collective action problems. That is, we sometimes need coercion to get people to contribute to creating things that benefit all (or many) and that all or many genuinely want, but that absent coercion, insufficient numbers of people will contribute to, so these things will not come about. Also, we need to avoid domination by potential free riders. (Thanks to Jane Mansbridge for this point.)

10. The arguments in this chapter are complemented by those of Melvin Rogers (2020) in "Race, Domination, and Republicanism" and by an outline of fundamental principles for justice in the twenty-first century in Allen et al. (2022) *A Political Economy of Justice*.

11. As Jane Mansbridge points out to me, this brings out the significance of Thucydides's critique of Pericles in the *History of the Peloponnesian War* when the historian says that Athens was a democracy in name only because all the power was really in the hands of one man, namely, Pericles (book 2.65). Mansbridge astutely observes that Thucydides was seeking to refute the democracy's claim to have achieved a depersonalization of power. It's also notable that in the early modern period some monarchies were thought not to be personal but instruments of God or legitimated by their pursuit of justice or the common good. The idea emerged that the monarchy was not the specific person of the monarch, and this facilitated the emergence of modern conceptions of the state.

12. This is not quite the same as Rawls's idea that the basic liberties must be protected equally for all even if, due to inequalities in resources, not all have equal value of political liberty. The rich will have more value from the political liberties available to them. Rawls's solution to the gap between political liberties and actual empowerment is the application of the difference principle to the functioning of the basic liberties. He writes, "Taking the two principles together, the basic structure is to be arranged to maximize the worth to the least advantaged of the complete scheme of equal liberty shared by all" (sec. 32). I am articulating the further idea that there should be no avenue of lever pulling available exclusively to the rich and only to the rich, even if it is possible for the rich to do more with the levers available to be pulled.

13. Ober (2008), in *Democracy and Knowledge*, provides the most comprehensive empirical and theoretical articulation of the importance of epistemic egalitarianism to the success of democracy. See also Farrell and Shalizi (2015).

14. This has been recognized recently in the United States by the Presidential Commission for the Study of Bioethical Issues, which has made collaboration between experts and lay citizens a key feature of its work. See, for instance, the Commission's report *New Directions* (2010).

15. This ideal of equal agency is the cornerstone of Aristotle's concept of rectificatory justice, which he argues for in *Nicomachean Ethics*, book 5.4, and which I explicate in both *World of Prometheus* (2000, chap. 11) and *Talking to Strangers* (2004, 128–30). I have made this idea a core element of my own democratic theory.

16. As Jane Mansbridge points out, a fuller conception of reciprocity would include cocreation. Cocreation is the fifth facet of equality that I consider, and I address it below. The project of responsiveness also has the goal of doing things together than one cannot do alone. In the section of the Declaration most closely tied to reciprocity, however, the focus is primarily on redress of grievances, and I follow that structure here.

17. My account here, articulated fully in my *Talking to Strangers* (2004), is very close to Rawls's argument about the importance of a "sense of justice."
18. On campaign finance, Rawls put on the table years ago the question of what to do when accumulations of financial capital are converted into forms of political domination and undermine the fair value of political liberty (*Theory of Justice*, sec. 36). While efforts in the US to control private giving to political campaigns run into conflicts with the liberty of free expression, a reorganization of voting mechanisms around ranked-choice voting would redirect campaign funds into more socially productive uses, reducing the power of money in politics without infringing on rights of expression. See also Sodonis and Witte (2012).
19. See, for instance, Hacker (2011); Gilens (2012); and Scanlon (2018), who analyze how income and wealth inequality have come to affect American politics, with the political preferences of the wealthy elite dominating decision-making.
20. This is my revision to Hayek via a focus on several kinds of self-ordering system and the relations among them. While this might on first blush sound like Michael Walzer's argument in *Spheres of Justice* (1983), and while there are many points of similarity and alignment between my argument and Walzer's, our arguments are fundamentally distinct in the following way. Walzer sets out to offer an account of distributive justice, where the social goods of different spheres of social life each have principles of distribution pertinent to those spheres. The principles don't flow from any conception of human or natural rights (as Walzer points out in his introduction). He writes: "Hence in the pages that follow I shall imitate John Stuart Mill and forego (most of) the advantages that might derive to my argument from the idea of personal—that is, human or natural—rights. Some years ago, when I wrote about war, I relied heavily on the idea of rights. For the theory of justice in war can indeed be generated from the two most basic and widely recognized rights of human beings—and in their simplest (negative) form: not to be robbed of life or of liberty. What is perhaps more important, these two rights seem to account for the moral judgments that we most commonly make in time of war. They do real work. But they are only of limited help in thinking about distributive justice."
    In my argument, in contrast, I do not seek a theory of distributive justice, in the first instance, but a theory of, in effect, relational justice, where the relevant relationship sought is one of political equality, and the content of that is indeed captured by the basic and most widely recognized rights of human beings. I take distributive questions to be secondary to relational questions. As a result, the kinds of issues that emerge for attention in the political, social, and economic domains in my argument are often different than those that emerged for Walzer. The interesting exception is in our chapters on membership, where our concerns are highly aligned.
21. This is a central debate among Hayek, Nozick, and Rawls. Like Rawls, I take just proceduralism to yield substantive justice. We also differ, though. Rawls argues that the goal is to move from principles of justice (derived procedurally from the original position) to the "institutions" of the just society. I would argue that the goal is to equip people with principles that permit them to be constant revisers of the "chartering rules" that structure the basic structure. Like Rawls, I do seek to articulate universal principles, but I more emphatically expect (like Michael Walzer) that the concrete instantiation of those principles in specific demographic circumstances may well be highly various.
22. Of course, politics is not limited to dissensus; it also involves consensus, as Mansbridge points out in *Beyond Adversary Democracy* (1980). But it is always necessary to "come to consensus," which means starting from or passing through "dissensus."
23. See Sethi and Somanathan (2004) on impacts of segregation even in absence of discrimination.
24. A point made controversially by Arendt in "Lessons from Little Rock" (1959).

25. Robert Nozick (1973) provides the classic argument about the relation between liberty and economic difference or inequality, with Wilt Chamberlain as his example. Of course, there is a difference between Nozick and Rawls. Rawls based the difference principle on the idea that in the original position (without envy) we would accept (indeed welcome) any inequalities that grew the pie, and that the least advantaged sectors also had to benefit because we might end up there. But the difference principle kicked in only after the liberties were guaranteed and then after equal opportunity was guaranteed (two layers of priority).

26. Rawls had little to say about the organization of the firm, though Elizabeth Anderson has recently made important contributions on this topic, especially with her book *Private Government* (2017), which, like *Justice by Means of Democracy*, also rests on a reorientation toward political equality.

27. The method sketched here for proceeding from ideals to subideals to design principles to rules for action was used in Allen, Heintz, Liu, et al. (2020) and Allen, Fung, Weenick, et al. (2018).

28. Allen (2004, 85–91) initiates a conversation about the role of ideals for guiding action in relation to democracy's imperfections. The ideals identified here could be considered an extension of that argument.

Chapter Three

1. In my view, this is where Hayek made his central mistake.
2. This definition is drawn from Allen, Heintz, Liu, et al. (2020). HELLO
3. Energy: *Federalist Papers*: 22, 23, 26, 37, 69, 71, 73, 77–78. Republican safety: *Federalist* 70. See also Michels ([1911] 1962); Rahman (2017).
4. Declaration of Independence: "It is the right of the people to alter or to abolish ..."; US Constitution, Article 5: amendment process; *Federalist Papers* 39, 40, 43, 85.
5. My treatment here draws on Lukes (1974); *Federalist* 15; Rousseau ([1762] 2004).
6. The Georgia Land Lottery used lottery for distribution of homesteads in the nineteenth century; the California Redistrict Commission currently selects some commission members via lottery.
7. For a general review of different voting procedures, with a focus on the role of supermajority requirements as a decision mechanism, see Schwarztberg (2013).
8. On the early recognition that enslavement was creating factionalism, see, for instance, this excerpt from the Continental Congress debates on the Articles of Confederation, July 30, 1776:

> LYNCH. If it is debated, whether their *slaves* are their *property*, there is an end of the confederation. Our *slaves* being our property, why should they be taxed more than the land, sheep, cattle, horses, &c.? Freemen cannot be got to work in our Colonies; it is not in the ability or inclination of freemen to do the work that the negroes do. Carolina has *taxed* their negroes; so have other Colonies their lands.
> DR. FRANKLIN. *Slaves* rather weaken than strengthen the State, and there is therefore some difference between them and sheep; sheep will never make any insurrections.
> RUTLEDGE. I shall be happy to get rid of the idea of slavery. The *slaves* do not signify *property*; the old and young cannot work. The property of some Colonies is to be *taxed*, in others, not. The Eastern Colonies will become the carriers for the Southern; they will obtain wealth for which they will not be taxed."

9. See *Federalist* 51, 63, 69, 77. The concept of enterprise liability in corporate law travels similar conceptual territory. See Keating (2001).

10. Current reality does not meet this standard. As Bartels (2010) has shown, policy outcomes in US politics currently track the policy preferences of those at the top end of the socioeconomic ladder.

11. Smith (1976–2000), *Letters of Delegates to Congress*: Abigail Adams to John Adams, March 31, 1776; John Adams to Abigail Adams, April 14, 1776; John Adams to James Sullivan, May 26, 1776.

12. In personal communication, Jane Mansbridge asked: "When the US passes a law that affects people in China, is this oppression?" Fully working out how to understand the relation between natural and actual polities will no doubt involve clarifying degrees of impact by actual polities on natural polities and modes of distinguishing between fair and unfair, equitable and inequitable processes causing that impact.

13. The hardest challenge here, of course, is how globally consequential issues like climate change can be addressed via this conceptual framework. As we watch the world struggle to form meaningful international treaties and the like to address the problem, we are watching a process by which civic participants and government leaders are negotiating the question of just how natural and actual polities might be brought into alignment.

14. Hamilton sketches the theoretical point in *Federalist* 17; policing and agriculture are his examples of policy domains best handled at the state level. The fact that a right to education was included in nearly all state constitutions supports the point that they explicitly assigned education to the state level as well. See Rebell (2018).

15. The effort to align actual and natural polities could be understood as contributing to the "all-affected" literature, about how to ensure that political decision-making includes all those who are affected by a decision. See Warren (2017) for a review of the literature.

16. See Mansbridge (2017) on recursive representation.

17. This section adapts and reworks a portion of my 2019 essay in the *Atlantic*, "The Road from Serfdom" (Allen 2019).

18. This references the comment by then–Senate Majority Leader Mitch McConnell in February 2017 that "winners make policy; losers go home." See Savransky (2017).

Chapter Four

1. This is an alternative answer to Rousseau's famous question of why, though man was born free, he is everywhere in chains.

2. This is a rough-and-ready summary of the meanings of these terms as they have developed across a rich tradition of analysis of social capital and social ties. See Granovetter (1973); Putnam (2000).

3. For the economy, the benefits of a connected society include

   • improvements in education because of a broader diffusion of the linguistic, intellectual, and social resources that support learning in the first place as well as impacts on personal decisions about whether to invest in education (Jackson 2009; Lareau 2011; Ludwig, Ladd, and Duncan 2001);
   • increases to social mobility because a better diffusion of information allows people to see opportunities and fit themselves to them (Granovetter 1973; Jackson 2009);
   • increases to creativity because diverse solution approaches are more likely to be brought into conversation with one another (Page 2007);
   • more efficient knowledge transmission because information travels faster across bridging connections (Granovetter 1973; Jackson 2009).

For democratic politics, the benefits of a connected society include

- improved social awareness and public discourse because citizens have more exposure to the impacts on others of different policy questions and, with improved information flows across social ties, citizens are less likely to consider the beliefs of others to be simply incorrect (Sethi and Yildiz 2012);
- more efficient policy planning because policy makers can more easily draw on local knowledge to ensure alignment of policies with on-the-ground realities (Ober 2008);
- the creation of "latent publics" because social connections across communities help communities discover new kinds of alliances (Dewey [1927] 2012);
- a background cultural expectation of connectedness that sets into even sharper relief "disconnected," "out of touch" policy approaches, such as that used in the UK by the Tories when they developed National Health Service reform without consultation with the holders of local knowledge.

For personal well-being, the benefits of a connected society include

- an increased sense of agency because of access to a larger opportunity network (Allen 2004);
- increased opportunity to develop important relational skills, not merely those that support the intimacy of bonding relations but also the skills of the interpreter, mediator, and greeter, which serve to build and use bridging relationships (Allen 2004);
- the opportunity to protect and enjoy one's own culture without falling into isolation (Sidanius et al. 2008).

For the general benefits of egalitarianism, see Pickett and Wilkinson (2011).

4. Two recent books (Gest 2022; Mounk 2022) make aligned arguments.

5. The quotation continues thus: "Racism, as I have noted, has been the great national tragedy.... When old-line Americans, for example, treat people of other nationalities and races as if they were indigestible elements to be shunned and barred, they must not be surprised if minorities gather bitterly unto themselves and damn everybody else. Not only must *they* want assimilation and integration; *we* must want assimilation and integration too."

6. Experience of Carola Suarez-Orozco as narrated to author by Marcelo Suarez Orozco, October 6, 2014.

7. This commission was charged "to recommend what steps should be taken to develop the Canadian Confederation on the basis of an equal partnership between the two founding races [French and English], taking into account the contribution made by the other ethnic groups to the cultural enrichment of Canada and the measures that should be taken to safeguard that contribution." Report of the Royal Commission on Bilingualism and Biculturalism (A. Davidson Dunton, Co-chairman; Andre Laurendeau, Co-chairman), General Introduction, xxi. http://epe.lac-bac.gc.ca/100/200/301/pco-bcp/commissions-ef/dunton1967-1970-ef/dunton1967-70-eng.htm.

   In 1971, following on the work of this commission, the Canadian federal government decided to pursue a policy of multiculturalism, not biculturalism, which in the early 1980s enshrined particular multicultural rights, for instance, language rights, in an amended constitution. Constitution Act 1982 (Canada), http://www.solon.org/Constitutions/Canada/English/ca_1982.html.

8. Taylor's own powerful essay was supplemented by comments from other philosophers, among them Kwame Anthony Appiah, Jürgen Habermas, and Michael Walzer, and the

volume was quickly translated into Italian, French, and German, thus launching "multi-culturalism" as a fully multinational subject of exploration and policy development.

9. The 1993 dissolution of Czechoslovakia into two nations, the Czech Republic and Slovakia, each encompassing a distinct linguistic and ethnic group, was a case in point, as was the subsequent disintegration of Yugoslavia.

10. See note 3 above and also a further elaboration of the argument about the egalitarian effect of bridging ties in Allen (2013).

11. Boston Latin School is now using a similar version of this admissions method.

12. See also Carnevale and Smith (2016) on the relationships among diversity, innovation, and economic benefit.

13. Maloney and Zellmer-Bruhn (2006), 705: "Specifically, we propose that structural and procedural features can be combined and manipulated to mitigate the potential problems associated with heterogeneity and distance, and more importantly, to enhance the likelihood that the benefits are realized."

14. In conditions of mismatch, it's important that people be prepared to create "swift norms": Maloney and Zellmer-Bruhn (2006).

15. Underlying data from Putnam (2000):

Faced fundamental legal challenge (percent decline from membership peak to 1997)	Did not face fundamental legal challenge (percent decline from membership peak to 1997)
• American Association of University Women (−84%) • American Bowling Congress (−72%) • B'nai B'rith (−75%) • Business and Professional Women's Foundation (−89%) • Eagles (−72%) • Eastern Star, Order of the (−73%) • Elks (−46%) • General Federation of Women's Clubs (−84%) • Hadassah (−15%) • Jaycees (−58%) • Kiwanis (−42%) • League of Women Voters (−61%) • Lions (−58%) • Masons (−71%) • **Moose (female members) (−3%)** • Moose (male members) (−35%) • National Parent Teacher Associations (−60%) • Odd Fellows (−94%) • Optimists (−24%) • Rotary (−25%) • Shriners (−59%) • Women's Bowling Congress (−66%) • Women's Christian Temperance Union (−96%)	Gender integrated: • American Legion (−47%) • 4-H (−26%) • Grange (−79%) • NAACP (−46%) • Red Cross (volunteers) (−61%) Mixed gender history: • **Veterans of Foreign Wars (−9%)** Gender segregated but legally sheltered: • **Boy Scouts (−5%)** • **Girl Scouts (−15%)** • **Boy Scouts and Girl Scouts combined (−8%)** • Boy Scouts and Girl Scouts adult leaders (−18%) • **Knights of Columbus (−6%)**

Note: Boldface indicates membership decline of less than 10% over period, in contrast to group median of 58%.

16. I have made this argument in an extended fashion in an unpublished paper, "The Art of Association," that tracks the changes in the law of association between 1970 and 1990 and the impacts of those legal changes on the social organizations in which Putnam is interested. As the changed legal landscape demanded gender integration, the clubs suffered because the knowledge that they had inculcated in club members did not serve them well in the context of gender and racial integration. This means, though, that the problem affecting the clubs was, contra to the explanations offered by Putnam, their failure to adapt bodies of social knowledge to new legal and institutional landscapes that had, appropriately, evolved in a more democratic direction.

17. These are classroom norms provided by Adrienne Stang, Cambridge Public Schools, for a January 2021 professional development session for educators at Harvard Graduate School of Education focused on effective pedagogy for "hard histories."

18. Some answers to this question can be found in the psychological literature, for instance, a stress on the "openness to experience" factor in the five-factor model of personality (McCrae and Costa 1987) in Homan et al. (2008), and "a global mindset" in Maloney and Zellmer-Bruhn (2006). See also Allen and Parham (2015).

19. Sugrue (2016) provides a good overview of those demographic transitions.

20. This is a point underscored by Sugrue (2016, 70): "The color of America will certainly change by 2040, but the meaning of race and ethnicity in the future depends to a great extent on policy decisions today."

Chapter Five

1. See Rawls, *Theory of Justice*, section 36, on the forms of compensation that are necessary to preserve the fair value for all of equal political liberties in the face of wealth inequality.

2. For a theory of the public sphere based on this concept of overlapping social networks, in which the nation-state qua "polity" has a special place, see Allen (2015).

3. This is an evolution beyond the idea of "rooted cosmopolitanism" advanced by Appiah (2006) and for which I argue in Allen and Parham (2015).

4. Abraham Lincoln, undated fragment, often speculatively assigned to 1858. Available in *Collected Works of Abraham Lincoln*, vol. 2 (Ann Arbor, MI: University of Michigan Digital Library Production Services, 2001).

5. For an innovative approach to understanding the operations of social dynamism, see Farrell, Shalizi, and Allen (2022).

6. I note that exclusion is a form of domination when those who are "included" and those who are "excluded" are both incorporated in a single social system, for instance, a global economy driven by those in the category of the "included." Relationships of domination have often been misrepresented as simpler relationships of inclusion and exclusion. This tends to result in a misdiagnosis of what is required to rectify the position of those in the "excluded" category. Typically, the necessary rectification will not be inclusion alone but a more significant restructuring of relationships between those in each group in order to achieve non-domination. See Allen (2005).

7. See also Shelby (2015) for an interesting use of these ideas for contemporary discussions of relative empowerment and disempowerment within the citizenry.

8. Of course, some would also argue that it might be worth reintroducing frictions to the movement of capital.

9. The Global Compact on Migration, passed by the United Nations in December 2018, also focuses on achieving alignment between the interests of the different stakeholders in migration policy in order to reduce friction. It seeks to achieve this alignment not

through market transactions but through inclusive and participatory decision-making processes. See United Nations General Assembly (2018).

10. Cf. López-Guerra (2020), who offers a provocative argument that every citizen ought to be able to sponsor as many migrants from abroad as they might otherwise bring into the polity by way of childbirth. That is, every citizen would have a right to "make new citizens," and they could exercise this right either through birth or through sponsorship.

11. Posner and Weyl (2014) start each chapter of their book with a utopian fiction imagining the world that would obtain if their policies were in place. Some of these narrative elements introduce ideas that go beyond what would actually necessarily follow from their policies. In this sense, they conjure up romanticizing fantasies.

12. The Canadian refugee sponsorship program has had problems of this kind when it featured individual sponsorship; a newer Dutch model avoids similar financial relationships because of the problems that arise from financial entanglement of the two parties.

13. See Kopplin (2017) on recent investigations into au pair programs in the US.

14. See Galenson (1984) for an analysis of what indentured servants gained and lost via indenture.

15. Canada has established this goal of admitting migrants each year at a rate of 1 percent of its existing population. To provide a sense of scale here, a 1 percent admission rate in the US would mean about three million people a year. Currently, the US admits one million legal immigrants a year. International students are currently admitted on what is effectively a sponsorship model; the country currently manages the admission of approximately one million foreign students annually. A target of 1 percent of population would, therefore, be a significant upward movement of effort. The goal would not be to get there overnight but to begin to build from the existing figure of one million (or two million, if we wish to count the students) toward three million over a period of five to ten years as the society becomes better equipped to manage migration through a sponsorship program and with the intentionality exhibited in the Canadian program.

16. This is also the existing structure of foster care programs, which give evidence of both the benefits of this approach and the dangers of abuse.

17. For a good review of the role of mutual aid societies within the US, see Beito (2000); Kaufman (2002, 286); and Skocpol (2003). Many of the associations they discuss are transnational; for instance, the Odd Fellows and the histories outlined here also have their European counterparts. Beito (2000) in particular focuses on the provision of social benefits.

18. Economist Glen Weyl is answering the call. See Weyl (2022a, 2022b).

Chapter Six

1. The important triadic model of collaboration among these three sectors developed by Bowles and Carlin (2021) is at the base of the political economy I sketch here. It has also been captured in the work of Glen Weyl (e.g., 2022a, 2022b). Bowles and Carlin call their model "shrinking capitalism." I call it "embedded liberalism." Weyl calls it "pluralism." A name has yet to stabilize for this paradigm.

2. If you protect the basic liberties, both negative and positive, social difference will emerge, and "difference" is another word for "inequality." To paraphrase Tim Scanlon (2021), the important question is whether the emergent differences are justified or not. To make this determination, I rely on the principle of difference without domination. If the relevant inequality subjects individuals or groups to the arbitrary reserve control of others, or in other ways undermines political equality, then that inequality is problematic

and needs to be redressed, undone, or mitigated, depending on circumstances. The goal is a world in which social difference does not articulate with domination of any one person, or any group, by any other person or group.

Scanlon, in his essay, identifies six kinds of inequality to which we might object: inequality of status, unacceptable control of some by others; interference with equality of opportunity; interference with the fairness of political institutions; unequal provision of benefits owed to all; and institutions that generate unequal incomes without adequate justification. Notably, the first four objections capture problems of political or social inequality; the last two, problems of material inequality. This underscores how important political equality is within a picture of human flourishing. The goal of economic policy, or political economy, should be to treat political empowerment or equality as what we're aiming for, and then to ask the question of how we also work toward social and economic egalitarianism in support of political empowerment. To reiterate, the reason to prioritize institutional, social, and economic bases for political equality or empowerment is that this concept fully captures human purposiveness.

3. I paraphrase from Rawls ([1993] 2011, 6): "Social and economic inequalities are to satisfy two conditions: first, they are to be attached to positions and offices open to all under conditions of fair equality of opportunity; and second, they are to be to the greatest benefit of the least advantaged members of society."

4. See also Bartels (2010), who has shown how, in the case of the US, policy outcomes closely track the policy preferences of the wealthy.

5. On health-insurance-related job lock, see Gruber and Madrian (1994).

6. Economists in the US have begun to focus on "place-based" models of economic policy. See, for instance, Reich and Jacobs (2014); Shambaugh and Nunn (2018). On housing, mobility, and productivity, see Inchauste et al. (2018).

7. R. Henderson, "Reimagining Capitalism," lecture for the Edmond J. Safra Center for Ethics, April 2017.

8. College graduates' civic engagement. data from the American Academy of Arts and Sciences. Figures calculated according to National Center for Education Statistics (2009, 2011).

Chapter Seven

1. Allen (2016c) makes this point about multitasking, building on Arendt (1958).

2. Allen (2004, chap. 6) develops this point, drawing on Thomas Hobbes.

3. On the operations of acceptance, see Woodly (2015).

4. Downey (forthcoming) offers an important new theory of democracy delegation.

5. For a thorough treatment of the means-ends relationships required by Gandhian nonviolence, see Mantena (2012, 2018).

6. Heather Gerken has provided compelling arguments about how decentralized structure of political decision-making can empower minorities within a democracy, with reference to gay rights movements (in Gerken 2014) and race (in Gerken 2020).

7. This is a technique taught and trademarked by a civic organization called The Citizens' Campaign.

8. In sum, democracies can achieve wholeness by ensuring that society is held together by a comprehensive network of decision-making organizations that consistently meet the ethical demands of integration articulated by King. We don't need to work on our hearts only, but even more immediately on the practices and protocols of our organizations. As a matter of our organizational practices, without the need to achieve spiritual affinity

neighbor to neighbor, we can weave a holistic fabric of non-domination for civil society and achieve affirmation of freedom and life.

In *Talking to Strangers* I argue that a democracy might achieve "wholeness" via pursuit of an ethics of political friendship that, like King's ethical demands for integration, scaffolds practices of non-domination. Like King in "Ethical Demands," I focus in *Talking to Strangers* not on law but on the ethical realm, the topic of how each of us can transform our daily practices of interaction with others and thereby transform our world, advancing a project for the completion of democracy. Therefore, my argument, like King's, is open to criticisms that I fail to concretize adequately the institutional and organizational forms necessary to bring non-domination genuinely into being. Similarly, both our arguments have been criticized (although wrongly, I think) for an excessive reliance on a utopian fantasy of a prospective emergence of something like spiritual affinity. See, for instance, Hooker (2016), for a critique of *Talking to Strangers* that proceeds along this line.

In fact, it is possible to close the gap between King's ethical argument (and mine too) and the creation of concrete practices of non-domination in the lived reality of democracies. Drawing on King's account of practices of non-domination as entailing an orientation toward well-being (and not instrumentalization), full inclusion in decision-making, and noninjury, we can close that gap. His explicit focus on the positive liberties, and on the requirement for full participation in the social and political decisions that establish the constraints in which we can exercise our freedom, opens up a zone of action. Alongside our political institutions, civil society organizations—both commercial and noncommercial—crowd the landscape of any democracy's collective life. Some significant number of these make socially meaningful or impactful decisions that frame the horizons of possibility of our shared world. We could pursue a "constructive policy of wholeness" by pursuing organizational transformation throughout the landscape of civil society, guided by the three principles articulated by King.

9. Clare Donohue Meyer, personal communication.
10. For Madison and Hamilton, the necessity of a republican politics directed toward the common good and not merely petty, factional squabbles over parochial interests requires cognitive skills unavailable to the vast majority of the public. Here is Madison in *Federalist* 10: "The man whose situation leads to extensive inquiry and information" would be a more "competent judge" of "the nature, extent, and foundation" of the common interest "than one whose observation does not travel beyond the circle of his neighbors and acquaintances."

Bibliography

Acemoğlu, Daron, and James Robinson. 2015. "The Rise and Fall of General Laws of Capitalism." *Journal of Economic Perspectives* 29 (1): 3–28.

Alexander, Marcus, and Fotini Christia. 2011. "Context Modularity of Human Altruism." *Science* 334 (6061): 1392–94.

Alinsky, Saul. 1971. *Rules for Radicals*. New York: Random House.

Allen, Danielle. 2000. *World of Prometheus: The Politics of Punishing in Democratic Athens*. Princeton, NJ: Princeton University Press.

———. 2004. *Talking to Strangers: Anxieties of Citizenship since* Brown v. Board of Education. Chicago: University of Chicago Press.

———. 2005. "Invisible Citizens: On Exclusion and Domination in Ralph Ellison and Hannah Arendt." In *Nomos XLVI: Political Exclusion and Domination*, edited by Melissa S. Williams and Stephen Macedo. New York: New York University Press.

———. 2012a. "Ai Wei Wei and the Art of Protest." *The Nation*, August 29. https://www.thenation.com/article/archive/ai-weiwei-and-art-protest/.

———. 2012b. "Art of Association: The Formation of Egalitarian Social Capital." Annual Equality Lecture for British Sociological Association, April 15, 2012, British Library Conference Centre, London. https://www.youtube.com/watch?v=hZJA6uOS-jk.

———. 2013. "A Connected Society." *Soundings* 53 (Spring): 103–13.

———. 2014a. "Talent Is Everywhere: Using Zip Codes and Merit to Enhance Diversity." In *Beyond Affirmative Action*, edited by Richard D. Kahlenberg. New York: Century Foundation.

———. 2014b. *Our Declaration: A Reading of the Declaration of Independence in Defense of Equality*. New York: Norton/Liveright.

————. 2014c. "A False Conflict between Liberty and Equality." *Washington Post,* October 26, 2014. http://wapo.st/11GI6HE.

————. 2015. "Reconceiving the Public Sphere: The Flow Dynamics Model." In *From Voice to Influence: Understanding Citizenship in a Digital Age,* edited by Danielle Allen and Jennifer S. Light. Chicago: University of Chicago Press.

————. 2016a. "Toward a Connected Society." In *Our Compelling Interests: The Value of Diversity for Democracy and a Prosperous Society,* edited by Earl Lewis and Nancy Kantor. Princeton, NJ: Princeton University Press.

————. 2016b. "Equality and American Democracy." *Foreign Affairs,* January/February. https://www.foreignaffairs.com/articles/2015-12-14/equality-and -american-democracy

————. 2016c. *Education and Equality.* Chicago: University of Chicago Press.

————. 2016d. "What Is Education For?" *Boston Review,* May 9. http://bostonre view.net/forum/danielle-allen-what-education.

————. 2017. *Cuz: The Life and Times of Michael A.* New York: Norton/Liveright.

————. 2018. "Integration, Freedom, and the Affirmation of Life." In *To Shape a World: Essays on the Political Philosophy of Martin Luther King, Jr.,* edited by Tommie Shelby and Brandon Terry. Cambridge, MA: Harvard University Press.

————. 2019. "The Road from Serfdom." *Atlantic,* December 2019. https:// www.theatlantic.com/magazine/archive/2019/12/danielle-allen-american -citizens-serfdom/600778/.

————. 2020. "Difference without Domination," in *Difference without Domination: On Justice in Diverse Democracies,* edited by Danielle Allen and Rohini Somanathan. Chicago: University of Chicago Press.

————. 2021. *Democracy in the Time of Coronavirus.* Chicago: University of Chicago Press.

Allen, Danielle, Yochai Benkler, Leah Downey, Rebecca Henderson, and Josh Simons, eds. 2022. *Political Economy of Justice.* Chicago: University of Chicago Press.

Allen, Danielle, Archon Fung, Meredith Weenick, et al. 2018. "Pursuing Excellence on a Foundation of Inclusion." Presidential Task Force on Inclusion and Belonging Report, Harvard University. https://www.seas.harvard.edu /media/75346/download.

Allen, Danielle, Adam Gerard, Danielle Cerny, et al. 2021–2022. "One Commonwealth Agendas: Good Jobs Agenda." AllenforMA. https://allenforma.com /agendas/.

Allen, Danielle, Stephen Heintz, Eric Liu, et al. 2020. "Our Common Purpose: Reinventing American Democracy for the 21st Century." American Academy of Arts and Sciences Report. https://www.amacad.org/ourcommonpurpose /report

Allen, Danielle, and David Kidd. 2023. "Civic Learning for the 21st Century: Disentangling the 'Thin' and 'Thick' Elements of Civic Identity to Support Civic

Education." In *Handbook of Philosophy of Education*, edited by Randall Curren. New York: Routledge.

Allen, Danielle, and Jennifer S. Light, eds. 2015. *From Voice to Influence: Understanding Citizenship in a Digital Age*. Chicago: University of Chicago Press.

Allen, Danielle, and Angel Parham. 2015. "Achieving Rooted Cosmopolitanism in a Digital Age." In *From Voice to Influence: Understanding Citizenship in a Digital Age*, edited by Danielle Allen and Jennifer S. Light. Chicago: University of Chicago Press.

Allen, Danielle, and Justin Pottle. 2018. "Democratic Knowledge and the Problem of Faction." Knight Foundation White Paper Series: Trust, Media, and Democracy. https://kf-site-production.s3.amazonaws.com/media_elements/files/000/000/152/original/Topos_KF_White-Paper_Allen_V2.pdf.

Allen, Danielle, and Robert Reich, eds. 2013. *Education, Justice, and Democracy*. Chicago: University of Chicago Press.

Allen, Danielle, and Rohini Somanathan. 2020. *Difference without Domination: Pursuing Justice in Diverse Democracies*. Chicago: University of Chicago Press.

American Academy of Arts and Sciences. 2009. *Introducing the Humanities Indicators: An Online Prototype of National Data Collection in the Humanities*. Cambridge, MA: American Academy of Arts and Sciences.

———. 2013. *The Heart of the Matter*. Cambridge, MA: American Academy of Arts and Sciences.

American Council of Learned Societies. 1985. *A Report to the Congress of the United States on the State of the Humanities and the Reauthorization of the National Endowment for the Humanities*. New York: American Council of Learned Societies.

Anderson, Benedict. 1983. *Imagined Communities: Reflections on the Origin and Spread of Nationalism*. London: Verso.

Anderson, Elizabeth. 1999. "What Is the Point of Equality?" *Ethics* 109 (2): 287–337.

———. 2007. "Fair Opportunity in Education: A Democratic Equality Perspective." *Ethics* 117 (4): 595–622.

———. 2010. *The Imperative of Integration*. Princeton, NJ: Princeton University Press.

———. 2017. *Private Government: How Employers Rule Our Lives (and Why We Don't Talk about It)*. Princeton, NJ: Princeton University Press.

Appiah, Kwame Anthony. 2006. *Cosmopolitanism: Ethics in a World of Strangers*. New York: Norton.

Arendt, Hannah. 1958. *The Human Condition*. Chicago: University of Chicago Press.

———. 1959. "Reflections on Little Rock." *Dissent* 6 (1): 45–56.

———. 1968. *Men in Dark Times*. San Diego: Harcourt Brace.

Autor, D. 2014. "Skills, Education, and the Rise of Earnings Inequality among the 'Other 99 Percent.'" *Science* 344 (6186): 843–51.

Bachen, Christine, Chad Raphael, Kathleen M. Lynn, Kristen McKee, and Jessica Philippi. 2008. "Civic Engagement, Pedagogy, and Information Technology on Web Sites for Youth." *Political Communication* 25 (3): 290–310.

Banaji, Shakuntala. 2011. "Framing Young Citizens: Explicit Invitation and Implicit Exclusion on Youth Civic Websites." *Language and Intercultural Communication* 11 (2): 126–41.

Banerjee, A., and R. Somanathan. 2001. "A Simple Model of Voice." *Quarterly Journal of Economics* 116 (1): 189–227.

Bartels, Larry. 2010. *Unequal Democracy: The Political Economy of the New Gilded Age*. Princeton, NJ: Princeton University Press.

Beito, David T. 2000. *From Mutual Aid to the Welfare State: Fraternal Societies and Social Services, 1890–1967*. Chapel Hill: University of North Carolina Press.

Beitz, Charles. 1989. *Political Equality*. Princeton, NJ: Princeton University Press.

Bennett, Lance, Chris Wells, and Deen Freelon. 2009. "Communicating Citizenship Online: Models of Civic Learning in the Youth Web Sphere." Civic Learning Online Project. http://www.engagedyouth.org.

Bennett, Lance, and Michael Xenos. 2005. "Young Voters and the Web of Politics 2004: The Youth Political Web Sphere Comes of Age." CIRCLE Working Paper no. 42. https://circle.tufts.edu/sites/default/files/2019-12/WP42 _YouthPoliticalWebSphereComesofAge_2005.pdf.

Berlin, Isaiah. (1958) 1990. *Four Essays on Liberty*. Oxford: Oxford University Press.

Berman, Elizabeth Popp. 2014. "Thinking Like an Economist: On Expertise and the U.S. Policy Process." Occasional Paper Series, Institute for Advanced Study, no. 52. https://www.ias.edu/sites/default/files/sss/papers/paper52.pdf.

Bertrand, Marianne, and Sendhil Mullainathan. 2004. "Are Emily and Brendan More Employable Than Lakisha and Jamal? A Field Experiment on Labor Market Discrimination." *American Economic Review* 94 (4): 991–1013.

Bhabha, Homi K. 1994. *The Location of Culture*. New York: Routledge.

———. 2011. "Cultural Diversity and Cultural Differences." *Atlas of Transformation*. http://monumenttotransformation.org/atlas-of-transformation /html/c/cultural-diversity/cultural-diversity-and-cultural-differences-homi-k -bhabha.html.

Bidart, Frank. 1997. *Desire*. New York: Farrar, Straus & Giroux.

Bleakley, Hoyt, and Joseph P. Ferrie. 2013. "Up from Poverty? The 1832 Cherokee Land Lottery and the Long-Run Distribution of Wealth." NBER Working Paper no. 19175. Cambridge, MA: National Bureau of Economic Research.

Borrit, Gabor. 1994. *Lincoln and the Economics of the American Dream*. Urbana: University of Illinois Press.

Bourdieu, Pierre. 1977. *Outline of a Theory of Practice*. Translated by Richard Nice. Cambridge, UK: Cambridge University Press.

———. 1986. "The Forms of Capital." In *Handbook of Theory and Research for the Sociology of Education*, edited by J. Richardson. Westport, CT: Greenwood Press.

Bowles, Samuel, and Wendy Carlin. 2021. "Shrinking Capitalism: Components of a New Political Economy Paradigm." CEPR Discussion Paper no. DP16515. https://ssrn.com/abstract=3928826.

Bowles, Samuel, Glenn C. Loury, and Rajiv Sethi. 2014. "Group Inequality." *Journal of the European Economic Association* 12 (1): 129–52.

Bratman, M. 1992. "Shared Cooperative Activity." *Philosophical Review* 101 (2): 327–41.

———. 2009. "Modest Sociality and the Distinctiveness of Intention." *Philosophical Studies* 144 (1): 149–65.

Brighouse, Harry, and Marc Fleurbaey. 2010. "Democracy and Proportionality." *Journal of Political Philosophy* 18 (2): 137–55.

Bromberg, Philip M. 2011. *The Shadow of the Tsunami: And the Growth of the Relational Mind*. New York: Routledge.

Brubaker, Roger. 2004. *Ethnicity without Groups*. Cambridge, MA: Harvard University Press.

Campbell, D. E. 2009. "Civic Engagement and Education: An Empirical Test of the Sorting Model." *American Journal of Political Science* 53 (4): 771–86.

Carens, Joseph. 2010. *Immigrants and the Right to Stay*. Cambridge, MA: MIT Press.

———. 2013. *The Ethics of Immigration*. New York: Oxford University Press.

Carnevale, Anthony, and Nicole Smith. 2016. "The Economic Value of Diversity." In *Our Compelling Interests: The Value of Diversity for Democracy and a Prosperous Society*, edited by Earl Lewis and Nancy Kantor. Princeton, NJ: Princeton University Press.

Caruana, R., A. Crane, S. Gold, and G. LeBaron. 2021. "Modern Slavery in Business: The Sad and Sorry State of a Non-field." *Business & Society* 60 (2): 251–87.

Cauchon, Dennis, and Paul Overberg. 2012. "Census Data Shows Minorities Now a Majority of U.S. Births." *USA Today*, May 17, 2012.

Christman, John. 1991. "Liberalism and Individual Positive Freedom." *Ethics* 101 (2): 343–59.

———. 2005. "Saving Positive Freedom." *Political Theory* 33 (1): 79–88.

———. 2009. *The Politics of Persons: Individual Autonomy and Socio-historical Selves*. Cambridge, UK: Cambridge University Press.

CIRCLE Staff. 2013. "The Youth Vote in 2012." CIRCLE Fact Sheet. https://circle.tufts.edu/sites/default/files/2019-12/youth_vote_2012.pdf.

Cohen, G. A. 1988. *History, Labour and Freedom: Themes from Marx*. Oxford: Clarendon Press.

———. 1995. *Self-Ownership, Freedom and Equality*, Cambridge, UK: Cambridge University Press.

———. 2006. "Capitalism, Freedom and the Proletariat." In *The Liberty Reader*, edited by David Miller. Oxford: Clarendon.

———. 2009. *Rescuing Justice and Equality*. Cambridge, MA: Harvard University Press.

———. 2011. "Freedom and Money." In *On the Currency of Egalitarian Justice and Other Essays in Political Philosophy*, edited by M. Otsuka. Princeton NJ: Princeton University Press.

Cohen, Marshall. 1960. "Berlin and the Liberal Tradition." *Philosophical Quarterly* 10 (40): 216–27.

Coleman, J. 1988. "Social Capital in the Creation of Human Capital." *American Journal of Sociology* 94 (suppl.): S95–S120.

Committee on Prospering in the Global Economy of the Twenty-First Century, National Academy of Sciences, National Academy of Engineering, Institute of Medicine. 2007. *Rising above the Gathering Storm: Energizing and Employing America for a Brighter Economic Future*. Washington, DC: National Academies Press.

Conant, Jennet. 2017. *Man of the Hour: James B. Conant, Warrior Scientist*. New York: Simon and Schuster.

Constant, Benjamin. (1819) 1988. "The Liberty of the Ancients Compared with That of the Moderns." In *The Political Writings of Benjamin Constant*, edited by Biancamaria Fontana. Cambridge, UK: Cambridge University Press.

Dawood, Y. 2008. "The Anti-domination Model and the Judicial Oversight of Democracy." *Georgetown Law Journal* 96:1411–85.

Dee, T. 2003. "Are There Civic Returns to Education?" CIRCLE Working Paper no. 8. College Park, MD: The Center for Information and Research on Civic Learning and Engagement.

Dewey, John. (1927) 2012. *The Public and Its Problems*, edited and with an introduction by Melvin Rogers. University Park: Pennsylvania State University Press.

Downey, Leah. 2021. "Delegation in Democracy: A Temporal Analysis." *Journal of Political Philosophy* 29 (3): 305–29.

———. 2022. "Governing Money Democratically: Re-chartering the Federal Reserve." In *Political Economy of Justice*, edited by Danielle Allen, Yochai Benkler, Leah Downey, Rebecca Henderson, and Josh Simons. University of Chicago Press.

———. Forthcoming. *When Democracies Make Money*. Princeton, NJ: Princeton University Press.

Du Bois, W. E. B. 1903. *The Souls of Black Folk*. New York: Library of America.

Edmondson, A. 1999. "Psychological Safety and Learning Behavior in Work Teams." *Administrative Science Quarterly* 44 (2): 350–83.

Educating for American Democracy (EAD). 2021. "Educating for American Democracy: Excellence in History and Civics for All Learners." iCivics, March 2, 2021. https://njcss.weebly.com/uploads/1/3/0/2/13026706/edu cating-for-american-democracy-report-excellence-in-history-and-civics-for-all -learners.pdf.

Ellison, Ralph. (1952) 1980. *Invisible Man*. New York: Vintage.

Emerson, T. I. 1964. "Freedom of Association and Freedom of Expression." *Yale Law Journal* 74:1–35.

Eng, David, and Shinhee Han. 2000. "A Dialogue on Racial Melancholia." *Psycho-analytic Dialogues* 10 (4): 667–700.

———. 2006. "Desegregating Love: Transnational Adoption, Racial Reparation, and Racial Transitional Objects." *Studies in Gender and Sexuality* 7 (2): 141–72.

Farrell, Henry, and Cosma Shalizi. 2015. "Pursuing Cognitive Democracy." In *From Voice to Influence: Understanding Citizenship in a Digital Age*, edited by Danielle Allen and Jennifer S. Light. Chicago: University of Chicago Press.

Farrell, Henry, Cosma Shalizi, and Danielle Allen. 2022. "Evolutionary Theory and Endogenous Institutional Change." Unpublished manuscript.

Federalist Papers. Avalon Project of the Lillian Goldman Law Library at Yale Law School. https://avalon.law.yale.edu/subject_menus/fed.asp.

Ferguson, Michaele. 2012. *Sharing Democracy*. Oxford: Oxford University Press.

Finnemore, Martha, and Michelle Jurkovich. 2020. "The Politics of Aspiration." *International Studies Quarterly* 64 (4): 759–69.

Foa, Roberto Stefan, and Yascha Mounk. 2016. "The Danger of Deconsolidation: The Democratic Disconnect." *Journal of Democracy* 27 (3): 5–17.

Foner, Eric. 2011. *The Fiery Trial: Abraham Lincoln and American Slavery*. New York: W. W. Norton.

Forst, Rainer. 2011. *The Right to Justification: Elements of a Constructivist Theory of Justice*. Translated by Jeffrey Flynn. New York: Columbia University Press.

———. 2014. "Two Pictures of Justice." In *Justice, Democracy and the Right to Justification: Rainer Forst in Dialogue*, edited by Rainer Forst. New York: Bloomsbury.

Frank, Jill. 2005. *A Democracy of Distinction: Aristotle and the Work of Politics*. Chicago: University of Chicago Press.

Fraser, Nancy. 1990. "Rethinking the Public Sphere: A Contribution to the Critique of Actually Existing Democracy." *Social Text* 25/26:56–80.

———. (1992) 1996. "Rethinking the Public Sphere: A Contribution to the Critique of Actually Existing Democracy." In *Habermas and the Public Sphere*, edited by Craig Calhoun. Cambridge, MA: MIT Press.

Fraysse, Olivier. 1994. *Lincoln, Land and Labor: 1809–1860*. Translated by Sylvia Neely. Urbana: University of Illinois Press.

Futtema, Célia, Fábio de Castro, Maria Clara Silva-Forsberg, and Elinor Ostrom 2002. "The Emergence and Outcomes of Collective Action: An Institutional and Ecosystem Approach." *Society and Natural Resources* 15 (6): 503–22. Reprinted in *Ambiente & Sociedade* 10:107–27.

Galenson, David. 1984. "The Rise and Fall of Indentured Servitude in the Americas: An Economic Analysis." *Journal of Economic History* 44 (1): 1–26.

Gardner, Howard. 1983. *Good Work: When Excellence and Ethics Meet*. New York: Basic Books.

———. 2011. *Frames of Mind: The Theory of Multiple Intelligences*. New York: Basic Books.

————. 2015. "In Defense of Disinterestedness." In *From Voice to Influence: Understanding Citizenship in a Digital Age*, edited by Danielle Allen and Jennifer S. Light. Chicago: University of Chicago Press.

Gerber, E., and J. Jackson 1993. "Endogenous Preferences and the Study of Institutions." *American Political Science Review* 87 (3): 639–56.

Gerken, Heather. 2014. "The Loyal Opposition." *Yale Law Journal* 123:1958–94.

————. 2017. "Federalism 3.0." *California Law Review* 105 (6): 1695–1724.

————. 2020. "Second-Order Diversity: An Exploration of Decentralization's Egalitarian Possibilities." In *Diversity, Justice, and Democracy*, edited by Danielle Allen and Rohini Somanathan. Chicago: University of Chicago Press.

Gest, Justin. 2022. *Majority Minority*. Oxford: Oxford University Press.

Giddens, A. 1981–1985. *A Contemporary Critique of Historical Materialism*, vols. 1–2. Berkeley: University of California Press.

————. 1984. *The Constitution of Society: Outline of the Theory of Structuration*. Berkeley: University of California Press.

Gilder Lehrman Institute. n.d. "Abraham Lincoln and the Tariff." http://www .abrahamlincolnsclassroom.org/abraham-lincoln-in-depth/abraham-lincoln -and-the-tariff/.

Gilens, Martin. 2012. *Affluence and Influence: Economic Inequality and Political Power in America*. Princeton, NJ: Princeton University Press.

Glaeser, Edward L., Giacomo Ponzetto, and Andrei Shleifer. 2006. "Why Does Democracy Need Education?" NBER Working Paper no. 12128. Cambridge, MA: National Bureau of Economic Research.

Goldin, Claudia, and Lawrence Katz. 2008. *The Race between Education and Technology*. Cambridge, MA: Belknap.

Gould, Carol. 2004. *Globalizing Democracy and Human Rights*. Cambridge, UK: Cambridge University Press.

————. 2009. "Structuring Global Democracy: Political Communities, Universal Human Rights, and Transnational Representation." *Metaphilosophy* 40 (1): 24–41.

————. 2014. *Interactive Democracy: The Social Roots of Global Justice*, chapters. 4, 11–15. New York: Cambridge University Press.

————. 2016. "Democratic Management and International Labor Rights." In *Global Justice and International Labour Rights*, edited by Yossi Dahan, Hanna Lerner, and Faina Milman-Sivan. New York: Cambridge University Press.

Granovetter, Marc S. 1973. "The Strength of Weak Ties." *American Journal of Sociology*, 78 (6): 1360–80.

Green, Thomas A. 1985. *Verdict according to Conscience: Perspectives on the English Criminal Trial Jury, 1200–1800*. Chicago: University of Chicago Press.

Gruber, Jonathan, and Brigitte C. Madrian. 1994. "Health Insurance and Job Mobility: The Effects of Public Policy on Job-Lock." *Industrial and Labor Relations Review* 48 (1): 86–102.

Gutmann, Amy, ed. 1998. *Freedom of Association*. Princeton, NJ: Princeton University Press.

———. 1999. *Democratic Education*. Princeton, NJ: Princeton University Press.

———. 2015. "What Makes a University Education Worthwhile?" In *The Aims of Higher Education: Problems of Morality and Justice*, edited by Harry Brighouse and Michael McPherson. Chicago: University of Chicago Press.

Habermas, J. (1962) 1991. *The Structural Transformation of the Public Sphere*. Translated by Thomas Burger with the assistance of Frederick Lawrence. Cambridge, MA: MIT Press.

Hacker, Jacob. 2011. "The Institutional Foundations of Middle-Class Democracy." *Policy Network* 6:33–37.

Hanchard, Michael. 2018. *The Spectre of Race: How Discrimination Haunts Western Democracy*. Princeton, NJ: Princeton University Press.

Hardin, Russell. 1982. *Collective Action*. Baltimore: Johns Hopkins University Press.

———. 1995. *One for All: The Logic of Group Conflict*. Princeton, NJ: Princeton University Press.

Hare, Christopher, and Keith T. Poole. 2014. "The Polarization of Contemporary American Politics." *Polity* 46 (3): 411–29.

Hattam, V., and J. Lowndes. 2007. "The Ground Beneath Our Feet: Language, Culture, and Political Change." In *Formative Acts: American Politics in the Making*, edited by Stephen Skowronek and Matthew Glassman. Philadelphia: University of Pennsylvania Press.

Hayek, F. A. 1937. "Economics and Knowledge." *Economica* 4:33–54.

———. (1944) 1994. *The Road to Serfdom*. Chicago: University of Chicago Press.

———. 1945. "The Use of Knowledge in Society." *American Economic Review* 35:519–30.

Hayward, Clarissa. 2000. *De-facing Power*. Cambridge, UK: Cambridge University Press.

Henderson, Rebecca. 2020. *Reimagining Capitalism in a World on Fire*. New York: Public Affairs.

———. 2022. "Interrogating Corporate Purpose: Values-Based Firms and the Struggle to Build a Just and Sustainable World." Paper presented at the Edmond J. Safra Center Workshop on the Political Economy of Justice, February 2020. Manuscript on file with author.

Hess, Diana. 2009. *Controversy in the Classroom: The Democratic Power of Discussion*. New York: Routledge.

Hess, Diana, and Paula McAvoy. 2012. *The Political Classroom: Ethics and Evidence in Democratic Education*. New York: Routledge.

Hillygus, Sunshine. 2005. "The Missing Link: Exploring the Relationship Between Higher Education and Political Engagement." *Political Behavior* 27 (1): 25–47.

Hirschman, Albert O. 1970. *Exit, Voice, and Loyalty: Responses to Decline in Firms, Organizations, and States.* Cambridge, MA: Harvard University Press.

———. 1992. *Rival Views of Market Society and Other Recent Essays.* Cambridge, MA: Harvard University Press.

Hirschman, Sarah. 2009. *People and Stories: Who Owns Literature? Communities Find Their Voice through Short Stories.* Bloomington, IN: iUniverse.

Homan, Astrid C., John R. Hollenbeck, Stephen E. Humphrey, Daan Van Knippenberg, Daniel R. Ilgen, and Gerben A. Van Kleef. 2008. "Facing Differences with an Open Mind: Openness to Experience, Salience of Intragroup Differences, and Performance of Diverse Work Groups." *Academy of Management Journal* 51 (6): 1204–22.

Honneth, Axel. 1992. "Integrity and Disrespect: Principles of a Conception of Morality Based on a Theory of Recognition." *Political Theory* 20 (2): 187–201.

———. 2014. *Freedom's Right: The Social Foundations of Democratic Life.* Cambridge, UK: Polity.

Hooker, Juliet. 2016. "Black Lives Matter and the Paradoxes of U.S. Black Politics: From Democratic Sacrifice to Democratic Repair," *Political Theory* 44 (4): 448–69.

Howe, Daniel Walker. 1984. *The Political Culture of the American Whigs.* Chicago: University of Chicago Press.

Hussar, William J., and Tabitha M. Bailey. 2014. *Projections of Education Statistics to 2022, Forty-First Edition.* National Center for Education Statistics. http://nces.ed.gov/pubs2014/2014051.pdf.

Hutson, James L. 1998. *Securing the Fruits of Labor: the American Concept of Wealth Distribution, 1765–1900.* Baton Rouge: Louisiana State University Press.

Inchauste, G., J. Karver, Y. S. Kim, and M. A. Jelil. 2018. *Living and Leaving: Housing, Mobility and Welfare in the European Union.* Washington, DC: World Bank.

Jackson, Matthew O. 2009. "Social Structure, Segregation, and Economic Behavior." Presented as the Nancy Schwartz Memorial Lecture in April of 2007. http://papers.ssrn.com/abstract=1530885.

———. 2019. *The Human Network: How Your Social Position Determines Your Power, Beliefs, and Behaviors.* New York: Pantheon.

Jarvenpaa, S. L., K. Knoll, and D. E. Leidner. 1998. "Is Anybody Out There? Antecedents of Trust in Global Virtual Teams." *Journal of Management Information Systems* 14 (4): 29–64.

Jarvenpaa, S. L., and D. E. Leidner. 1999. "Communication and Trust in Global Virtual Teams." *Organization Science* 10 (6): 791–815.

Jeffries, Julia. 2022. "Culturally Relevant Teaching and Curriculum Building in White Social Studies Teachers." PhD diss., Harvard University.

Jenkins, Henry. 2009. *Confronting the Challenges of Participatory Culture: Media Education for the 21st Century.* John D. and Catherine T. MacArthur Foundation Reports on Digital Media and Learning. Cambridge, MA: MIT Press.

Jenkins, Henry, Mizuko Itō, and danah boyd. 2015. *Participatory Culture in a Networked Era: A Conversation on Youth, Learning, Commerce, and Politics*. Malden, MA: Polity.

Kamm, Frances. 1993. *Death and Whom to Save from It*. Vol. 1 of *Morality, Mortality*. New York: Oxford University Press.

Kang, Sheena. 2012. "A History of Participatory Politics." Essay for the "Youth, New Media and Citizenship" workshop, as part of the MacArthur Research Network on Youth Participatory Politics. Unpublished manuscript.

Katz, Lawrence. 2010. "Long-Term Unemployment in the Great Recession." Testimony for the Joint Economic Committee U.S. Congress Hearing on Long-Term Unemployment: Causes, Consequences and Solutions. https://scholar .harvard.edu/files/lkatz/files/long_term_unemployment_in_the_great_reces sion.pdf.

Katz, Michael S. 1976. *A History of Compulsory Education Laws*. Bloomington, IN: Phi Delta Kappa.

Kaufman, Jason. 2002. *For the Common Good? American Civic Life and the Golden Age of Fraternity*. New York: Oxford University Press.

Keating, Gregory C. 2001. "The Theory of Enterprise Liability and Common Law Strict Liability." *Vanderbilt Law Review* 54 (3): 1285–1335.

Keohane, Nannerl. 2012. "The Liberal Arts as Signposts in the 21st Century." *Chronicle of Higher Education*, January 29. http://chronicle.com/article /The-Liberal-Arts-as-Guideposts/130475/.

King, Martin Luther, Jr. (1963) 1986a. "The Ethical Demands for Integration." In *A Testament of Hope: The Essential Writings and Speeches of Martin Luther King, Jr.*, edited by James Melvin Washington. New York: HarperOne.

———. (1968) 1986b. "A Testament of Hope." In *A Testament of Hope: The Essential Writings and Speeches of Martin Luther King, Jr.*, edited by James Melvin Washington. New York: HarperOne.

Kirp, D. 2014. "The Benefits of Mixing Rich and Poor." *New York Times*, May 10. http://opinionator.blogs.nytimes.com/2014/05/10/the-benefits-of-mixing -rich-and-poor.

Kolodny, Niko. 2014. "Rule over None 1: What Justifies Democracy." *Philosophy and Public Affairs* 42 (3): 195–229.

Koppelman, A. 2004. "Should Noncommercial Associations Have an Absolute Right to Discriminate?" *Law and Contemporary Problems* 67 (4): 27–57.

Kopplin, Zack. 2017. "'They Think We Are Slaves': The U.S. Au Pair Program Is Riddled with Problems—and New Documents Show That the State Department Might Know More Than It's Letting On." *Politico*, March 27. https:// www.politico.com/magazine/story/2017/03/au-pair-program-abuse-state -department-214956/.

Kulikoff, Allan. 1992. *The Agrarian Origins of American Capitalism*. Charlottesville: University Press of Virginia.

————. 1993. "The American Revolution and the Making of the American Yeoman Classes." In *Beyond the American Revolution: Further Exploration in the History of American Radicalism,* edited by Alfred Young. DeKalb: Northern Illinois University Press.

————. 1996. "Was the American Revolution a Bourgeois Revolution?" In *"The Transforming Hand of Revolution": Reconsidering the American Revolution as a Social Movement,* edited by Ronald Hoffman and Peter J. Albert. Charlottesville: University Press of Virginia.

————. 2000. *From British Peasants to Colonial American Farmers.* Chapel Hill: University of North Carolina Press.

Laborde, Cecile, and John Maynor, eds. 2008. *Republicanism and Political Theory.* Oxford: Blackwell.

Laden, Anthony. 2013. "Learning to Be Equal." In *Education, Justice, and Democracy,* edited by Danielle Allen and Robert Reich. Chicago: University of Chicago Press.

Lane, Melissa. 2020. "The Idea of Accountable Office in Ancient Greece and Beyond." *Philosophy* 95 (1): 19–40.

Lansing, J. Stephen. 2006. *Perfect Order: Recognizing Complexity in Bali.* Princeton, NJ: Princeton University Press.

Lareau, Annette. 2011. *Unequal Childhoods: Class, Race, and Family Life.* 2nd ed. Berkeley: University of California Press.

Lebron, Christopher. 2014. "Equality from A Human Point of View." *Critical Philosophy of Race* 2 (2): 125–59.

Levinson, Meira. 2012. *No Citizen Left Behind.* Cambridge, MA: Harvard University Press.

Levitsky, Stephen, and Daniel Ziblatt. 2019. *How Democracies Die.* New York: Penguin.

Li, J., and D. C. Hambrick. 2005. "Factional Groups: A New Vantage on Demographic Faultlines, Conflict, and Disintegration in Work Teams." *Academy of Management Journal* 48 (5): 794–813.

Lincoln, Abraham. 1953. *The Collected Works of Abraham Lincoln, 1809–1865.* Edited by Roy P. Basler. Springfield, IL: Abraham Lincoln Association.

Linder, D. O. 1984. "Freedom of Association after *Roberts v. United States Jaycees.*" *Michigan Law Review* 82 (8): 1878–1903.

López-Guerra, Claudio. 2020. "Immigration, Membership, and Justice: On the Right to Bring Others in the Polity." In *Difference without Domination: Pursuing Justice in Diverse Democracies,* edited by Danielle Allen and Rohini Somanathan. Chicago: University of Chicago Press.

Loury, Glenn C. 1977. "A Dynamic Theory of Racial Income Differences." Discussion Paper no. 225, Northwestern University Center for Mathematical Studies in Economics and Management Science.

———. 2002. *The Anatomy of Racial Inequality*. Cambridge, MA: Harvard University Press.

———. 2020. "Relations before Transactions: A Personal Plea." In *Difference without Domination: Pursuing Justice in Diverse Democracies*, edited by Danielle Allen and Rohini Somanathan. Chicago: University of Chicago Press.

Ludwig, J., H. F. Ladd, and G. J. Duncan. 2001. "Urban Poverty and Educational Outcomes." *Brookings-Wharton Papers on Urban Affairs* 200:147–201.

Lukes, Steven. 1974. *Power: A Radical View*. London: Macmillan.

Macedo, Stephen, Yvette Alex-Assensoh, Jeffrey N. Berry, Michael Brintnall, David E. Campbell, Luis Ricardo Fraga, et al. 2005. *Democracy at Risk: How Political Choices Undermine Citizen Participation and What We Can Do about It*. Washington, DC: Brookings Institution.

Malin, Heather, Parissa J. Ballard, Maryam Lucia Attai, Anne Colby, and William Damon. 2014. "Youth Civic Development and Education: A Consensus Report." Stanford University Center on Adolescence and University of Washington, Seattle, Center for Multicultural Education. https://education.uw.edu/sites/default/files/cme/images/Civic%20Education%20report.pdf.

Maloney, Mary M., and Mary Zellmer-Bruhn. 2006. "Building Bridges, Windows and Cultures: Mediating Mechanisms between Team Heterogeneity and Performance in Global Teams." *Management International Review* 46 (6): 697–720.

Mandell, Daniel. 2020. *The Lost Tradition of Economic Equality in America, 1600–1880*. Baltimore: Johns Hopkins University Press.

Mansbridge, Jane J. 1980. *Beyond Adversary Democracy*. Chicago: University of Chicago Press.

———. 2017. "Recursive Representation in the Representative System." HKS Working Paper no. RWP17-045. https://ssrn.com/abstract=3049294.

Mantena, Karuna. 2012. "Another Realism: The Politics of Gandhian Nonviolence," *American Political Science Review* 106 (2): 455–70.

———. 2018. "Showdown for Nonviolence: The Theory and Practice of Nonviolent Politics." In *To Shape a World: Essays on the Political Philosophy of Martin Luther King, Jr.*, edited by Tommie Shelby and Brandon Terry. Cambridge, MA: Harvard University Press.

Markell, Patchen. 2022. *Politics against Rule: Hannah Arendt and the Human Condition*. Unpublished manuscript.

Marshall, George. 1947. "The Marshall Plan Speech." https://www.marshallfoundation.org/wp-content/uploads/2014/06/Marshall_Plan_Speech_Complete.pdf.

McCarty, Nolan, Keith T. Poole, and Howard Rosenthal. 2006. *Polarized America: The Dance of Ideology and Unequal Riches*. Cambridge, MA: MIT Press.

McChrystal Group. 2020. "Fusion Cell Playbook." https://mg-website-api-live.s3.amazonaws.com/documents/201207_Fusion_Cell_Playbook_-_Edit.pdf.

McCrae, R. R. 1987. "Creativity, Divergent Thinking, and Openness to Experience." *Journal of Personality and Social Psychology* 52 (6): 1258–65.

McCrae, R. R., and P. T. Costa. 1987. "Validation of the Five Factor Model of Personality across Instruments and Observers." *Journal of Personality and Social Psychology* 52 (1): 81–90.

Meissner, Doris. 2019. "Rethinking US Immigration Policy: New Realities Call for New Answers." Migration Policy Institute. https://www.migrationpolicy.org /research/rethinking-us-immigration-policy-new-realities-call-new-answers.

Meyerson, D., K. E. Weick, and R. M. Kramer. 1996. "Swift Trust and Temporary Groups." In *Trust in Organizations*, edited by R. M. Kramer and T. R. Tyler. Thousand Oaks, CA: Sage.

Michaels, Walter Benn. 2007. *The Trouble with Diversity: How We Learned to Love Identity and Ignore Inequality*. New York: Henry Holt.

Michels, Robert. (1911) 1962. *Political Parties: A Sociological Study of the Oligarchic Tendencies of Modern Democracy*. New York: Free Press.

Mill, John Stuart (1859) 2006. *"On Liberty" and Other Writings*. Cambridge, UK: Cambridge University Press.

Miller, David. 1983. "Constraints on Freedom." *Ethics* 94 (1): 66–86.

———. 2009. "Democracy's Domain." *Philosophy and Public Affairs* 37 (3): 201–28.

———. 2016. *Strangers in Our Midst: The Political Philosophy of Immigration*. Cambridge, MA: Harvard University Press.

Mills, Charles W. 1997. *The Racial Contract*. Ithaca, NY: Cornell University Press.

———. 2009. "Critical Race Theory: A Reply to Mike Cole." *Ethnicities* 9 (2): 270–81

Moglen, S. 2013. "Sharing Knowledge, Practicing Democracy: A Vision for the Twenty-First-Century University." *Education, Justice, and Democracy*, edited by Danielle Allen and Rob Reich. Chicago: University of Chicago Press.

Mounk, Yascha. 2022. *The Great Experiment: Why Diverse Democracies Fall Apart and How They Can Endure*. New York: Penguin.

Murtha, T. P., S. A. Lenway, and R. P. Bagozzi. 1998. "Global Mind-Sets and Cognitive Shift in a Complex Multinational Corporation." *Strategic Management Journal* 19 (2): 97–114.

Museum of the American Revolution. 2020. *When Women Lost the Vote*. https:// www.amrevmuseum.org/virtualexhibits/when-women-lost-the-vote-a -revolutionary-story.

Nam, C. 2015. "Technology as Connected and Critical Learning Practice." In *International Handbook of Progressive Education*, edited by M. Y. Eryaman B. C. Bruce. New York: Peter Lang.

National Academy of Sciences, National Academy of Engineering, and Institute of Medicine. 2007. *Rising above the Gathering Storm: Energizing and Employing America for a Brighter Economic Future*. Washington, DC: National Academies Press.

National Center for Education Statistics. 2009. *1993/03 Baccalaureate and Beyond Longitudinal Study*. https://nces.ed.gov/pubs2006/2006166.pdf.

———. 2011. *2008/09 Baccalaureate and Beyond Longitudinal Study*. https://nces.ed.gov/pubs2011/2011236.pdf.

National Commission on Excellence in Education. 1983. *A Nation at Risk: The Imperative for Educational Reform*. https://eric.ed.gov/?id=ED226006.

Nie, Norman H., Jane Junn, and Kenneth Stehlik-Barry. 1996. *Education and Democratic Citizenship in America*. Chicago: University of Chicago Press.

New York City Department of Education. 2013. *Office of English Language Learners: 2013 Demographic Report*. https://eric.ed.gov/?id=ED580312.

Nozick, Robert. 1973. "Distributive Justice." *Philosophy and Public Affairs* 3 (1): 45–126.

Ober, Josiah. 2007. "Natural Capacities and Democracy as a Good-in-Itself." *Philosophical Studies* 132 (1): 59–73.

———. 2008. *Democracy and Knowledge: Innovation and Learning in Classical Athens*. Princeton, NJ: Princeton University Press.

———. 2010. "What Is Democracy? What Is It Good For?" James Moffett Lecture, Princeton University, September 30.

———. 2017. *Demopolis: Democracy before Liberalism in Theory and Practice*. Cambridge, UK: Cambridge University Press.

Okin, Susan. 1991. *Justice, Gender, and the Family*. New York: Basic Books.

Olson, M. 1965. *The Logic of Collective Action: Public Goods and the Theory of Groups*, Cambridge, MA: Harvard University Press.

Ostrom, Elinor 1990. *Governing the Commons: The Evolution of Institutions for Collective Action*. Cambridge, UK: Cambridge University Press.

———. 1998. "A Behavioral Approach to the Rational Choice Theory of Collective Action." *American Political Science Review* 92 (1): 1–22.

Ostrom, Elinor, Thomas Dietz, Nives Dolšak, Paul C. Stern, Susan Stonich, and Elke U. Weber, eds. 2002. *The Drama of the Commons*. Washington, DC: National Academies Press.

Page, Scott E. 2007. *The Difference: How the Power of Diversity Creates Better Groups, Firms, Schools, and Societies*. Princeton, NJ: Princeton University Press.

Pettit, Philip. 1997. *Republicanism: A Theory of Freedom and Government*, Oxford: Oxford University Press.

———. 2001. *A Theory of Freedom*. Cambridge, UK: Polity.

———. 2008. "Freedom and Probability. A Comment on Goodin and Jackson." *Philosophy and Public Affairs* 36 (2): 206–20.

———. 2011. "The Instability of Freedom as Non-interference: The Case of Isaiah Berlin." *Ethics* 121 (34): 693–716.

———. 2012. *On the People's Terms: A Republican Theory and Model of Democracy*. Cambridge, UK: Cambridge University Press.

————. 2014. *Just Freedom: A Moral Compass for a Complex World*. New York: Norton.

Philip, T., and A. Garcia. 2013. "The Importance of Still Teaching the iGeneration: New Technologies and the Centrality of Pedagogy." *Harvard Educational Review* 83 (2): 300–319.

Pickett, Kate, and Richard Wilkinson. 2011. *The Spirit Level: Why Greater Equality Makes Societies Stronger*. New York: Bloomsbury.

Piketty, Thomas. 2014. *Capital in the Twenty-First Century*. Cambridge, MA: Harvard University Press.

Pitkin, H. 1988. "Are Freedom and Liberty Twins?" *Political Theory* 16 (4): 523–52.

Pocock, J. G. A. 1975. *The Machiavellian Moment: Florentine Political Thought and the Atlantic Republican Tradition*. Princeton, NJ: Princeton University Press.

Polanyi, Karl. (1944) 2001. *The Great Transformation: The Political and Economic Origins of Our Time*. 2nd ed. Boston: Beacon.

Posner, Eric A., and Glen Weyl. 2014. "A Radical Solution to Global Income Inequality: Make the U.S. More like Qatar," *New Republic*, November 6. https://newrepublic.com/article/120179/how-reduce-global-income-inequality-open-immigration-policies.

————. 2018. *Radical Markets: Uprooting Capitalism and Democracy for a Just Society*. Princeton, NJ: Princeton University Press.

Pranger, Robert J. 1968. *The Eclipse of Citizenship*. New York: Holt, Rinehart and Winston.

Presidential Commission for the Study of Bioethical Issues. 2010. "*New Directions: The Ethics of Synthetic Biology and Emerging Technologies*." https://papers.ssrn.com/sol3/papers.cfm?abstract_id=2445575.

Putnam, Robert D. 1993. *Making Democracy Work: Civic Traditions in Modern Italy*. Princeton, NJ: Princeton University Press.

————. 2000. *Bowling Alone: The Collapse and Revival of American Community*. New York: Touchstone.

————. 2007. "*E pluribus unum*: Diversity and Community in the Twenty-First Century." *Scandinavian Political Studies* 30 (2): 137–74.

Putnam, Robert D., and David E. Campbell. 2010. *American Grace: How Religion Divides and Unites Us*. New York: Simon & Schuster.

Rahman, K. Sabeel. 2017. *Democracy against Domination*. New York: Oxford University Press.

Ravallion, Martin. 2016. "The World Bank: Why It Is Still Needed and Why It Still Disappoints." Journal of Economic Perspectives 30 (1): 77–94.

Rawls, John. 1971. *A Theory of Justice*. Cambridge, MA: Belknap.

————. (1993) 2011. *Political Liberalism*. Expanded ed. New York: Columbia University Press.

————. 1999. *A Theory of Justice*. Rev. ed. Cambridge, MA: Belknap.

Rebell, Michael. 2018. *Flunking Democracy: Schools, Courts, and Civic Participation.* Chicago: University of Chicago Press.

Reich, M., and K. Jacobs. 2014. "All Economics is Local." *New York Times,* March 22. http://opinionator.blogs.nytimes.com/2014/03/22/all-economics-is-local /#more-152533.

Ricks, Thomas E. 2022. *Waging a Good War: A Military History of the Civil Rights Movement, 1954–1968.* New York: Farrar, Straus and Giroux.

Risse, Mathias. 2020. *On Justice: Philosophy, History, Foundations.* Cambridge, UK: Cambridge University Press.

Rodrik, Dani. 2016. "The Politics of Anger." *Project Syndicate,* March 9. https:// www.project-syndicate.org/commentary/the-politics-of-anger-by-dani -rodrik-2016-03.

Rodrik, Dani, and Charles Sabel. 2022. "Building a Good Jobs Economy." In *Political Economy of Justice,* edited by Danielle Allen, Yochai Benkler, Leah Downey, Rebecca Henderson, and Josh Simons. Chicago: University of Chicago Press.

Rodrik, Dani, and Stefanie Stantcheva. 2021. "A Policy Matrix for Inclusive Prosperity." NBER Working Paper no. 28736. Cambridge, MA: National Bureau of Economic Research.

Rogers, J., K. Mediratta, and S. Shah. 2012. "Building Power, Learning Democracy: Youth Organizing as a Site of Civic Development." *Review of Research in Education* 36 (1): 43–66.

Rogers, Melvin. 2020. "Race, Domination, and Republicanism." In *Difference without Domination: Pursuing Justice in Diverse Democracies,* edited by Danielle Allen and Rohini Somanathan. Chicago: University of Chicago Press.

———. Forthcoming. *The Darkened Light of Faith: Race, Democracy, and Freedom in African American Political Thought.* Princeton, NJ: Princeton University Press.

Rose, Julie. 2016. *Free Time.* Princeton, NJ: Princeton University Press.

Rothstein, R. 2013. "Racial Segregation and Black Student Achievement." In *Education, Justice, and Democracy,* edited by Danielle Allen and Rob Reich. Chicago: University of Chicago Press.

———. 2015. "If the Supreme Court Bans the Disparate Impact Standard It Could Annihilate One of the Few Tools Available to Pursue Housing Integration." Economic Policy Institute. http://www.epi.org/publication/if-the-supreme -court-bans-the-disparate-impact-standard-it-could-annihilate-one-of-the-few -tools-available-to-pursue-housing-integration/.

Rousseau, Jean-Jacques. (1762) 2004. *The Social Contract.* Harlow, UK: Penguin.

Salam, Reihan. 2018. *Melting Pot or Civil War? A Son of Immigrants Makes the Case against Open Borders.* New York: Sentinel.

Salter, Malcolm S. 2017. "Implications of Reciprocal Justice Theory for Corporate Purpose." Unpublished manuscript.

————. 2022. "Corporate Purpose in a Post-Covid World." In *Political Economy of Justice*, edited by Danielle Allen, Yochai Benkler, Leah Downey, Rebecca Henderson, and Josh Simons. Chicago: University of Chicago Press.

Sampson, R. 2013. "Division Street, U.S.A." *New York Times*, October 26. http://opin ionator.blogs.nytimes.com/2013/10/26/division-street-u-s-a/#more-150124.

Savransky, Rebecca. 2017. "McConnell: 'Winners Make Policy, Losers Go Home.'" *The Hill*, February 21. https://thehill.com/homenews/senate/320506-mccon nell-winners-make-policy-and-losers-go-home.

Saxenian, AnnaLee. 2006. *The New Argonauts: Regional Advantage in a Global Economy*. Cambridge, MA: Harvard University Press.

Scanlon, T. M. 2018. *Why Does Inequality Matter?* Oxford: Oxford University Press.

————. 2021. "Why Does Inequality Matter?" In *Combating Inequality: Rethinking Government's Role*, edited by D. Rodrik and O. Blanchard. Cambridge, MA: MIT Press.

Schlesinger, Arthur. 1992. *The Disuniting of America: Reflections on a Multicultural Society*. New York: Norton.

Schudson, Michael. 1998. *The Good Citizen: A History of American Civic Life*. Florence, MA: Free Press.

Schultz, George, and Pedro Aspe. 2017. "The Failed War on Drugs," *New York Times*, December 31. https://www.nytimes.com/2017/12/31/opinion/failed -war-on-drugs.html.

Schwartzberg, Melissa. 2013. *Counting the Many: The Origins and Limits of Supermajority Rule*. Cambridge, UK: Cambridge University Press.

Scott, James C. 1992. *Domination and the Arts of Resistance*. New Haven, CT: Yale University Press.

Sen, Amartya. 1985. "Well-Being, Agency and Freedom." *Journal of Philosophy* 82 (4): 169–221.

————. 1988. "Freedom of Choice: Concept and Content." *European Economic Review* 32 (2/3): 269–94.

————. 1992. *Inequality Reexamined*. Oxford: Oxford University Press.

————. 1999a. *Development as Freedom*. New York: Knopf.

————. 1999b. "Democracy as a Universal Value." *Journal of Democracy* 10 (3): 3–17.

————. 2002. *Rationality and Freedom*. Cambridge, MA: Harvard University Press.

Sethi, Rajiv, and Rohini Somanathan. 2004. "Inequality and Segregation." *Journal of Political Economy* 112 (6): 1296–1321.

Sethi, Rajiv, and Muhamet Yildiz. 2012. "Public Disagreement." *American Economic Journal: Microeconomics* 4 (3): 57–95.

Shachar, Ayelet. 2009. *The Birthright Lottery: Citizenship and Global Inequality*. Cambridge, MA: Harvard University Press.

————. 2020. *The Shifting Border: Legal Cartographies of Migration and Mobility*. Manchester: Manchester University Press.

Shambaugh, Jay, and Ryan Nunn, eds. 2018. *Place-Based Policies for Shared Economic Growth*. Washington, DC: Brookings Institution.

Shelby, Tommie. 2015. "Impure Dissent: Hip Hop and the Political Ethnica of Marginalized Black Urban Youth." In *From Voice to Influence: Understanding Citizenship in a Digital Age*, edited by Danielle Allen and Jennifer S. Light. Chicago: University of Chicago Press.

——. 2016. *Dark Ghettoes: Injustice, Dissent, and Reform*. Cambridge, MA: Harvard University Press.

Shorris, Earl. 2000. *Riches for the Poor: The Clemente Course in the Humanities*. New York: W. W. Norton.

——. 2013. *The Art of Freedom: Teaching Humanities to the Poor*. New York: W. W. Norton.

Shulman, George. 2008. *American Prophecy: Race and Redemption in American Culture*. Minneapolis: University of Minnesota Press.

Sidanius, Jim, Shana Levin, Colette van Laar, and David O. Sears. 2008. *The Diversity Challenge: Social Identity and Intergroup Relations on the College Campus*. New York: Russell Sage Foundation.

Simon, Herbert. 2014. "Response to Philippe van Parijs on Universal Basic Income." *Boston Review*, October. http://bostonreview.net/forum/basic-income-all /herbert-simon-ubi-and-flat-tax.

Singh, Perna, and Matthias vom Hau. 2016. "Ethnicity in Time: Politics, History, and the Relationship between Ethnic Diversity and Public Goods Provision." *Comparative Political Studies* 49 (10): 1–3.

Skinner, Quentin. 2008. "Freedom as the Absence of Arbitrary Power." In *Republicanism and Political Theory*, edited by Cecile Laborde and John Maynor. Oxford: Blackwell.

Skocpol, T. 2003. *Diminished Democracy: From Membership to Management in American Civic Life*. Norman: University of Oklahoma Press.

Slauter, Eric. 2011. "Life, Liberty, and the Pursuit of Happiness: How Did These Words Become the Most Important Part of the Declaration of Independence? The Answer Starts with a Small Band of Motivated Americans." Boston.com, July 3. http://archive.boston.com/news/politics/articles/2011/07/03/life _liberty_and_the_pursuit_of_happiness/.

Small, Mario. 2009. *Unanticipated Gains: Origins of Network Inequality in Everyday Life*. Oxford: Oxford University Press.

Smith, Paul H., ed. 1976–2000. *Letters of Delegates to Congress, 1774–1789*. 25 vols. Washington, DC: Library of Congress. https://memory.loc.gov/ammem /amlaw/lwdg.html.

Sodonis, Tyler, and Joe Witte. 2012. "The Supply Side: Alternative Reform Approaches to Campaign Finance." *Fair Vote*, January 26. https://www.fair vote.org/citizens-united-rebuttal.

Soifer, A. 1998. *Law and the Company We Keep*. Cambridge, MA: Harvard University Press.

Song, Sarah. 2018. *Immigration and Democracy*. Oxford: Oxford University Press.

Stevenson, Bryan, and Sarah Lewis. 2018. "Truth and Reconciliation: An Interview." *Aperture*. https://aperture.org/editorial/truth-reconciliation-bryan-stevenson-sarah-lewis/.

Stout, Jeffrey. 2003. *Democracy and Tradition*. Princeton, NJ: Princeton University Press.

Suarez-Orozco, Marcelo, and Mariela Pæz. 2008. *Latinos: Remaking America*. Berkeley: University of California Press.

Sugrue, Thomas. 2016. "Less Separate, Still Unequal: Diversity and Equality in 'Post–Civil Rights' America." In *Our Compelling Interests: The Value of Diversity for Democracy and a Prosperous Society*, edited by Earl Lewis and Nancy Kantor. Princeton, NJ: Princeton University Press.

Sundquist, Eric. 2012. "The Humanities and the National Interest." *American Literary History* 24 (3): 590–607.

Swann, W. B., Jr. 1983. "Self-Verification: Bringing Social Reality into Harmony with the Self." In *Social Psychological Perspectives on the Self*, edited by J. Suis and A. G. Greenwald. Hillsdale, NJ: Lawrence Erlbaum.

———. 1996. *Self-Traps: The Elusive Quest for Higher Self-Esteem*. New York: Freeman.

Swann, W. B., Jr., V. S. Y. Kwan, J. T. Polzer, and L. P. Milton. 2003. "Fostering Group Identification and Creativity in Diverse Groups: The Role of Individuation and Self- Verification." *Personality and Social Psychology Bulletin* 29 (11): 1396–1406.

Swann, W. B., Jr., J. T. Polzer, D. C. Seyle, and S. J. Ko. 2004. "Finding Value in Diversity: Verification of Personal and Social Self-Views in Diverse Groups." *Academy of Management Review* 29 (1): 9–27.

Szreter, S., and M. Woolcock. 2004. "Health by Association? Social Capital, Social Theory, and the Political Economy of Public Health." *International Journal of Epidemiology* 33 (4): 650–67.

Taylor, Charles. 1979. "What's Wrong with Negative Liberty." In *The Idea of Freedom*, edited by A. Ryan. Oxford: Oxford University Press.

———. 1994. *Multiculturalism: Examining the Politics of Recognition*. Princeton, NJ: Princeton University Press.

Tessema, Mikael. 2020. "'We Need Equity, Not Equality': The Status of Equity and Equality in Theories of Procedural Justice." Thesis, Harvard University.

Tuck, Richard. 2019. "Active and Passive Citizens," lecture given at King's College London. https://www.youtube.com/watch?v=uuNzVzT3h_w.

Turner, J. C. 1985. "Social Categorization and Self-Concept: A Social Cognitive Theory of Group Behavior." In *Advances in Group Process: Theory and Research*, edited by E. J. Lawler. Greenwich, CT: JAI Press.

United Nations General Assembly. 2018. *Report of the United Nations High Commissioner on Refugees. Part II: Global Compact on Refugees*. 73rd session, supplement no. 12.

United States Census. 2019. CPS Historical Migration/Geographic Mobility Tables. Table A-1, "Annual Geographic Mobility Rates, by Type of Movement: 1948–2019." https://www2.census.gov/programs-surveys/demo/tables/geo graphic-mobility/time-series/historic/tab-a-1.xls.

United States Supreme Court. 1958. NAACP v. Alabama ex rel Patterson. 357 U.S. 449.

———. 1961. International Association of Machinists et al., Appellants, v. S. B. Street et al. 367 U.S. 740.

———. 1963. NAACP v. Button. 371 U.S. 415.

———. 1973. Tillman v. Wheaton-Haven Recreation Assn, Inc. 410 U.S. 431.

———. 1976. Runyon et Ux., DBA Bobbe's School v. McCrary et al. 427 U.S. 160.

———. 1984. Roberts v. Jaycees. 468 U.S. 609.

———. 1987. Board of Directors, Rotary International v. Rotary Club of Duarte. 481 U.S. 537.

Van Oorschot, W., W. Arts, and J. Gelissen. 2006. "Social Capital in Europe: Measurement and Social and Regional Distribution of a Multifaceted Phenomenon." *Acta Sociologica* 49 (2): 159–67.

Verba, Sidney, and Kay Lehman Schlozman. 1995. *Voice and Equality: Civic Voluntarism in American Politics.* Cambridge, MA: Harvard University Press.

Viehoff, Daniel. 2014. "Democratic Equality and Political Authority." *Philosophy and Public Affairs,* 42 (4): 337–75.

Waldron, Jeremy. 2017. *One Another's Equals: the Basis of Human Equality.* Cambridge, MA: Belknap.

Walzer, Michael. 1983. *Spheres of Justice: A Defense of Pluralism and Equality.* New York: Basic Books.

———. 2008. "On Promoting Democracy." *Ethics and International Affairs* 22 (4): 351–55.

Warren, Mark E. 2001. *Democracy and Association.* Princeton, NJ: Princeton University Press.

———. 2017. "The All Affected Interests Principle in Democratic Theory and Practice." Institute for Advanced Studies (IHS), Vienna. http://irihs.ihs .ac.at/4306/.

Washington, George. 1792. "From George Washington to Alexander Hamilton, 26 August 1792," Founders Online, National Archives. http://founders.archives .gov/documents/Washington/05-11-02-0015.

Weyl, Glen. 2022a. "Why I Am a Pluralist." RadicalXChange (blog), February 10. https://www.radicalxchange.org/media/blog/why-i-am-a-pluralist/.

———. 2022b. "The Political Philosophy of RadicalXChange." In *Political Economy of Justice,* edited by Danielle Allen, Yochai Benkler, Leah Downey, Rebecca Henderson, and Josh Simons. Chicago: University of Chicago Press.

Wilentz, Sean. 2002. "America's Lost Egalitarian Tradition." *Daedalus* 131 (1): 66–80.

Williams, Bernard. 2001. "From Freedom to Liberty: The Construction of a Political Value." *Philosophy and Public Affairs* 30 (1): 3–26.

———. 2009. "The Idea of Equality," in *In the Beginning Was the Deed: Realism and Moralism in Political Argument*, selected, edited, with introduction by Geoffrey Hawthorn. Princeton, NJ: Princeton University Press.

Witt, John. 2012. *Lincoln's Code: The Laws of War in American History*. New York: Free Press.

Woodly, Deva. 2015. *The Politics of Common Sense: How Social Movements Use Public Discourse to Change Politics and Win Acceptance*. Oxford: Oxford University Press.

Wuthnow, Robert. 1996. *Sharing the Journey: Support Groups and the Quest for a New Community*. Florence, MA: Free Press.

———. 2002. Loose Connections: Joining Together in America's Fragmented Communities. Cambridge, MA: Harvard University Press.

Xenos, Michael, and Lance Bennett. 2007. "The Disconnection in Online Politics: The Youth Political Web Sphere and US Election Sites, 2002–2004." *Information, Communication, and Society* 10 (4): 443–64.

Yoshikawa, Hirokazu. 2012. *Immigrants Raising Citizens: Undocumented Parents and Their Young Children*. New York: Russell Sage Foundation.

Young, Iris Marion. 1990. *Justice and the Politics of Difference*. Princeton, NJ: Princeton University Press.

———. 1994. "Gender as Seriality: Thinking about Women as a Social Collective." *Signs* 19 (3): 713–38.

———. 1996. "Communication and the Other: Beyond Deliberative Democracy." In *Democracy and Difference: Contesting the Boundaries of the Political*, edited by S. Benhabib. Princeton, NJ: Princeton University Press.

Index

accountability: in ancient Athens, 73; elections as means of, 68, 74, 80
Acemoğlu, Daron, 188, 192
actual polities, 87–90
Adams, Abigail, 81, 191
Adams, John, 82–83
African Americans, 50, 105, 124, 154, 179, 217
American founders: critiques of, 70, 81; designing of government by, 70, 77–78; and political economy, 5, 131, 136–37. *See also* Declaration of Independence; US Constitution
Anderson, Benedict, 204
Anderson, Elizabeth, 171
Anti-Federalists, 93–94
antiracism, 112
Arendt, Hannah, 159
Aristotle, 8, 9, 11, 80, 136, 161
Articles of Confederation, 91–92
assimilation, 107–13, 209
association, freedom of/right to: domination and inequality resulting from, 46, 48–51; Jim Crow system and, 49–50; legal impacts on, 119–20, 247n15; legal norms concerning, 60–61; marriage and, 50–51; public and political aspect of, 34; social difference resulting from, 46, 48, 50–51; value of, 17, 21, 35- 42
Athens. *See* Greece
autonomy: as component of well-being, 26–27, 31, 33; in connected society, 113;

democracy linked to, 34–35; domination contrasted with, 239n25; as fundamental moral need, 32; Mill and, 236n9; political participation and, 27–29, 33, 48; private, 21, 23–30; public, 25–30; right of association and, 34; social conditions for, 31–33, 113

ballot access, 39, 85
Beccaria, Cesare, v, 161
behavioral economics, 236n1
beliefs: influence of rules on content of, 11; as rules for action, 7–8, 10, 60
benevolent autocracies, 99
Bentham, Jeremy, 140
Berlin, Isaiah, 21–22, 24, 210, 236n10
Berman, Elizabeth Popp, 20
Bhabha, Homi, 110
Bidart, Frank, 11, 128
Bill of Rights, 34
#BlackLivesMatter, 224
Black Panthers, 240n6
blind spots: in economics, 6; in political economy, 6, 16, 20, 25; in Rawls's *Theory of Justice*, 25–30; in theory of justice, 6; in twentieth-century political thinking, 20–25, 29
Bolsonaro, Jair, 20
bonding ties, 52–53, 103–4, 107, 112–13, 124–25
Borges, Jorge Luis, 128
Bourdieu, Pierre, 10–11

Brexit, 6, 20, 141, 228
bridging ties: benefits of, 105, 107; bonding ties in relation to, 104; in connected society, 53–54, 103–7, 112–16, 120–26; cultural framework for, 120–26; defined, 53; distributive justice in conflict with, 149; in empowering economies, 159–60, 180–82; social structure as basis of, 104, 113–16

campaign finance, 6, 36, 39, 44, 85, 242n18
Canada, 109–10, 152, 154–55, 245n6, 248n15
caste systems, 46, 51, 154, 156–57
central banks, 184–85
checks and balances, 74–76, 80, 91–92
citizenship: earlier models of, 215–19; epistemic/intellectual challenge of, 203–8, 220–21; multitasking as challenge of, 201–3, 219–20; new model for, 200, 201, 219–27; relational challenge of, 208–14
civic education, 122, 192–93, 199, 202, 206, 216, 220, 226
civil rights movement, 89, 108, 217
civil society/social domain: alternative theory of justice in, 30, 45; capacities, skills, and knowledge for, 117–26; connected society as subsidiary ideal of, 52, 54–55, 103; design principles for, 103, 113–21, 200; difference without domination in, 45–48, 101, 102, 164; effects of rights protection on, 45–46, 49–50, 52; egalitarian participatory constitutional democracy and, 101; immigration policy and, 134–36; institutional and organizational reforms of, 249–50n8; Jim Crow system's effect on, 49; justice as end/purpose of, 72; King on restructuring of, 84–85, 249–50n8; linking of political and economic domains with, 47, 58, 67, 115, 131–32; membership in, 134–35, 139–45; network effects in, 103; power sharing in, 86; rules and norms of, 107, 113–21; subsidiary ideals and, 63, 130–31, 133, 149–52, 156. See also membership, sociopolitical; social policy
Civil War, 151
classical liberalism. See liberalism
climate change, 87
cocreation, 41, 43, 211, 241n16
Cohen, G. A., 59
collaboration, 78–79, 95, 123, 141, 160, 178–81, 190, 225. See also compromise

common schools, 108
compromise, 42, 95–98, 193. See also collaboration
Congress, US. See US Congress; US House of Representatives; US Senate
connected society/social connectedness, 101–28; assimilation compared to, 107–13; autonomy in, 113; benefits of, for economic domain, 244n3; benefits of, for personal well-being, 245n3; bonding ties in, 103–4, 112–13, 124–25; bridging ties in, 53–54, 103–7, 112–16, 120–26; capacities, skills, and knowledge for, 117–26; and conception of the people, 127; cultural design for, 115–21; defined, 53–54; design principles for, 103, 113–21; difference without domination as goal of, 52–53, 55, 103, 112–13, 155–56; egalitarianism in, 104, 106; institutional design for, 113–15; multiculturalism compared to, 107, 109–13; network effects in, 105–6, 112; polypolitanism and, 130–31, 155–56; Rawls and, 48; rules and norms for, 113–21; social policy for cultivating, 54; social ties in, 52–53; as subsidiary ideal of civil society, 52, 54–55, 103
consequentialism, 8
Constant, Benjamin, 21–23, 201, 203
Constitution, US. See US Constitution
contract, freedom of/right to, 46
co-ownership of political institutions, 37, 43–44, 78
cosmopolitanism, 139–40, 142–45, 146. See also polypolitanism
Crenshaw, Kimberlé, 110
critical race theory, 18, 236n5
cultural domain, rules and norms of, 115–21

decision-making/governance: basic elements of, 73; checks and balances in, 75–76, 80; in democracies, 36, 38–41, 73–74, 76, 205; epistemic egalitarianism in, 36, 40, 76; experts' role in, 36, 40; laypeople's role in, 36, 40; natural and actual polities in, 87–90; unity as precondition of, 96–97. See also power
Declaration of Independence: conception of the people in, 71–72, 81–82; critique of, 81–82; facets of political equality in, 240n6; pragmatism undergirding, 9–10,

240n8; pursuit of happiness as basis of, 10, 82–83, 206, 240n8

democracy: autonomy linked to, 34–35; collaboration in, 78–79; co-ownership of political institutions in, 43; decision-making/governance in, 36, 38–41, 73–74, 76, 205; deliberative, 217–18, 222–23; depersonalization of power in, 38–39, 69–81, 90–96, 204, 208, 241n11; education's significance for, 190; energy in, 69, 90–99; epistemic/intellectual challenge of, 203–8; existential challenge of, 201–3; foreign interventions on the part of, 99–100, 138; in governance of firms, 170–78; inclusion in, 69, 81–90, 159; instrumental value of, 239n2; intrinsic value of, 35, 239n2; justice best served by, 4, 7, 32, 33, 72, 92, 99–100; as open-ended project, 9–10, 70, 98, 128; origins of, 70–71; political equality dependent on, 33, 35; pragmatism linked to, 8–10, 128; relational challenge of, 208–14; revisability of, 9–10; safety of and in, 69, 90–99; types of, 39; unity as basis of healthy functioning of, 96–98, 226; virtuous cycles in, 47, 160; well-being linked to, 7, 9–10, 32, 229. *See also* citizenship; co-ownership of political institutions; egalitarian participatory constitutional democracy; people, the

demography, 126–27

depersonalization of power, 38–39, 69–81, 90–96, 204, 208, 241n11

Dewey, John, 7, 206

difference. *See* social difference

difference principle, 17–18, 54, 58, 163–64, 194, 236n3, 243n25

difference without domination: connected society and, 52–53, 55, 103, 112–13, 155–56; as criterion for determining legitimacy of social processes, 163, 248n2; defined, 51, 102; in democratic governance of firms, 171–72; in economic domain, 45–48, 55–56, 131–32, 135–36, 159, 162–66, 194; immigration policy and, 56–57; justice guided by principle of, 45–47; liberal political philosophy based on, 58–60; protection of liberties/rights designed to result in, 52–53, 55–56; republican safety linked to, 91; rules and norms conducive

to, 46–47, 50, 60–61, 107; segregation as counter example to, 49–50; in social domain, 45–48, 101, 102, 164. *See also* non-domination

distributive justice, 18, 133, 144, 145, 146, 149, 156–57, 192, 242n20

diversity: capacities, skills, and knowledge relevant to, 122–24; and social cohesion, 117–20

Diversity Challenge, The (Russell Sage), 124

domination. *See* difference without domination; non-domination

Douglass, Frederick, 191

Du Bois, W. E. B., 28, 48, 59, 91, 203, 224

due dependence, 74, 79–80, 91, 95, 96

due responsibility, 79–80, 91, 95

economic/income/wealth inequality, 18, 56–57, 140, 158, 169, 172–73, 186–88, 243n25

economics/economics domain: alternative approach to, 55–56, 160–66, 186, 188; alternative theory of justice in, 30, 45; behavioral, 236n1; benefits of connected society for, 244n3; blind spots in, 6; design principles for, 159–60, 166, 186, 200; difference without domination in, 45–48, 55–56, 131–32, 159, 162, 194; distributive questions in, 16–18, 49, 55–56, 160, 163–64; dominance of, in sociopolitical thinking, 19–20, 25, 158–59; education and, 186–93; effects of rights protection on, 45–46, 49–50, 52, 55–56; empowering civic participation as purpose of, 131–32, 136–39; foreign policy and, 170; immigration policy and, 134–45; inclusion as goal of, 159; instrumental value of, 159; Jim Crow system's effect on, 49; legislative oversight of, 184–85; linking of political and social domains with, 47, 58, 67, 115, 131–32; measurements of, 177; middling-class, 131, 137, 161; negative liberties associated with, 24–25; paradoxical results arising from protection of, 46; policy domains of, 164–65; political equality and, 45–48; polity form antecedent to form of, 155; power sharing in, 86; quasi-Rawlsian welfarism in, 16–18; Rawls's difference principle and, 54; relational vs. transactional perspective in, 162–66, 172, 182–83, 192–93; rules for action in, 13;

economics/economics domain (*cont.*)
rules for action undergirding, 4–5;
sociopolitical membership and, 134–45;
subsidiary ideal in, 55, 63, 132; universalization in, 19–20; utilitarian welfarism in,
16–18, 20. *See also* empowering economies; political economy
education: access to, 188; assimilation as goal
of, 108; civic, 122, 192–93, 199, 202, 206,
216, 220, 226; economic domain and,
186–93; humanities and social sciences
in, 191; natural and actual polities for,
89–90; Plato's conception of civic, 201–3;
political equality as goal of, 191–93;
as public good, 41; significance of, for
democracy, 190
egalitarian empowerment, 45, 53, 56, 102, 106,
127, 195
egalitarianism: connected society characterized by, 104, 106; as difference without
domination, 103; network effects and,
103. *See also* epistemic egalitarianism;
political equality
egalitarian participatory constitutional
democracy, 67–100; assuring safety of
and in, 90–99; constitutional democracy
without egalitarian participation, 81,
86; defined, 68; depersonalization of
power in, 69–81; design principles for,
69; energy in, 90–99; inclusion in, 81–90;
institutional mechanisms of, 73–74;
populist rejection of, 193; power sharing
in, 86; reciprocity associated with, 41–42;
steering function of the people in, 68–69;
as subsidiary ideal of civil society, 101; as
subsidiary ideal of political domain, 4,
44, 62–63; voting systems in, 68, 209.
See also epistemic egalitarianism
elections: ballot access for, 39, 85; as means
of accountability, 68, 74, 80. *See also*
Electoral College; voting systems
Electoral College, 77–78
Ellison, Ralph, *Invisible Man*, 109
empowering economies, 158–95; bridging
ties in, 159–60, 180–82; defined, 159; democratic steering necessary for, 160, 166,
180, 182–86; design principles for, 159–60,
166, 186; difference without domination
resulting in, 45–48, 55–56, 131–32, 135–36;
and exploitative economies, 135–39; and

good-jobs economy, 176–80, 183–85;
labor and, 167–70; political and social
membership as basis of, 133, 135; political
economy guided by principle of, 159;
power-sharing liberalism as basis for, 160,
179; reconception of firm governance and,
170–78; rules and charters for, 160; as subsidiary ideal of economic domain, 55, 132
energy, in democratic participation, 69,
90–99
enslavement, 82–83, 132, 137, 167
epistemic egalitarianism, 36, 39–41, 76
equality, types of, 32. *See also* economic/in-
come/wealth inequality; egalitarianism;
moral equality; political equality
eudaemonism, 7, 240n6. *See also* well-being
European Union (EU), 141
executive branch, 92–93; basic elements of
governance in, 73; legislative branch's
relations with, 78, 93–94; power of, 69,
92–94
experts: and democratic decision-making,
36, 40; role of, in empowering economies, 160

factionalism, 95–96, 215. *See also* polarization
fair fighting, 219, 222–24, 226
Fair Housing Act, 60–61
federalism, 89
Federalist Papers, v, 69, 70, 72, 74, 91, 95, 215
Federalists, 93
Federal Reserve, 184
feminism, 18
filibuster, 91
firms: democratic governance in, 171–72;
purpose-driven, 173–75
flourishing. *See* well-being
forbearance, 78, 79, 95, 97, 98, 219, 224
Fourteenth Amendment, 89
frame shifting, 224
Franklin, Benjamin, 82

Gandhi, Mohandas, 212, 224
Gates, Theaster, 224
Georgia land lottery, 137, 177
Germany, political right in, 20
GI Bill, 180
Glaeser, Edward L., 190
Global Compact on Migration, 247n9
Goldin, Claudia, 186–87

good-jobs economy, 167, 176–80, 183–85
Gould, Carol, 171, 172
governance. *See* decision-making/
    governance
Granovetter, Mark, 112
Great Recession (2008), 167
Greece, 7, 39, 70–71, 73, 151, 201–3, 206, 241n11
grievances. *See* redress of grievances

habeas corpus, 93
Habermas, Jürgen, 218
habits. *See* rules and norms (practical and
    context-specific)
Hamilton, Alexander, 74, 78–79
happiness: Declaration of Independence
    and, 10, 82–83, 206, 240n8; individual
    determination of, 9; pragmatism and,
    8–9; utilitarian conception of, 241n8.
    See also well-being
Hare, Christopher, 169
Hayek, Friedrich, 4–5, 22
Henderson, Rebecca, 173–75
Henry, Patrick, 26
Hillygus, Sunshine, 189
Hirschman, Albert, 137, 170
Hobbes, Thomas, 71
Homestead Act, 177
homophily, 51
House of Representatives, US, 77, 95
housing, 53, 60, 113–15, 146, 167–68, 179, 195, 220
Hume, David, 140
hybridity, 110–11

Ibsen, Henrik, *A Doll's House*, 37
identity, personal, 110–11
immigrants: and assimilation, 109; political
    voice of, 144–45, 147, 151, 154–55, 168–69;
    in Silicon Valley, 181
immigration policy: as economic issue,
    135–36; political, economic, and social
    ramifications of, 56–57, 132–33; polypoli-
    tanism and, 149–55; quotas in, 248n15;
    as social issue, 134–35; and sociopolitical
    membership, 57, 133–45, 149–52; VIP
    proposal for, 133, 145–49. *See also* mem-
    bership, sociopolitical; sponsorship, of
    migrants/refugees
inclusion, in democracy, 69, 81–90, 159
income inequality. *See* economic/income/
    wealth inequality

indentured servitude, 147–48
individualism, 21
inequality. *See* economic/income/wealth
    inequality; equality; racial inequality
integration, 85, 108, 153–54, 208–14, 249–50n8
intersectionality, 110–11

Jackson, Andrew, 216
Jackson, Matthew, 112
Jacobs, Ken, 115
James, William, 7–8, 10, 60
Jefferson, Thomas, 82, 161
Jim Crow system, 49–50, 98, 108, 217
justice: core principles of, 14, 31; democracy
    best form of government for, 4, 7, 32, 33,
    72, 92, 99–100; design principles for, 30,
    35–47; difference without domination as
    guiding principle of, 45–47; as end/pur-
    pose of civil society, 72; ideals undergird-
    ing, 12, 31–35; non-sacrificeability of, 24;
    non-sacrificeability of positive and nega-
    tive liberties as guiding principle of, 30,
    35; political equality as guiding principle
    of, 4, 6–7, 30, 35–44, 47, 242n20; Rawls's
    conception of, 17–19, 29; reciprocity as
    fundamental to, 41–43; reconceptualiza-
    tion of, 29; subsidiary ideals of, 12, 14,
    62; substantive, 91, 92; in utilitarian eco-
    nomic perspective, 18; well-being as goal
    of, 30, 31, 99. *See also* distributive justice;
    redress of grievances

Kant, Immanuel, 7–8, 21
Katz, Larry, 186–87
Kennedy School of Government, Harvard
    University, 16
Keynesian social democracy, 13, 186
King, Martin Luther, Jr., 84, 191, 208–14, 224,
    240n6, 249–50n8
Kirp, David, 114
Knights of Columbus, 153
Knights Templar, 153

labor and labor markets: and democratic
    governance of firms, 171–72; in empower-
    ing economies, 167–70; free, 56, 132, 137,
    167–70, 179–80; immigration, member-
    ship, and mobility policies for, 131, 136,
    139, 141–42, 144–45, 148–49, 152–54, 156,
    167–70, 181; immigration and, 57; impact

labor and labor markets (*cont.*)
of connectedness on, 104; measurements of, 167; policy-making focus on, 54; political voice of, 57, 144–45, 168–70
land, organization and use of, 49, 53, 54, 113, 116, 137, 161, 180, 194, 228
land lottery, 137, 177
Latinx peoples, 105, 124
laypeople, and democratic decision-making, 36, 40
League of Women Voters, 216
legislative branch: basic elements of governance in, 73; economic policy-setting function of, 184–85; executive branch's relations with, 78, 93–94; health and functionality of, 94–95; power of, 93
Levitsky, Daniel, 78–79
liberalism: critiques of, 57–58; Declaration of Independence and, 240n8; dominant policy paradigm of, 16; negative vs. positive liberties in, 20–25; reconstruction of, 58; republican (eighteenth-century), 239n26; rules for action in, 13. *See also* neoliberalism; power-sharing liberalism
liberties and rights: of ancients vs. moderns (political vs. private), 21–25, 237n17; Anderson's tri-partite theory of freedom, 171; basic, 21; defined, 237n12; empowering economies' protection of, 160; intrinsic value of, 159; paradoxical results arising from protection of, 48–50, 102; Rawls and, 22–29, 237nn17–20, 241n12; relationship of positive and negative, 20–26, 33–34, 237n17; tradeoff among positive and negative, 24. *See also* negative liberties; positive liberties/rights
Lincoln, Abraham, v, 93, 98, 132, 137, 240n6
linking ties, 53, 104, 171
Loury, Glenn, 162–64

majority vote, 68
Mansbridge, Jane, 241n9, 241n11, 241n16
marriage, 50–51
Marshall, George, 159, 161
Marshall Plan, 159, 170
Marx, Karl, 5
Masons, 153–54
material inequality. *See* economic/income/wealth inequality

membership, sociopolitical: of civil associations (*see also* membership, sociopolitical); cosmopolitanism as paradigm for, 139–40, 142–45, 146; cultural unification and, 143; design principles for, 139, 145, 152, 200; effects of rights protection on, 56–57; immigration and, 57, 133–45, 149–52; nationalism as paradigm for, 139–40, 142–43, 146; political equality as guiding principle for, 145, 149; polypolitanism and, 57, 63, 130–31, 133, 149–56; social and economic effects of, 134–45; subsidiary ideal for, 63. *See also* immigration policy
Memorial to Peace and Justice, Montgomery, Alabama, 224
methodological individualism, 112
microaggressions, 213
middling-class economy, 131, 137, 161
migration. *See* immigration policy
military, privatization of, 37, 43
Mill, John Stuart, 8, 21, 206, 235n5, 235n6, 236n9, 240n8
Mills, Charles, 236n5
minoritarian positions: American founders' concern for, 77–78; assimilation process for, 109; intersection of political, social, and economic domains for, 59; mechanisms for protecting, 68, 77–78, 91, 98; theories of justice and, 59
Montesquieu, Charles-Louis de Secondat, Baron de La Brède et de, 74
moral equality, 32, 35
Morrison, Toni, v
Movement for Black Lives, 224
Mrs. Murphy's exception, 60–61
multiculturalism, 107, 109–13, 245n6, 245n7
multitasking, by democratic citizens, 201–3, 219–20
mutual aid associations, 153–54

nationalism, 139–40, 142–43, 146
National Security Agency, 93
Native Americans, 82, 137, 139, 180
natural polities, 87–90
negative liberties: non-sacrificeability of, 30, 33, 35; positive liberties in relation to, 21–26, 33–34, 48–49, 203, 210–11
neoinstitutionalism, 112
neoliberalism, 13, 164

network effects: in connected society, 105–6, 112; distribution of goods and resources conditioned by, 105–6; and egalitarianism, 103; social fabric upheld by, 103

network theory, 112

Nineteenth Amendment, 216

non-domination: overview of, 37–38; political equality based on, 36, 37–38. *See also* difference without domination

nonrandom processes, 162–63

non-sacrificeability of positive and negative liberties, justice guided by principle of, 30, 35

nonviolence, 211–13, 224, 226

norms. *See* rules for action

Nozick, Robert, 243n25

Obama, Barack, 187

Occupy Wall Street, 224

Oddfellows, 153

Okin, Susan, 59

Orban, Viktor, 20

participatory democracy, 236n11

people, the: American founders' conceptions of, 71–72, 81–82, 215–16; in ancient Athens, 73; and civil society/social connectedness, 127–28; conceptions of, 38, 69, 71, 127–28, 143, 204; democratic concept of, 204; divisions/classes of, 77–78; immigration as challenge to, 143; legislative branch as representative of, 94; ownership of political institutions by, 37, 43–44, 78; power of, 69; steering function of, 68–69, 76–77, 80

Pericles, 202, 206, 241n11

Pettit, Philip, 37–38

Pickett, Kate, 148

Piketty, Thomas, 172–73, 187–88

Plato, 7–8, 201–3, 206, 215

Plessy v. Ferguson, 119

Pocock, J. A., 236n11

polarization, 79, 169. *See also* factionalism

political domain. *See* political institutions/political domain

political economy: alternative approach to, 4, 12–13, 200, 228–29; basis of, 4–5; blind spots in, 6, 16, 20, 25; economics' dominance in, 19–20, 25, 158–59; empowering economies as guiding principle of, 159;

political equality as basic principle for, 4; pressing problems of, 158; reinvention of, 3, 29–30; role of law in, 161; theory of justice as guide for, 5–6; universalizing vs. specific approaches in, 20

political equality: alternative types of, 150–52; benefits of, 26–27; and co-ownership of political institutions, 37, 43–44; democracy as necessary form of government for, 33, 35; distributive justice in conflict with, 133, 156–57; diverse methods of determining, 138; economics and, 45–48; educational approach conducive to, 191–93; empowerment associated with, 34, 137; epistemic egalitarianism and, 36, 39–41; equal access to political participation as condition for, 36, 39, 85; facets of, 36–44, 240n6; intrinsic value of, 32–33, 159; issues associated with, 6; justice guided by principle of, 4, 6–7, 30, 35–44, 47, 242n20; non-domination as condition for, 36, 37–38; non-sacrificeability of, 99, 102, 129, 131, 133, 137; political economy based on, 4; Rawls's conception of, 26–27; reciprocity linked to, 36–37, 41–43; social policy and, 45–48; sociopolitical membership guided by principle of, 145, 149; in a theory of justice, 30; well-being associated with, 4, 6, 27, 30, 33, 138. *See also* positive liberties/rights

political friendship, 43, 209, 250n8

political institutions/political domain: autonomy safeguarded by, 31–32; checks and balances in, 74–75, 91–92; co-ownership of, 37, 43–44, 78; design principles for, 69, 200; and difference without domination, 46; egalitarian participatory constitutional democracy as subsidiary ideal of, 4, 44, 62–63, 98–99; establishing and maintenance of rules and norms by, 67; fundamental role of, 72; institutional and organizational reforms of, 249–50n8; land, labor, and capital organized by, 161; linking of social and economic domains with, 47, 58, 67, 115, 131–32; political equality and, 36–37, 44; power sharing in, 85; safety of and in, 69, 90–99; subsidiary ideals in, 62–63, 68, 130–31

political liberties. *See* positive liberties/rights

political participation: autonomy in relation to, 27–29, 33, 48; cultural homo-/heterogeneity and, 29; economic effects of, 192; educational tracks and, 189–90; equal access to, 36, 39, 85; instrumental value of, 26; intrinsic value of, 28; nondomination and, 38; and well-being, 239n23. *See also* membership, sociopolitical; participatory democracy; political voice

political parties, 96, 216

political philosophy, 7–12

political voice: critique of US Constitution concerning, 84; of immigrants, 144–45, 147, 151, 154–55, 168–69; of labor, 57, 144–45, 168–70; polypolitanism and, 57, 151, 154, 156. *See also* political membership/participation

polity forms. *See* actual polities; natural polities; regime types

polypolitanism, 130–57; and connected society, 125, 130–31, 155–56; defined, 130, 151; as model of sociopolitical membership, 57, 63, 130–31, 133, 149–56; negative effects of, 151; policy for institutionalizing, 152–55; and political voice, 57, 151, 154, 156; as subsidiary ideal of social domain, 63, 130–31, 133, 149–52, 156

Ponzetto, Giacomo, 190

Poole, Keith, 169

popular sovereignty. *See* depersonalization of power; people, the

populism, 192–93

positive liberties/rights: intrinsic value of, 32–33; King's advocacy for, 210; negative liberties in relation to, 21–26, 33–34, 48–49, 203, 210–11; sacrificeability/non-sacrificeability of, 22–24, 26, 29–30, 33, 35; substantive, 91. *See also* political equality

Posner, Eric, 133, 139–42, 145, 147, 156

power: basic elements of, 73; checks and balances concerning, 75–76, 80, 91–92; depersonalization of, 38–39, 69–81, 90–96, 204, 208, 241n11; of the people, 69; sharing of, 81–87. *See also* decision-making/governance

power-sharing liberalism: as alternative to current and traditional rules for action, 13; empowering economies and, 160, 179;

ideals, principles, and norms of, 15, 58–60; individual-based, not group-based, model of, 59–60; in Netherlands and Lebanon, 59

pragmatism, 7–12; Declaration of Independence and, 240n6, 240n8; democracy linked to, 8–10, 128; and formulation of design principles, 60, 62; judgment as key feature of, 10; method of, 7–8; and well-being, 8–9, 11

primogeniture laws, 161

Prince Hall Masons, 154

prisons, privatization of, 37, 43

privatization, of military and prisons, 37, 43

pro bono defense, 39, 85

proceduralism, 47, 90, 92, 237n15, 242n21

prophecy, 219, 224–25

public good(s), 28, 41, 71, 116, 193

purpose-driven firms, 173–75

purposiveness, of human beings, 32–33, 206–8, 221–23, 225–27, 249n2

Putnam, Robert, 116–19

quasi-Rawlsian welfarism, 16–18

racial inequality, 105, 158

ranked-choice voting, 85, 95

Rawls, John: critiques of, 22–30, 34, 47–48, 59, 171, 194; and deliberative democracy, 218; difference principle of, 17–18, 54, 58, 163–64, 194, 236n3, 243n25; goals of, 17; impact of, 11–12; *The Law of Peoples*, 99; and political/positive liberties/rights vs. private/negative liberties/rights, 22–29, 34, 48, 50, 156, 237nn17–20, 241n12; and proceduralism, 237n15, 242n21; and theory of justice, 47–48, 59, 235n4, 242n21; *A Theory of Justice*, 11, 16–19, 22–24, 59, 171; universalist perspective of, 18–19; utilitarianism as target of, 17–18; veil of ignorance postulated by, 18–19, 59

reciprocity: political equality linked to, 36–37, 41–43; and redress of grievances, 37, 42

Reconstruction, 98, 179

redistricting, 43

redress of grievances, 37, 42

regime types, 99, 155

Reich, Michael, 115

republican liberalism, 239n26

republican liberty, 236n10
republican safety, 69, 90–99
Robinson, Jim, 188, 192
Rodrik, Dani, 164, 176–78, 180, 182–83, 185–86, 188, 193, 210
Rohingya genocide, 88
Rome, 71
Roosevelt, Franklin, 93
Royal Commission on Bilingualism and Biculturalism (Canada), 109–10, 245n6
rules and norms (practical and context-specific): difference without domination as goal of, 46–47, 50, 60–61; in economic realm, 4–5, 13; for empowering economies, 160; of governance, 78–79; historical examples of, 13; ideals and principles undergirding, 12, 62; impact of, 11; as means of making procedure substantive, 47; origin and development of, 4–5, 67; political institutions' role in establishing, 67; proposal for alternative, 12–15; in social domain, 107, 113–21. *See also* rules for action
rules for action: alternative to current, 12–13; beliefs as, 7–8, 10, 60; pragmatism and, 10–11, 62. *See also* rules and norms

Sabel, Charles, 176–78, 180, 182–83, 185–86, 193, 210
Salter, Malcolm, 173, 175–76
Saxenian, AnnaLee, 181
Scanlon, Tim, 248n2
Schlesinger, Arthur, Jr., 108–10
Schudson, Michael, 215
segregation, 49–50, 56, 105–6, 108, 119, 212
self-interest, 219, 221, 222
Sen, Amartya, 207, 223, 240n2, 240n8
Senate, US, 77–78, 91
September 11, 2001, attacks, 93
seriality, 110–11
Sethi, Rajiv, 162
sex trafficking, 147
Shelby, Tommie, 236n7
Shleifer, Andrei, 190
Silicon Valley, 181–82
Simon, Herbert, 43
small businesses, 61
Smith, Adam, 4–5, 140
social capital, 19, 52, 104, 112, 116–20

social connectedness. *See* connected society/social connectedness
social contract theories, 71, 170
social democracy. *See* Keynesian social democracy
social difference: domination and inequality resulting from, 46, 50, 51; freedom of association leading to, 46, 50; patterns of, 11; pros and cons of, 46. *See also* difference without domination
social domain. *See* civil society/social domain
social justice: common understanding of, 18
social policy: alternative approach to, 53; difference without domination as goal of, 53–54; political equality and, 45–48
social ties, 52–53, 104. *See also* bonding ties; bridging ties; linking ties
society. *See* civil society/social domain; connected society/social connectedness
sponsorship, of migrants/refugees, 146–48, 152–55, 169, 248n10, 248n12
stakeholder capitalism, 173, 177, 179, 193–95
Stantcheva, Stefanie, 164
state: the good determined by, 29–30; personal autonomy protected by, 27
state-of-nature theories, 71
STEM (science, technology, engineering, and math) education, 186–87, 189–92
Stevenson, Bryan, 224
Stowe, Harriet Beecher, 224
subsidiary ideals: connected society as, 52, 54–55; domain-specific, 62–63; egalitarian participatory constitutional democracy as, 4, 44, 62–63, 68, 98–99; empowering economies as, 55, 132; of justice, 12, 14, 62; polypolitanism as, 57, 130–31, 133, 149–52
Sullivan, James, 83
Supreme Court, US, 119

taxation, redistributive, 17, 164, 185
Taylor, Charles, *Multiculturalism*, 109–10
Tea Party, 240n6
theory of justice: blind spots in, 6; defined, 5; political economy guided by, 5–6; political equality's role in, 30; Rawls and, 235n4; sociobiology's claims contrasted with, 235n3; well-being as goal of, 5, 235n4
thouness, 211–13, 222, 224, 225, 226

Thucydides, 241n11
tolerance, 78, 95, 98, 219, 224
transportation, 53, 113–15, 119, 167–68, 179, 195
Treaty of Versailles, 143
Truman, Harry, 93
Trump, Donald, 6, 20, 228
Tuck, Richard, 150

United Nations, 143
unity, as basis of political self-governance, 96–98, 226
Universal Declaration of Human Rights, 135
universalism, 18–20
University of California, Los Angeles, 124
US Congress, 93, 95. *See also* US House of Representatives; US Senate
US Constitution: checks and balances established by, 74–75; conception of the people in, 81, 83; critiques of, 81, 83–84; distribution of power established in, 83–84, 89; and egalitarian participatory constitutional democracy, 70. *See also* American founders
US House of Representatives, 77, 95
US Senate, 77–78, 91
US Supreme Court, 119
utilitarian economic welfarism, 16–18
utilitarianism: and happiness, 241n8; quantitative bias of, 19; as target of Rawls, 17–18

veil of ignorance, 18–19, 59
virtue ethics, 8
Visas between Individuals Program (VIP), 133, 145–49, 152

voting systems: Electoral College rules and, 78; minority-protecting, 68; ranked-choice, 85, 95; steering function of the people determined by, 68–69. *See also* majority vote

Walzer, Michael, 99–100, 242n20
war on drugs, 88–89
Washington, George, 79, 95–96
wealth inequality. *See* economic/income/wealth inequality
welfare, 194–95
well-being: autonomy as component of, 26–27, 31, 33; democracy linked to, 7, 9–10, 32, 229; identity and, 111; individual determination of, 31; justice as means of achieving, 30, 31, 99; negative liberties associated with, 21; philosophy guided by focus on, 7; political equality as basis for, 4, 6, 27, 30, 33, 138; political participation and, 239n23; pragmatism and, 8–9, 11; Rawls's conception of, 26–27; theory of justice aimed at achieving, 5, 235n4. *See also* happiness
Wells, Ida B., 191
Weyl, Glen, 87–88, 133, 139–42, 145, 147, 156
Wilkinson, Richard, 148
will formation, 204–5, 207–8
Wittgenstein, Ludwig, 7
women, voting rights of, 209, 216
World Bank, 19–20

Young, Iris, 110

Ziblatt, Daniel, 78–79